AMERICA THROUGH EUROPEAN EYES

JOURNAL OF A TOUR IN THE
STATE OF NEW YORK

JOURNAL

OF A

TOUR

THROUGH THE

STATE OF NEW YORK

IN THE YEAR 1830

WITH REMARKS ON AGRICULTURE

IN THOSE PARTS MOST ELIGIBLE FOR SETTLERS

BY

JOHN FOWLER

[1831]

AUGUSTUS M. KELLEY · PUBLISHERS

NEW YORK 1970

First Edition 1831

(London: Whittaker, Treacher & Arnot, 1831)

Reprinted 1970 by
AUGUSTUS M. KELLEY · PUBLISHERS
REPRINTS OF ECONOMIC CLASSICS
New York New York 10001

.   .   .   .

S B N   678 00582 6

L C N   74 100125

.   .   .   .

JOURNAL OF A TOUR

IN THE

STATE OF NEW YORK,

IN THE YEAR 1830;

WITH

REMARKS ON AGRICULTURE

IN THOSE PARTS MOST ELIGIBLE FOR SETTLERS:

AND RETURN TO ENGLAND BY

THE WESTERN ISLANDS,

IN CONSEQUENCE OF SHIPWRECK IN THE ROBERT FULTON.

BY JOHN FOWLER.

" It occupies me to turn back regards
  On what I've seen or pondered, sad or cheery;
  And what I write I cast upon the stream,
  To swim or sink."

                          BYRON.

LONDON:
WHITTAKER, TREACHER, AND ARNOT.

1831.

TO

THOMAS ATTWOOD, ESQUIRE,

THE

LIBERAL AND ENLIGHTENED ADVOCATE OF REFORM,

AND THE

FOUNDER OF POLITICAL UNIONS,

THOSE GREAT MORAL ENGINES, WHICH, BY CONCENTRATING

PUBLIC FEELING, SENTIMENT, AND ENERGY,

HAVE CONTRIBUTED TO

PRODUCE SUCH GLORIOUS RESULTS THROUGHOUT THE COUNTRY,

THESE PAGES ARE VERY RESPECTFULLY DEDICATED,

BY HIS FRIEND

AND ZEALOUS WELL-WISHER,

THE AUTHOR.

PREFACE.

LENGTHY prefaces, like lengthy parliaments, are now happily out of favour: if the reader is to be introduced to any thing worthy his notice, why detain him on the threshold? if not, 'tis but needlessly adding to his labour and disappointment.

I had once thought of offering apology for *not going earlier to press,* when it occurred to me that some complaisant critic or other might obligingly submit to me (young authors aforetime *have* known them as much concerned for their welfare) whether it would not have been better *to have dispensed with the ceremony altogether;* and thus, at one gentle flourish of his pen, have reduced my solicitude on this head to a mere dead letter. In other designs, surmises, and anticipations, I was but little more happy, until, at length, I have determined to abide steadfastly by the old adage, " the least said, the soonest mended ;" and a few more prefatory words shall suffice me.

The subsequent pages—as much of them at least as I lay claim to—were originally written, on a hasty Tour, for my own satisfaction and reference, and that of a limited circle of friends who felt interested in my proceedings ; but others, whose judgment and candour I appreciate, having expressed some gratification in the perusal of them, and numerous inquiries having been addressed to me, particularly upon the subject of agriculture and the prospects for emigrants in the State of New York, as also respecting our shipwreck,—in the hope that what I relate may not be found wholly devoid of interest or utility, I have been induced, with little correction or revision, to offer it, such as it is, to the public. This only recommendation I wish to advance in its favour:—It is presented by one who, to the extent of his opportunities, has endeavoured to investigate for himself,—who has no private or party feelings to gratify,—no smiles of patronage to court, or frowns to dread,—one who, in short, as he would scorn the meanness, has no earthly interest or motive to stoop to imposition, or in representing things otherwise than as they really are.

J. F.

ERRATA.

In a few copies of this edition will be found the following errors:—
Page 110, line 11, for attended *with*, read attended *by*.
  112, — 17, for *venemous*, read *venomous*.
  152. — 14, for *levelled*, read *leveller*.
  166, — 10, for bears resemblance, read bears *any* resemblance.
  172, — 4, for *then* disappeared, read *there* disappeared.
  182, — 18 and 20. for usual *time* are as *follows*, read usual *times* are as
                    follow.
  235. — 24, for getting under *way*. read *weigh*.
  252, — 22, for *Ponte* del Gada, read *Ponta* —and wherever it occurs after-
                    wards.

JOURNAL, &c.

VOYAGE TO NEW YORK.

June 24th, 1830.—Having for some time past been meditating a trip across the Atlantic, and circumstances at the present moment seeming rather to conspire to favour the project, about twelve o'clock this day I put myself on board the packet-ship York, Captain Thompson, bound from Liverpool to New York, with seven cabin and seven steerage passengers. Before clearing the river we were taken in tow by a steam-boat, which continued with us to the Floating Light, (a light ship moored about fifteen miles from Liverpool,) when the wind got more easterly, and we made good progress through the night.

25th.—Little worthy of remark. Those never afloat before, sick in their berths, and those who have, being yet without their *sea legs*, staggering about the deck in a way that *must* be tolerated here, but would not be thought over creditable on land; the vessel herself scarcely in proper trim, and all things bespeaking a recent departure from port, not omitting the intolerable *bilge water*, which drives me out of the cabin altogether. Light wind from the S.E.

26th.—At three, this morning, I was awoke, or
rather aroused, by the sound of very heavy rain. Went
on deck and found it pouring almost in torrents,
accompanied with thunder. The storm lasted little
more than an hour, when the sun arose in cloudless
beauty, and a gentle breeze from the S. carried us
along at the rate of four or five knots for the remainder of the day. A circumstance occurred which occasioned some amusement. One of the sailors, happening
to descend the hatchway, was not a little surprised
to observe a pair of legs obtruding from amongst the
packages, and judging they must have an owner, he
began to make investigation accordingly; but it was
not until some time had elapsed, and they had sustained a repetition of pretty harsh usage, that any
one could be found willing to assert proprietorship
over them. At length the owner erected himself, and,
after *examination had,* he turned out to be an Irish
ship-carpenter, who, on the morning of our leaving
Liverpool, having a disposition to visit New York,
and it being somewhat inconvenient to him to
make the necessary disbursements, had contrived to
stow himself away, as mentioned, and had thus remained about two days without food of any description, if I except the sailors' specific,—grog, a bottle
of which he had provided himself with before his con-
cealment; had he not been discovered he says it was
his intention to have kept below until he thought we
were about half seas over, when we surely could not
have refused to carry him through. He appears one
of those stupid, half-witted fellows to whom a change

of country can prove but of slight advantage, and
Captain Thompson has thrown a sad damp upon his
prospects by telling him that he will put him upon
the first homeward-bound vessel we can speak that
will take charge of him, so that it is questionable
even yet if Paddy effect his passage.

27th.—Passed three American ships, supposed bound
to Liverpool, but without speaking any of them; the
wind chopping about all day, occasionally carrying
us nine or ten knots, and as often not more than two.

28th.—The night has been stormy. Wind this morning N.W., making very poor way. We, however, consider ourselves clear of the Channel, and are beginning
to experience the fine bold swell of the Atlantic. Few
of the passengers have yet settled matters with their
stomachs, and appear on deck (those who come at
all) with most ghastly visages. Amongst those in the
cabin we have an elderly lady, sixty-four years of age,
whose only son, if not only surviving relative, has been
settled in America about fourteen years, and with
whom she is now going to close her days. She comes
from near Nottingham, and, though she has never
been at sea before, bears the voyage admirably, and
out of four, is quite the best lady passenger on board.
On my anticipating the pleasure she would derive
from meeting her son again, the tears started into her
eyes, and she replied, "Oh, Sir, if I did not feel it
beyond expression, do you think I could have been
induced, at my time of life, and all alone, to have
taken such a journey as this, and when we reach New
York I shall then have 700 miles to travel, but there

my boy will meet me, and——" She could proceed
no farther.   Heaven grant her the realization of every
hope which animates her aged breast.

We have not averaged to-day more than five knots,
and that a point or two out of our course: 'tis well we
are out of the Channel, or with the wind as it is, and
blowing fresh, we could make no way at all. Crept into
my berth about eleven o'clock.   Let not the landsman
suppose this getting into a comfortable bed for a night
of undisturbed repose; 'tis quite another thing I
assure him: but let him fancy a small room (though
called a *State Room*) some three feet by six, and six
feet high, in which are placed, one above the other,
two tolerable-sized kneeding troughs, and he will then
have as good an idea as is necessary of a dormitory
at sea.   This said berth is not boarded at the bottom,
(would it were,) but made in the ordinary way with
sacking, only braced down the middle instead of the
sides, leaving, when at all relaxed, a most comfortless
hollow in that part, into which, of course, you roll
immediately you enter, and, except when the lurching
of the ship throws you for a moment upon the side,
must there remain until you turn out altogether; probably, if you happen to occupy the lower berth, with
the over-workings of some uneasy stomach incon-
veniencing you from above.   At any rate there is the
incessant dashing of the waves close to your head,
—the noise of the helm, trampling on deck, and many
et ceteras to break in upon sound slumber.   When
you rise, if shaving be the first operation, and the
motion of the vessel considerable, it may probably be

about half an hour before you can accomplish it, chiefly by holding on with one hand whilst using the razor with the other, and you may consider yourself pretty fortunate if the floor of your apartment be not swimming with the contents of sundries capsized in the interim. This is perhaps rather the worst side of the picture, though most "that go down to the sea in ships" have to pass through it; in fact, to a landsman, from beginning to end, 'tis no place of comfort : it may be *endured* we know, and so may a prison ; and often have I thought, with Johnson, if there be a choice of evils, the latter has it.

29*th.*—Very little wind from the S.W. Spoke an Irish brig bound to Belfast. Paddy escapes transfer. The ship Ganges, of Philadelphia, which left Liverpool with us, and of which we have generally kept ahead, passed us this morning : her cargo is light, whilst ours, I believe, is the heaviest ever conveyed by any packet from Liverpool to New York; consequently, with light winds, she beats us, and, *vice versâ,* when blowing fresh, we beat her, being able to carry more sail. About noon, the wind got more in our favour, and, until the evening of the following day, we made our course at the rate of six or eight knots. It then changed right ahead, and at night increased to a gale.

July 1*st.*—This morning it blows tremendously, and just as unfavourably, rather increasing than diminishing throughout the day and night.

2*nd.*—4 *a. m.* The storm still rages furiously and rolls us about, as if, at times, it were ready to roll us over, to the no small discomfiture of the lady part

of our cargo, who I can perceive would gladly exchange their present situation for very humble accommodation on land, and no wonder; the sea, in a storm,
and to be upon it, (herein consists all the difference,)
may well excite apprehension in the female mind.
I have seen some of the other sex unable to contemplate it with any great degree of composure, and the
satisfaction of being on a good seaworthy vessel is
sensibly felt by all.   Let none ever be induced, from
the consideration of a trifling saving of expense, or
any other motive, to cross the Atlantic in one which
has not been recommended to them by those on whose
judgment, and sincerity too, (for the deceptions practised upon the ignorant by the charterers of vessels
are infamous,) they can fully rely.   The hazards and
privations of sailors are enough, at any rate, without
adding to the list of evils a crazy or even suspicious
barque.   At noon it began to moderate, and before
night the wind nearly died away.

   3rd.—Strange contrast.   This morning we are
becalmed, and the same ocean which yesterday was
rearing its waves around us, and drenching us with
its yeasty spray, is now, excepting a long swell at
intervals, as quiescent as a lake, and without a ripple
breaking its surface.   It is also much warmer, though
accompanied with an unpleasant drizzling rain.   Took
breakfast at the cabin table, for the first time since
coming on board, the smell (stench) of the *bilge water,*
now beginning to subside, having hitherto induced
me greatly to prefer the deck.   Fare excellent.   Tea,
coffee, boiled ham and eggs, anchovies, pickled shad,

cold tongue and other meat, bread, of the finest American flour, baked fresh every day, biscuits, &c. &c· The hours for meals are :—Breakfast, at eight ; lunch, at twelve ; dinner, at three ; tea, coffee, or supper, just to your choice, at eight. We have a cow on board, which furnishes an abundant supply of milk ; four or five fine sheep ; half a dozen small pigs; some geese, and ducks and fowls unnumbered. Poultry, however, soon become very poor stuff at sea. I know of no animals which do not suffer by sailing excepting pigs; they appear to thrive quite as well as on land. Our wines and spirits are first rate, champaign especially ; ale and London porter equally good, and all supplied unsparingly. In short, whoever could find in his heart to desire more after this fashion, than is furnished in the New York packets, deserves to be treated to a bread and water diet for the remainder of his days; though, as one not estimating these matters over highly, I still hold there are drawbacks enough to counterbalance all the good recorded, and I could partake of less sumptuous fare on land with a far keener relish. Tastes, however, vary ; and I know those, whom I verily believe, without further induce-ment by this admirable bill of fare, might be tempted across the Atlantic. I once saw a little Scotchman under similar circumstances, who, had the voyage continued as many months as it did weeks, would surely not long have survived it. Throughout the twenty-four hours there was scarcely a successive five minutes that he did not occupy either in eating, drinking, or sleeping, and, to do him justice, never did I see so

many good things so unprofitably bestowed. John
Abernethy would at once have called him a "perfect
beast." Rain all day.

4th.—During the night a breeze has sprung up just
from the quarter we would not have had it, and it is
again blowing fresh. Spoke an English brig bound
for Liverpool. This is the anniversary of the American declaration of independence, the signing of
which memorable deed took place on the 4th July,
1776, and is consequently fifty-four years ago. Libe-
rated the cork of an extra bottle of champaign upon
the occasion.

5th.—Rain all night. Wind from the same quarter
(N. W.) Spoke a brig from New Orleans, bound to
Hamburgh.

6th.—The finest day since leaving port, though
nearly becalmed. Fell into chat with an intelligent
person from the Sister Isle. Amongst other things he
tells me that the quality of *flax* is much deteriorating
in Ireland, in consequence of the farmers having got
into the habit of using lime to their land, which they
were not formerly accustomed to do ; and that now
nearly all their finest flax comes from Holland. I
know nothing myself of the matter, but if it be so,
it is worthy of notice. A beautiful evening. Some
of our party on deck; I believe for the first time since
putting to sea.

7th.—After a fine morning, about noon it came on
to rain, and blow fresh ; and this evening we are
going near ten knots :—great work with our weight
of lading.

8th.—It has rained all night; but the wind has been favourable, and continues easterly this morning. We hope to have made one-third of our way. Evening, quite a gale ; scudding with close-reefed sails ; most unseasonable weather ; far more like March or November than July. I pity the poor farmers in England if it be no better with them.

9th.—Wind still favourable (N. N. E. ;) but excessively cold.

10th to 13th.—Wind got more ahead, and we made but little progress. The past has been a tempestuous night; the ship rolling and pitching so that we could scarcely keep in our berths. Capt. T. remarks that latterly his summer have been much more boisterous and unpleasant than his winter voyages. Have had our lower studding-sail-boom carried away. What little way we are making is quite out of our course.

14th.—Wind still ahead, but more moderate ; and the sea gone down considerably. So far an improvement upon yesterday, when we were pitched about, lumber-like, and to no purpose. Have discovered, partly by accident, that our mainyard has been seriously injured, in fact, nearly broken through by the gale; had it given way during its continuance, the loss of the mainsail would have been inevitable, with, probably, much other damage. All hands busily employed in rigging out another ; and this evening, by dint of great exertion, we have hoisted it aloft, and attached the sail to it as before. We now only wait a fair wind.

15th.—Rain all night. Wind dead ahead. Three weeks out to-day.

16th.—Wind turning a trifle in our favour, and doing something better than standing still, which is more than we have been able to say for several days past. Took a bath this morning, (a luxury I have much missed since coming on board,) by getting over the bows of the vessel, and stationing one of the men aloft, whilst another supplied him with water, *fresh from the ocean*, to shower upon me; no finer *sea bathing* could be desired, though I seem to be the only one manifesting the least partiality for it. We have had a drizzling rain, or rather very dense fog, through the day, a kind of weather generally experienced about the banks of Newfoundland, which we are now nearly approaching, our latitude being 43½, and longitude 45. This evening the wind ahead again.

17th. Morning. Wind ahead and enveloped in fog. Spoke a very fine brig, the Mary, from Baltimore ; could not learn distinctly where she was bound. Evening. Wind a little more to the south; going about six knots.

18th.—Still a dense fog, which obliges us to keep a sharp look-out for sails, and also for ice-bergs, frequently met with here at this season of the year, of prodigious size, to the destruction of many vessels The packet-ship, *Liverpool,* a few years ago, on her first voyage, or intended voyage to Liverpool from New York, struck upon one of them at mid-day, and went down in fifteen minutes ; the crew and all saved by taking to the boats, and landed at Newfoundland, from whence they returned to New York. Made several attempts to obtain soundings, but without success. Vivid and incessant lightning from eight in the evening till after midnight.

19*th*.--Wind S. W. by W.; as adverse as it can blow. Fog, with occasional heavy rain. Have not had an observation for days; but find a bottom with a line of forty-three fathoms, and consider ourselves about the middle of the banks. Twelve *p. m.* nearly a calm, and very vivid lightning again.

20*th.*—Wind this morning from the E. N. E. though so light as to be of little service to us. It has, however, pretty much dispelled the fog, and rendered it more agreeable in that respect. Passed a number of brigs, &c., chiefly French, engaged in fishing. The season commences in April, and ends in November, in which time the quantity taken is incredible. We have been trying to hook one, but as we are going two or three knots, of course, stand but little chance.

21*st.*—Just off the banks, and nearly becalmed; otherwise a charming day. One of the finest I ever passed at sea. The sky perfectly cloudless, and the horizon singularly clear and distinct, so as we rarely— never—see it in England. It is indeed a most welcome change after the wretched *Bank weather* we have been groping through, and has not failed to produce a very sensible effect upon the animal spirits of every living thing on board, as something, however, too fair to last, towards evening, clouds and squalls succeed; the wind ahead; and to-night we are tossed about just after the old fashion.

22nd.—Stormy. Wind ahead. As great a contrast to yesterday as is well possible.

23rd.—Finer. And the wind so that we have made a tolerable *slant* throughout the day.

24th.—After noon we had a brisk wind from the east, carrying us eight knots, which towards evening increased to ten or eleven. About ten o'clock it began to rain very heavily, and became excessively dark. An hour afterwards, on a sudden, the wind chopped round to the west, and commenced blowing furiously from that quarter; had but just time to get the sails in ere it turned us end for end. Rain all night.

25th.—Morning. Wind ahead. Evening more northerly, and very cold. Making pretty good way.

26th.—After two o'clock this morning a famous breeze sprung up from the N.E.: going nine or ten knots. About three days, at this rate, would land us at New York, but I am scarcely sanguine enough to anticipate such unwonted despatch. I hope, at all events, our voyaging may terminate with the month, though, considering the winds and weather we have had, so far from having any thing to complain of, the wonder is how we have got on so well. Our ponderous cargo, too, has been against us.

27th.—Had a good wind until noon to-day, when it became completely calm, so incessant and sudden are the changes at sea, the more so on approaching land, and our latitude to-day being 41° 5′, and longitude 66°, leaves us about 320 miles to run to our destined port. A shark was playing round us for an hour or two in the morning, apparently about ten

feet in length. Shortly before observing him, myself
and another had been talking of a bathe; a performance we were well satisfied to dispense with afterwards. A shark, in seizing its prey, has to turn on
its side, the under jaw being so much shorter than the
upper one, as to prevent it taking it in the ordinary
position in which it swims.—Evening. Wind from
N.W. making five to seven knots.

28th.—Very foggy. In the midst of the Nantucket
shoals. Soundings at thirty-three fathoms. Mates
and crew busily employed in painting, scraping, and
scouring the ship; repairing and blacking the rigging,
&c.; getting all in the trimmest possible order to
enter port. Passed very near one of the *Havre* packets.
Should doubtless, now, discover many vessels if the
atmosphere were clearer.

29th.—Still foggy. Fair wind from the E. Have
been out five weeks to-day. Got an imperfect observation, by which we suppose ourselves nearly in the
latitude of New York, and are, consequently, steering
due west. Spoke a brig from Portland bound to the
West Indies.

30th.—A gale from the S.E. all night, which has
been sending us along at the rate of nine or ten knots,
but, as an abatement to so much good luck, has
deprived us of our foretopsail, shivering it to pieces.
Surely such *summer* weather was never seen before! Men aloft diligently on the look-out for land,
but the horizon is so thick that we may be almost
close upon it ere we can discover it, and unless it
clear up, shall soon be obliged to *lay to.* Nine

o'clock : it has become clearer, and one of the mates from aloft has just sung out, " *Land O !*"   Thrice welcome sound !   It is, doubtless, some part of Long Island, and thus satisfied, we are crowding all the sail we can.

Evening.—At length riding safely at anchor within *Sandy Hook*, sixteen miles from New York, so that we may fully anticipate a termination of our voyage to-morrow.   About two hours before we anchored two boats came alongside of us, the one for the letter-bag, the other for the newspapers for the different reading rooms.   Their first inquiries were after the health of our *most gracious Majesty*, whom we could only report alive when we left; more, I imagine, than the next packet will be able to do. Shortly after despatching these boats, a pilot boarded us.   It is the finest evening we have had for long, so that we have distinctly seen them sending up rockets from the Castle Gardens in New York, the scene of nightly displays of fire-works, I am told, during the summer months, and a very favourite resort for the fashionables of the city.   Most of our party making merry with champaign, rejoiced at the coming prospect.

31st.—A brilliant morning, but no wind.   Are beginning to feel it very warm.   The pilot reports it the hottest summer they have had since the year 1822, for some days the thermometer in the shade having stood at 93°;—appalling intelligence after the temperature we have been exposed to for the last five weeks, muffled up in top-coats and cloaks, and shivering even then, and now finding our lightest summer attire almost oppressive.—Scarcely a breath of air until four o'clock, when we had just enough to put us in motion for the city, the approach to which is very fine, heightened by the beauty of the day and the extreme clearness of the atmosphere. The shores on each side, though a good deal wooded, have, nevertheless, a rich and cultivated appearance, often ornamented with a handsome villa, and every where well guarded with fortifications. Governor's Island, nearer the city, also a military station, is a beautiful object, and soon the Battery, Castle Gardens, many of the churches and public buildings, and Brooklyn on the heights, with crouds of shipping in the Bay, arrest the attention, and cannot fail to excite deep interest in the mind of a stranger; but I was withdrawn from the contemplation of this imposing scene to be introduced to one still more agreeable: two of my friends, having observed our approach, had come off in a boat to give me a welcome to their shores, which I was within a little of reaching before they knew any thing of my intention of visiting them, the ship by which I had been *advised of* having only arrived on the preceding day, though it had the start of us from Liverpool nearly a week. Mutual congratulations exchanged, I accompanied them ashore, and shortly after crossed the river to the residence of a friend in Brooklyn, situated immediately opposite to New York. Upon ascending the elevation on which it is partly built, I was much struck with the fineness and extent of the view which it commanded, embracing the whole of

the city, the bay, the vessels in the East River, as it
is termed, (though more properly I should think a
strait or *sound,*) Governor's and other Islands, the
Highlands of the Hudson, as well as the shores of New
Jersey. The houses in the principal streets have a
particularly neat and elegant appearance: they are
chiefly built of wood, and painted white, with green
latticed blinds on the outside; and most of them I
observe are furnished with conductors. For the entire
length of some of the streets, weeping willows are
planted on each side, which, independent of being
very ornamental, afford a delightful shade to the
fronts of the houses, and protect the foot-paths even
from a noon-day sun. It was late before I returned
to the city, which I had engaged to do with a friend,
who had taken up his quarters at a boarding-house
(seemingly more in fashion here than hotels) in V——
W.-street; but I am sorry to say it proved much too
early for my comfort, having scarcely retired to bed
ere I found myself assailed by those most loathsome
of nocturnal annoyances, bugs, and have arisen this
morning, (1*st August)* with one of my organs of vision
nearly closed, besides divers other injuries, altogether
a very pretty figure to make my *début* in a foreign
city. Madame hostess, however, promises another
room to-night, and strict search during the day, so
I try my luck once more.—Chiefly in-doors, and
little to remark.

2*nd.*—Of the past night I shall only observe that it,
was infinitely worse than its predecessor, the vile
vermin compelling me to effect a precipitate retreat

from my apartment, and indeed from the domicile altogether, into the street, before one o'clock this morning ; and what, with the loss of two entire nights' rest, and being swelled and inflamed from head to foot, into the bargain, I feel now as good for nothing as, under such circumstances, I may well be supposed to do. But enough—'tis as poor a subject for others as myself.—This being the first business day since my landing, my first business upon it was to obtain a permit from the Custom-house to bring my luggage ashore, for which article I was charged 20 cents. The officers here, since the *tariff* came so extensively into operation, are more precise and troublesome than in England, first obliging you to swear, or affirm, to the contents of your packages, and afterwards subjecting them to as scrupulous a search as if no such ceremony had been exacted.—Found the passengers, officers, and crew of our vessel, natives as well as strangers, complaining grievously of the heat of the weather, though the thermometer in the shade was scarcely standing at 80° ; but the contrast between that and 58° and 60°; which we had it for the chief part of our passage, is too considerable to accommodate one's-self to, very agreeably, at so short a notice.

Dined with my friends at Brooklyn, and, after my two nights' experience of the state of things in the city, and an assurance that I might go elsewhere and fare no better, was well satisfied to accept of their very pressing invitation to continue where I was, and pre-serve what remained to me of my English blood, for some worthier opportunity and assailants.

3rd.—Rose this morning vastly refreshed, and feeling myself again. In the course of the day made a pretty extensive perambulation of the city, of which, however, I shall not, at present, attempt any description ; as a whole I was highly pleased with it. The City-hall and the Exchange are indeed noble edifices. Many of the banks, hotels, and other public places, are very spacious and elegant; and the Battery, Castle Gardens, Broadway, &c., are well worthy the admiration they so generally excite ; but, as a striking defect, I noticed a great want of uniformity in the building of the houses, and, in the business streets particularly, of a total inattention to neatness, if I may not add cleanliness. At a future opportunity, and upon further acquaintance, will return to the subject again, and offer a somewhat more respectful notice of this great city.—Revisited Brooklyn in the evening, of which, the more I see, the more I admire it. It is nothing less than a charming situation, interesting in itself, and so completely removed from the noise, dust, and bustle of the town, and yet through the medium of the steam-boats regularly crossing the river every five minutes during the day, seeming to possess every advantage of a residence in it. Its present population amounts to 15,000, but it is very rapidly increasing, and will, no doubt, continue to do so, many of the principal merchants, &c. now giving it a decided preference to the upper parts of the city. After a day spent there, what a luxury to ascend its beautiful heights, inhale the fresh and pure breezes from the water, and feast the eye with all the varied attractions which the scene unfolds! I have found it so, at least, ere yet I have scarcely known it. Much of the land in the neighbourhood of Brooklyn appears to be devoted to the raising of fruits and vegetables for its own and the New York markets; prodigious quantities of which are taken across the water daily, as, also, from other parts of the island. I have counted eleven waggons driven off one steam-boat at a time; and a friend, who was with me, told me there were frequently more. It is besides a place of considerable trade; contains tanneries, distilleries, cotton and linen cloth manufactories, rope-walks, market-houses, and a great number of stores, warehouses, &c. There are several places of worship, a Lancasterian school, and other very respectable seminaries.—Thermometer at noon to day 81°. A thunder-storm in the evening, which greatly relieved the air. Night temperate and pleasant.

4th.—Previous to setting out on my intended excursion to the western part of the state, wishing to see something of Long Island, and having given a relative, resident near Flushing, a promise of spending a few days with him, took my place this afternoon upon a steam-boat, plying daily to different parts of of the Sound, to *Whitestone*, about eighteen miles distant from New York. We had a pretty numerous party on board. The day was beautiful, and the scenery along the banks of the river of a very interesting character. About midway between New York and Whitestone we passed by Horll Gatt, or Hurl Gate, (by some even less respectfully designated) a narrow, crooked, and dangerous strait, occasioned by huge projecting rocks, which very much contract the bed of the river, and produce tremendous whirlpools and eddies, formerly to the loss of many vessels which attempted the passage, though no accident of the kind has recently occurred, the navigation being better understood : to strangers, however, it has still rather a formidable appearance. At high water the rocks are nearly covered, and the current but little ruffled.

On arriving at Whitestone, a mere landing, I was met by a conveyance, which my friend had kindly despatched for me, and soon set down at his abode.—W—— left England about ten years ago, married into one of the most respectable families on the island, purchased a nice farm, and is now settled in the midst of his wife's relations, and surrounded by as fine a little group of his own as I have often seen ; doubtless as happy as such a pleasing combination of circumstances can render him, and assuring me, that, if an estate in England were left to him, he would not cross the Atlantic again to take possession of it. I know not, indeed, wherein would consist the inducement.

In the morning, the *5th*, I accompanied him over his farm, which comprises near two hundred acres of land, with an excellent house, outbuildings, &c. The quality of the soil, like most in the island, is rather light, but, with the aid of manure, produces excellent crops of all descriptions of grain and various kinds of fruit. He has a beautiful young peach orchard, containing one thousand trees, now loaded with fruit,

selling in New York market, at from a dollar to a dollar
and a half per bushel; twenty or thirty acres occupied with apples, which thrive remarkably well, and
are worth two dollars per barrel, of two bushels and a
half. There are nearly fifty acres of woodland upon
the farm, in which I observed a good deal of fine
timber of different sorts, viz. the common, the white,
and the red oaks, cedar, hickory, sassafras, birch,
chesnut, and locust; the latter a wood much in request, and sells from sixty cents to a dollar per foot.
W—— has taken considerable pains with his stock,
and has a fine breed of cows, sheep, and pigs, with
some very handsome and valuable young horses:—
quite entered into the spirit of farming.

The morning was very sultry, and whilst walking we
remarked an unusual heat in the ground, so much so as
when off the turf to be quite unpleasant to the feet.
About mid-day it began to cloud over, became exceedingly dark, and a thunder-storm succeeded, which,
whilst it lasted, was a complete *tornado*, more violent,
W—— tells me, than he has known for years. It
has done great damage amongst the fruit and other
trees in the neighbourhood, torn some large ones up
by the roots, and broken almost every branch off
others. In half an hour after it was over the sun broke
out again as bright as ever, and, though it rained very
heavily during the storm, upon going out the only remaining moisture I could perceive was upon the leaves
of a few Swedish turnips which were growing in the
garden. So essential to vegetation are frequent
showers in this island in the hot months. In a dry

summer they suffer much.—As a thing which has attracted my attention since coming into the country, I
may notice the endless variety of the insect tribe with
which the creation every where teems, many of them
unknown in England, and generally too insignificant
to occasion inconvenience.   Omitting bugs, to be met
with in most countries and horrible every where, the
most troublesome on the list is the musqueto, much
resembling our gnat, only larger, but the bite of
which is venomous in the extreme; and even if you
can manage to keep them off by day, their perpetual
buzzing around you is very annoying ; and at night,
unless you envelop yourself or the entire of your bed
in a net, and exclude all light from the apartment,
you are tormented with them beyond measure ; and
what with locusts, crickets, tree-toads, kater-dids,
grasshoppers, &c. &c., the din and bustle of the
country, though of a very different kind, seems
scarcely less than that of the town, and strikes by no
means agreeably, as contrasted with the melody of the
feathered choir in England, scarcely one of which
has any note in America.   'Tis true, the winter effectually suppresses the nuisance, a remedy, you will
say, as bad as the disease; and a stranger might
deem it unworthy of notice at any time, but let him
make his first landing here in the month of July or
August, and I will venture to say, unless he be both
deaf and invulnerable, he does not pronounce it so
afterwards.

6th.—Much of this and the succeeding day were
occupied in visiting farms in the neighbourhood, and

in making such memorandums on agricultural subjects, as appeared to me most interesting ; briefly as
follows :—First stating that Long Island (called also
Nassau Island) belongs to the state of New York;
that it is about 115 miles long from east to west, and
20 broad; that is, at its greatest breadth, not averaging
more than ten. It is bounded on the south by the
Atlantic, and on the north by Long Island Sound,
which separates it from the continent. Its eastern
extermity terminates in a point, and westward it extends into the *Narrows*, about eight miles below New
York. It is divided into three counties, King's
County, (the longest settled, I believe, in the state,)
Queen's County, and Suffolk County, the latter extending over two-thirds of the island.—The character
of the land in Long Island is very various ; but the
north side of it, for twenty or thirty miles up, comprises the best. Farms in this part are to be purchased
at from forty to one hundred dollars per acre, according to buildings and improvements upon them, &c.
To the south the soil is very sandy, and, in some parts,
not worth cultivation. The east is very much overgrown with pine forests.—Indian corn appears to be
considered the staple article of produce, yielding
from 25 to 50 bushels (of 56 lbs) per acre, and worth
from 50 to 60 cents per bushel. Wheat may average
20 bushels (of 61 lbs.) per acre, and the price 1 dollar.
Oats, 30 bushels, (of 30 lbs.) price 37½ cents. Barley,
25 bushels, (of 52 lbs.) price 62½ cents. Rye, 20
bushels, price 62½ cents. Clover seed not gathered.
Hay, from 30 to 40 cwt, per acre, price 8 to 10 dollars

per ton. Potatoes and turnips, much as in England, the price of the former 37½ cents per bushel; the latter not much grown for cattle. Horses, for farming purposes, are worth from 60 to 75 dollars; fancy horses, from 130 to 400 dollars. Milch cows, from 15 to 40 dollars. Sheep, (fat) 2 dollars; store sheep, 1 dollar. Pigs, (fed) 5 dollars per 100 lbs. weight. Beef, by the carcase, from 6 to 8 dollars per 100 lbs. hide and tallow given in. Butter usually sells for about 18 cents the lb.; no cheese made. Turkeys are worth 1 dollar. Geese, 50 to 75 cents. Ducks, the couple, 75 cents. Fowls, 62½ cents. Eggs, 12 cents per dozen; apples and peaches, already noticed, with melons, strawberries, cherries, and currants, are produced in abundance, and sold at remunerating prices.

The natural grasses of the island seldom grow stout enough to mow, but the artificial ones thrive well, and will average from 25 to 30 cwt. for four years, though, of course, this is much dependant upon the dryness or wetness of the season. Manure, or ashes, are every where requisite, and much used: a plentiful supply obtained from New York: the ultimate cost on the land about twenty dollars per acre. The salt marshes also, and frequent inlets from the sound, afford great quantities of marine vegetable manure, the salt grass being of little value for other purposes. Fallowing is not much practised. The land tilled about equally by horses and oxen.

The price given to farming men through the summer season (say for eight months) is from eight to twelve dollars per month; in the winter from four to six dollars per month, always boarding them,—the invariable practice throughout the country. Women, five dollars per month, the year round, and board. The usual hours of labour are from sun-rise to sun-set.

The most general kind of fencing is stone walls, the erection of which cost about 125 cents the rod; some have a stone foot, with post and rails above, raised at rather less expense.

The roads in the island, though a little too sandy, may, upon the whole, be considered good. The cost of repairing them to the farmer about five or six dollars to every hundred acres of land he occupies.

There are very ready conveyances to New York both by land and water,* principally by steam-boats: passage for a person 25 cents; freight for fruit, grain, &c. 3 cents per bushel. The expense of carting by land, (a load of hay, &c.) when a team and man are hired for the purpose, is one dollar and a half.

One great advantage attaching to Long Island, or the west end of it, as a situation for farming, is its contiguity to New York, in consequence of which it is always furnished with a superior market for its various productions, particularly butter, fruit, and vegetables; and oftentimes, in the blockade of winter,

* When I say by land, I mean, of course, to Brooklyn, at which place the sound, or river, is only three-quarters of a mile in width, and where, by means of floating slips, horses and carriages are driven without any difficulty upon the steam-boats, and conveyed across, in a few minutes, with as much facility as if upon a bridge. How is it that we do not adopt a similar plan at many of our ferries, where it could be used with so much advantage? At Runcorn, above Liverpool, for instance.

articles of bulk and weight may be conveyed to the
city, when, from the difficulty and expense of carriage,
they are prohibited from places more remote; wood,
potatoes, hay, and straw, upon these occasions, will
frequently return the farmer a profit of fifty or even a
hundred per cent.

There is a considerable quantity of game, &c. on
the island, (though decreasing,) consisting of quail,
some partridge, woodcocks, snipe, and rabbits, and,
at seasons, wild ducks innumerable; in the forests to
the east, deer are also found. The bays, with which
the island is much indented, abound with varieties of
excellent fish.

Upon the whole I should be inclined to say that
Long Island is rather a situation for an opulent farmer
than for one of limited means. The land, in the first
place, is much dearer than in other parts of the state,
and, in addition, it is cultivated at a greater expense.
Retired, or half-retired merchants are, therefore, commonly to be found amongst the proprietors, a class of
persons farming about as much for amusement as
profit, and, as " the old coachman loves the smack of
the whip," whenever they feel a taste for business, or
the city, they are, at any moment, ready to step
into it.

The island, for the most part, is considered healthy,
though the fever and ague is, by no means, unknown.

The day of my last date (7th August) has been the
hottest since my landing. Thermometer 85° in the
shade.

Took a boat for an hour or two's fishing in one of

the bays, though without any success as far as re
garded our own efforts, but boarding a smack we
hooked out of her well a number of fine *black fish*,
and, at the expense of a dollar or so, returned well
laden to the gentleman's from whose house we started,
and to his no small surprise, until we discovered the
manœuvre we had been practising ; though the fishing
here is often very good. The master of the smack
told us that he had about 1800 then in his well,
weighing from half a pound to five and six pounds
apiece. Lobsters are caught in great plenty, and
have been taken of the extraordinary weight of
twenty-five pounds each ! I myself saw the *claw* of
one which, when fresh, I am satisfied would have
weighed from seven to nine pounds.

Upon returning to W——'s in the evening I was
presented with a New York paper in which I was not
surprised to read as follows:—"The packet-ship Manchester, Captain Sketchley, from Liverpool, arrived
in town yesterday morning, bringing advices of that
long-anticipated event, the decease of his Majesty
George the Fourth. The bulletin issued on the occasion was as follows:—'Windsor Castle, 26th June,
1830. It has pleased Almighty God to take from
this world the King's most excellent Majesty. His
Majesty expired at a quarter-past three o'clock this
morning without pain. (Signed) H. Halford,—Mat-
thew John Tierney.' His Majesty was born 12th
August, 1762, and was consequently in the 68th year
of his age ; ascended the throne 29th January, 1820,
crowned 19th July, 1821, and died 26th June, 1830.

The Duke of Clarence immediately took the oaths of office as William the Fourth. He was born 23d August, 1765."——So for the present ends the career of the Georges!

8th.—Have felt the night oppressive; but which I attribute, in part, to sleeping with closed windows, (a thing, summer or winter, I scarce ever practise,) to exclude my musqueto enemies.

In the morning rode with —————— to Flushing *village;* in our way to which we called at ——————, the finest establishment I have seen in the island, and conveying every idea of comfort and independence. The house is built of wood, and, after the fashion here, has a spacious entrance hall, with the door at the side, which admits of windows along that part, and besides the outer door, mostly open, there are also latticed doors at each end. The floor is very neatly matted, and the hall, throughout, furnished pretty much as a parlour, with sofas, settees, &c. It is, beyond any comparison, the pleasantest summer room in the house. I know not why this style of building should not be more frequently adopted in England; it will by me, however, whenever I turn house builder. Here the effects of the *tornado,* mentioned on the 5th, were but too sadly apparent, and besides other damage we found the family much regretting, as well they might, the loss of a most beautiful weeping willow, which grew near the house, every branch of which had been stripped, and the bare stump only left standing.

Flushing is a neat, lively village, at the head

of the bay, containing a number of good houses, stores, some excellent hotels, and several places of worship. Dr. Spafford, in his *Gazeteer of the State of New York* thus refers to it:—" Within a few years the fashionables of the metropolis have made Flushing, which, indeed, has many attractions, quite a place of resort for the butterflies of fashion, at least for a part of the year, and it has, of course, genteel accommodations, and receives, for its day, many high encomiums on the pleasure of a trip to Flushing, the town, the bay and harbour, so like ' Venice and its bay.' But 'the fashions of this world pass away;' and I hope this resort may not make Flushing *too much like Venice,* before it take some other direction."

Under the same head is also the following notice:—"In this town (township) are still remaining two white oaks, which, with others long since destroyed, formed a shade, under which George Fox held a religious meeting in the year 1672. It is well known that George Fox was the founder of the sect of Friends, or Quakers, and that they erect no monuments to perpetuate remembrance. The Quakers, therefore, regard these trees with lively interest, and see in them all that monuments could teach, however splendid or costly."

Returned to W——'s to dine; soon after which, with many obliging regrets at the shortness of my stay, I again took my departure to Flushing, to meet the New York steam-boat. Varying the morning's route a little, we passed by what is considered, I believe, the most complete farm upon the island. It consists of two hundred acres of land, a very superior house, a good farm-house, and excellent outbuildings, being also well fenced, and in a high state of cultivation. It cost the original proprietor 75,000 dollars, and has lately been sold for 30,000 dollars. It is, however, wanting of wood, which greatly detracts from its value.

On arriving at New York, I crossed the ferry to Brooklyn, where I was politely welcomed by the friends whose hospitable roof I had so recently quitted. The temperature of to-day much as yesterday.

9th.—The night very fine and pleasant, as the morning continues. Making up letters for England, by the ship *Adeline*, leaving to-morrow, when I also hope to be off on my western journey.

10th.—A day of dissatisfaction, having passed it in the disappointed expectation of the arrival of a gentleman from Philadelphia, who had engaged to accompany me into Orange county:——come or not I start in the morning.

My worthy friends at Brooklyn are much troubled this evening on account of the serious indisposition of their infant, from an attack of *cholera morbus*, a disease which carries off a great number of children here at this season of the year. Two doctors* have been called in, who quite disagree as to the mode of treatment, and between them and the disease

* In this land of freedom *doctor* appears to be a title given and assumed nearly indiscriminately by all of the profession.

the little sufferer has, I fear, but a poor chance.
During the late hot weather the number of deaths
in the city alone amounted, in one week, to 204 ;
(the usual number about 80,) more than 70 of these
were under one year old, and 80 under five years
of age. Many of the churchyards bear melancholy
testimony to the mortality which at times has prevailed here; though no bodies are now permitted to
be interred, except in vaults, in the populous parts
of the city. The general habits of the people, as
regards the matter of health, as far as I have observed
them in public, I consider decidedly bad,—chewing
quantities of tobacco, drinking spirits, eating much,
and upon the same occasion, of meat, pastry, fruit,
and vegetables, and rising almost ere the repast be
swallowed, with other customs they may not thank
me to particularize, but the dispensing with which
I have no doubt would, at least, render *dyspepsia*, one
of their most fashionable maladies, and of the very
name of which I begin to weary, much less frequent
than it is.

11*th*.—At seven this morning I got upon the steam
boat *Albany*, to proceed up the Hudson river to
Albany, about 150 miles north of New York, designing thus to leave Orange county until my return,
but meeting with my Philadelphia friend just before
starting, I was persuaded to adhere to my original
plan of proceeding, and to land with him at Newburgh, sixty miles up the river, for the purpose of
visiting it now. —The fare to that place seventy-five
cents.

The *Albany* is the most splendid conveyance I ever moved in, in my life, though surpassed, I am told, by the *North America*, belonging to the same Company, and fully confirms every report I had heard of the vast superiority which the Americans display over us in the construction and arrangement of their steam-vessels,—in fact, of all vessels.

It is no uncommon thing for there to be 500 or 600 persons on board one of these boats at a time. This morning there might be about 350; some, like us, landing at intermediate places, of which there are twenty or more, but the greater part going through to Albany. The whole distance (150 miles) is usually performed in twelve hours, more or less.

In so rapid a transit it is impossible that I should describe places, or do any justice to the impressions excited by the varied and all-attractive scenery of this noble river. I could have wished not to have "thought down hours to moments," but to have prolonged moments to hours. I was so hurried on from the sublime to the beautiful, and again from the beautiful to the sublime, that before the image of one had impressed itself upon the mind, the other appeared to take possession, and every successive change but deepened the thrill of admiration and rapture. " On one hand are seen summits, crowned with forests, apparently impenetrable to the footsteps of cultivation, and on the other, beautiful and extensive lawns, checkered with the abodes of husbandry, and glowing in all the rich verdure of summer ; while, in the same circumstances

of vision, may be seen the fading view of some town
or city, and in perspective, a perpetual opening
scenery of forests and cultivation, plains and mountains, towns and villages, imparting to the beholder
all the charms of novelty, with the highest emotions
of the sublime."

Almost the name of every place, too, I heard articulated reminded me of some scene or circumstance
connected with that glorious struggle for independence, of which this was so frequently the theatre,
and I exulted within myself at beholding the hallowed
ground where the great and the brave had fought and
fallen, but to raise over their ashes a prouder monument than the "the storied urn, or animated bust,"
the deathless, the blood-bought altar of liberty! long,
long may it claim the homage, and the hearts of their
posterity.

Commencing the ascent of the river, I find the
various objects of interest to a stranger well and
accurately described in an excellent publication, with
which I supplied myself previous to leaving New
York ;* and to which, hurried as, upon this occasion,
my journey must necessarily be, I may have frequently
to refer.

The first place noticed is ' Weehawken, about six
miles from the city, on the west side of the river, the
ground on which Gen. Hamilton fell in a duel with
Col. Burr. It is a small spot on the margin of the
river, with huge rocks on three sides, effectually screen-

* "Traveller's Guide to the Middle and Northern States, and
Canada."

ing it from the observation of man, except from the
river; and probably has, for that cause, been selected
as a suitable place for settling affairs of honour.

' Till within a few years it contained a monument
erected to the memory of General Hamilton by the
St. Andrew's Society; but it has been removed. His
body was deposited in the ground attached to Trinity
Church in the city, where there is a handsome monument, inclosed in an iron railing.

' The *Palisadoes*, which make their first appearance
on the Hudson, about eight miles from New York,
are a range of rocks, from twenty to five hundred feet
in height, and extending from thence to Tappan, a
distance of about twenty miles. In some places they
rise almost perpendicularly from the shore, and form,
for several miles in extent, a solid wall of rock, diversified only by an occasional fishing hut on the beach
at their base, or wood slides down their sides,* and
sometimes by an interval of a few acres of arable land,
affording an opening for a landing place and a steep
road leading to their top. On the opposite side of
the river the land is varied by hill and dale, cultivated
fields and woods, with cottages and country seats.

' Twenty-four miles above New York the river expands and forms what is called *Tappan Bay*. The
little village of Tappan, a place of much note during
André's and Arnold's conspiracy, is situated on its
western shore. The spot of André's grave is still
pointed out near this village, though his remains, a

---

* For the purpose of conveying fire-wood from the top to the
bottom of the rocks.

few years since, were conveyed to England by order
of the British Government. The bay is from two to
five miles wide, and eight miles long. Above Tappan
village, on the eastern shore, is the village of *Tarrytown*, where André was captured by three American
militia-men.*

'Near the northern extremity of Tappan Bay, on the
eastern shore, is the *Sing Sing* state prison. It comprises 800 dormitories or solitary cells, is four stories
high, and occupies 50 by 500 feet of ground. From

* 'The names of the three men were John Paulding, Isaac Van
Wart, and David Williams. Paulding died some years ago, and
a monument was erected over his grave by the Corporation of New
York. Van Wart died more recently, and a monument to his
memory has been erected by the citizens of West Chester county.
The following inscriptions are copied from the pedestal of the
monument:

On the north side—
" Here repose the immortal remains of
ISAAC VAN WART,
An Elder of Greensburgh Church, who died on the 23rd of May, 1828, in
the 69th year of his age. Having lived the life, he died the death of a
Christian."

On the south side—
" FIDELITY.
" On the 23rd Sept. 1780, Isaac Van Wart, accompanied by John Paulding, and David Williams, all farmers of the county of West Chester, inter-
cepted Maj. André on his return from the American lines in the character
of a spy, and, notwithstanding the large bribes offered them for his release,
nobly disdained to sacrifice their country for gold,—secured and carried
him to the commanding officer of the district, whereby the dangerous
and traitorous conspiracy of Arnold was brought to light, the insidious
designs of the enemy baffled, the American army saved, and our beloved
country, now free and independent, rescued from most imminent peril."

On the east side—
" VINCIT AMOR PATRIÆ."
" Nearly half a century before this monument was built, the conscript
fathers of America had, in the Senate Chamber, voted that Isaac Van
Wart was a faithful patriot, one in whom the love of country was invin-
cible, and this tomb bears testimony that the record is true."

On the west side—
" The citizens of the county of West Chester erected this tomb in testimony of the high sense they entertained for the virtuous and patriotic conduct of their fellow-citizen, and as a memorial sacred to public gratitude."

each end of the main building, which stands parallel
with the river, in a westerly direction, are carried out
wings 300 feet in extent, forming a spacious inner
yard open only to the river. The wings, composed
of marble, are constructed for workshops, a chapel, a
kitchen, hospital, &c. The chapel is of sufficient
dimensions to hold 900 persons. The keeper's house,
on the south-eastern end of the main building, is also
constructed of marble. The number of convicts in
the prison in 1829, was about 600. Its erection was
commenced in 1825; and its cost is estimated at rising
of 200,000 dollars.

    ' The *Highlands*, or *Fishkill Mountains*, which first
appear about forty miles from New York, will attract
notice, not only from their grandeur and sublimity,
but also from their association with some of the most
important events of the revolution. This chain of
mountains is about sixteen miles in width, and extends
along both sides of the Hudson, to the distance of
twenty miles. The height of the principal has been
estimated at 1565 feet. According to the theory of
Dr. Mitchell, this thick and solid barrier seems, in
ancient days, to have impeded the course of the water,
and to have raised a lake high enough to cover all
the country to *Quaker Hill* and the *Laconic Mountains*
on the east, and to *Shawangunk* and the *Catskill
Mountains* on the west; extending to the *Little Falls*
of the *Mohawk*, and to *Hadley Falls* on the Hudson ;
but by some convulsion of nature, the mountain chain
has been broken, and the rushing waters found their
way to the now *New York Bay*. At the entrance of

the Highlands, on the south, is the site of an old fort on *Verplank's Point,* opposite to which stood the fort of *Stoney Point,* which was taken from General Wayne in 1778, and re-taken by him the same year. About two miles north of this, what is termed the *Horse-race* commences. This consists of an angle in the river, which, for a little more than a mile, takes an easterly direction, contracted to a very narrow space within bold and rocky mountains; one of which, *Anthony's Nose,* is 1,228 feet high, and is opposite the mouth of Montgomery Creek, overlooking Forts Montgomery and Clinton. These forts, under command of General Putnam, were captured by the British troops under Sir Henry Clinton, in 1777, when on his way to co-operate with General Burgoyne, the news of whose surrender, however, reached Sir Henry when he had proceeded as far as Kingston, fifty miles higher up, and changed his advance into a retreat. *Bloody Pond,* so called from its being the place in which the bodies of the slain were thrown after the defences of these forts, is in the rear of Fort Clinton.

' *West Point,* one of the most impregnable posts during the revolutionary war, is situated on the west side of the Hudson, near the entrance of the Highlands on the north. It formed one of the most important fastnesses of the American army during the eight years' contest with the British nation; and the consequence attached to it, in a military point of view, was evinced by the repeated but unsuccessful efforts of the enemy to obtain it.

' It was here that Arnold conceived the horrid pur-

pose of bartering his country for gold. This conspiracy, however, which aimed a death-blow at liberty
in the western hemisphere, resulted only in the universal contempt and ignominy of Arnold and the
lamented death of the unfortunate André.* There

* The circumstances connected with this event are of so peculiarly interesting and affecting a character, that, though rather a
long one, I cannot feel satisfied to withhold or abridge the following
extract. Those familiar with the history of the revolutionary war
must forgive me—those who are not *will* —" Benedict Arnold was
a native of the State of Connecticut, and from the first commence
ment of hostilities he had distinguished himself as a brave soldier,
and an enterprising and skilful commander. He had succeeded in
the bold and difficult attempt to invade the Canadas from the State
of Maine, where the sufferings of himself and soldiers had excited
the sensibility of the nation towards him. At Quebec, on Lake
Champlain, and at Saratoga, he had acted a distinguished part;
and, at the time of his appointment to the command of West
Point, which was in November, 1779, he bore an honourable testi-
monial of his attachment to his country, in the wounds which he
had recently received at the surrender of Burgoyne.

" The residence of General Arnold was at the house and farm of
Colonel Beverly Robinson, opposite West Point, on the east bank
of the Hudson :—(the house is still a conspicuous object.)—It was
here that General Arnold made the first proposals to surrender West
Point, and the forces under his command, to the British army. The
agents on the part of the British were Colonel Beverly Robinson
and Major John André, who held frequent communications with the
American General from on board the Vulture sloop of war, then
lying at Haverstraw Bay, about 10 miles below Stoney and Verplank's
Points.

" Major André, at that time 29 years of age, had from the natural
amiablenes of his character, and his superior accomplishments as
a citizen and a soldier, acquired the unreserved confidence of his
officers, and was emphatically considered the favourite of the British army. In early life he had formed an attachment with a lady
whom he addresses by the name of Delia, and to whom he had
devoted all the leisure afforded from the intervals of a mercantile
profession, until the news of her marriage with a more successful
rival, drove him, disappointed and unfortunate, to the bustling pursuits of the camp. His biographer remarks:—' There was something singularly interesting in the character and fortunes of André.

are here at present a number of dwelling-houses, and
a military academy, built on the plain which forms the

To an excellent undertanding, well improved by education and travel, he united a peculiar elegance of mind and manners, and the advantages of a pleasing person. His knowledge appeared without
ostentation. His sentiments were elevated, and inspired esteem, as
they had a softness that conciliated affection. His elocution was
handsome—his address easy, polite, and insinuating. By his merit
he had acquired the unlimited confidence of his General, and was
making rapid progress in military rank and reputation. But in the
height of his career, flushed with new hopes from the execution of
a project the most beneficial to his party that could be devised, he
is at once precipitated from the summit of prosperity, and sees all
the expectations of his ambition blasted, and himself ruined.'

"A night in the month of Sept., 1780, was chosen for the fatal interview between Arnold and André. Under the pretence of a cor-
respondence with the British General, on the subject of a treaty of
peace, Arnold had succeeded in enlisting in his service an intelligent and respectable citizen of the name of Smith. Under his direction a boat was despatched to the Vulture sloop of war, then
lying across the Bay of Haverstraw, about twelve miles distant, to
convey the British agent to the place appointed by Arnold for their
meeting. On examining the papers, it was found that a pass had
been sent for Colonel Beverly Robinson, and also a blank pass for
whomsoever should be selected for the important trust. In the
latter pass was inserted the name of John Anderson, under which
name André consented to be conveyed to the shore from whence he
was destined never to return. The place appointed for the interview was at the foot of a mountain called Long Clove, on the west
side of the Hudson. Hither General Arnold had repaired, and on
the arrival of André was found secreted in a thick grove of firs, the
scene of their subsequent conference. After considerable conversation,
which lasted till the dawn of day, it was found impracticable for André
to return without being discovered from the neighbouring forts of
Stoney and Verplank's Points. He was, therefore, conveyed to the
house of Smith, the person who had brought him to the shore, and
who afterwards accompanied him on his way to New York. At this
house he procured a coat in exchange for his military dress which he
had worn on shore, and on the evening of the day after his arrival,
set out in company with Smith, and under a pass from General
Arnold, for White Plains.

"The first night of their journey was spent at a Mr. M'Koy's, about
eight miles from the place of their departure. The next day they

bank of the river, 188 feet in height, to which a road ascends on the north side of the point. In the back

rode, without any interruption, as far as Pine's Bridge, across the Croton river, which empties into the Hudson on the west side, at the head of Tappan Bay. Here, having received the necessary in structions as to the road he was to take, André the next morning took leave of his guide, and pursued his journey. He had not proceeded more than six miles, when he was arrested by the three American militia-men, who, with others, were out ,on a scouting party between the out-posts of the two armies. These men stopped Major Andre in a narrow part of the road, at a place near Tarrytown, by suddenly seizing his horse by the bridle. Instead of immediately producing the pass which had been furnished him by General Arnold, André inquired where they belonged to? They answered, " To below." Not suspecting any deception, he replied, " So do I ;" and declaring himself to be a British Officer, he entreated that he might not be detained, being on pressing business. This declaration was followed by further inquiries, which excited still more suspicion, and at length induced a resolution on their part to detain him. Finding himself thus surprised and a prisoner, he made use of every persuasion to regain his liberty, and offered a very valuable gold watch for his release; but it was all to no effect.

" They asked for his papers, which being refused, they commenced searching him, and memorandums, in Arnold's handwriting, relating to the forces and defences of West Point, were found concealed in his boots.

" Despatches were immediately forwarded to Gen. Washington, together with a letter from Major André to General Arnold, apprizing him of his arrest and detention. In consequence of some mis take of the messenger, information of the circumstances reached Arnold some time before Washington was apprized at all of them. Upon the receipt of the letter Arnold seized the messenger's horse, and immediately proceeded down a precipice to the river, where boats were always ready to pass to and from West Point, and jumping into one of them, he directed the hands to row him down the river to the Vulture sloop of war. In the meantime information had been received by Washington, and scarce had Arnold passed Stoney and Verplank's Points, when Colonel Hamilton arrived at the latter place with orders to stop him.

" André was arrested on the 23rd Sept., and a Board of General Officers were immediately summoned, by order of General Wash. ington, for his trial. The circumstances of the case were the subject of much excitement in both the American and British armies, ground, and elevated on a mass of rocks 598 feet in height, is the site of *Fort Putnam*. Silence and decay now mark the spot of this once formidable fortress. Its mouldering ruins, however, convey a pretty correct idea of the impregnable barrier its ramparts once presented to the enemies of freedom.

'The *Military Academy*, here established by Congress, was first organized under the direction of the late General Williams, in 1802. Of the number of applicants for admission to this institution, a preference is usually given, first, to the sons of officers of the revolution, and, secondly, to the sons of deceased officers of the late war. None are admitted under the age of fourteen years, nor above twenty-two. The number of cadets is limited to 250, each of whom costs the Government 336 dollars annually; and the whole establishment is maintained at an annual expense of 115,000 dollars. In addition to the

and created much sympathy in favour of André. After an inquiry of a number of days, the court determined that André ought to be considered as a spy from the enemy, and that, agreeably to the law and usage of nations, he ought to suffer death. This sentence was protested against, on the ground that André had been admitted into the American camp under the protection of a flag, and at the immediate instance of Arnold, the commanding officer of the district, whose safe passport and return he had a right to demand. But the sentence was consented to be waved only on condition of delivering Arnold into the custody of the American army; which being refused by the British General, André was executed on the 2nd of October, 1780, at Tappan, or Orange Town, where his remains were deposited. When disinterred, for the purpose of being conveyed to England, it was discovered that the roots of a cypress had entwined their branches around the skull of the deceased.

"The four surviving children of Gen. Arnold have become pensioners of Great Britain, and receive annuities of £100 sterling each."

various sciences which are taught here, the cadets are
instructed in all the practical minutiæ of tactics; comprehending the lowest duties of the private soldier,
as well as the highest duties of the officer.   They are
also required to encamp for six or eight weeks in a
year; during which time they are instructed in the
manner of pitching and striking tents, in the various
infantry evolutions, and in all the details of the
camp.'

   ' Several of the buildings at West Point are elegant,
and among the number may be ranked a new and
spacious hotel.   It has been erected in a style and
on a scale which render it a great ornament to the
grounds.   It is substantially built of stone, painted
yellow, and the lower story is surrounded on its sides
with extensive piazzas, forming a delightful prome-
nade.   Its rear is upon the Hudson, and presents a
fine view up the river through the Highlands.   The
front faces the parade ground and the ground used
for the encampment.'

   ' Near the north-eastern extremity of the grounds, at
the projecting point forming the abrupt bend of the
river, stands a monument of white marble, consisting
of a base and short column, on the former of which
is simply inscribed on one side, " Kosciusko," it having been erected to the memory of that distinguished
patriot, who resided here.'

   ' On the bank of the Hudson, at the south-eastern
extremity of the parade ground, and several yards beneath, is a spot called Kosciusko's Garden, or Kos-
cuisco's Retreat.   It is the place to which the Polish

patriot was accustomed to retire to study, and which
was cultivated by his own hands. Though now neglected, the marks of cultivation are perceptible in
the regularity of the walks and the arrangement of
the trees. A more delightful spot for recreation or
repose cannot be imagined, nor one more suitable as
a retreat from the cares of the great world, or a
sanctuary for unfortunate patriotism or persecuted
virtue.'

' Passing the Highlands, the prospect changes into a
very agreeable contrast. The bay of Newburgh with
the village of the same name, and New-Windsor, and
on the opposite shore the village of Fishkill, with its
numerous adjacent manufactories and country seats,
together with a view of the Hudson for many miles
above, form a prospect which cannot fail to impart
much interest. The village of New-Windsor stands
on the margin of the river, seven miles from West
Point. It is calculated for a pleasant place of residence, but in business it must yield to the rival village of

' Newburgh. This is an incorporated village, situated on the declivity of a hill on the west side of
the Hudson, ten miles north from West Point, and
eighty-four south from Albany. It contains about
six hundred houses, and four thousand inhabitants.
From its situation it commands an extensive intercourse and trade with the country on the west, and,
by means of the Hudson river, with New York. This
place was for some time the head-quarters of the
American army during the revolutionary war; and

the "stone house" in which General Washington quartered is still standing.

'On the opposite side of the river (from Newburgh) is Beacon Hill, one of the highest summits of the Fishkill Mountains, where parties of pleasure frequently resort, in the summer season, to witness an extent of prospect including a part of the territories of five different states.   This hill is 1471 feet in height.

'Half a mile south is the New Beacon, or Grand Sachem, 1685 feet above the level of the Hudson. They are called Beacon Hills, from the circumstance that beacons were erected on their summits during the revolutionary war.   The continuation of this chain of mountains is lost in the Appalachian Range on the north-east, and extends south as far as the eye can reach.   Diminished in distance is seen West Point, environed by mountains, apparently reposing on the surface of the Hudson, and bathing their rocky summits in the clouds.'

We reached Newburgh between twelve and one o'clock, from whence we procured a man with a pair of horses and one of their light waggons to convey us across the county about twenty-five miles, for which we agreed to pay him four dollars.   After travelling over twelve miles of very bad road, through a barren, rocky, half cleared, uninteresting country, we arrived at Montgomery, a village with a few pretty good houses and stores, and, perhaps, about 800 inhabitants.   We were detained some little time at this place, in borrowing another waggon, the one we started with having broken down by the way, and declined further service.

About a mile before *making* Montgomery, we passed the house and farm of a *Mr. Waite*, who emigrated from Bristol a few years ago : he has about ninety acres of land, contiguous to his house, for which he gave thirty dollars per acre, and two hundred more at some little distance :—is looked upon as a good and extensive farmer.

As we drove along we observed many persons cutting and carrying their hay, in the midst of stumps and stones, and where an English farmer would have deemed it utterly impracticable to have performed either operation. They allow their hay to become much riper than we do, gathering it last of all, except their Indian corn crop, and it really appears poor dry and coarse stuff. The cattle I saw were of a very inferior description; the cows small—precise breed not easily determinable; sheep, just of the order that range our commons; and as to pigs, they were perfectly hideous; their heads large, legs long, sides very flat, and bristled along the back like a wild boar. I have not seen one handsome individual of this race, except in Long Island. With some partial exceptions, where the land was pretty much cleared of stumps and stones, it had a very uninviting aspect, so much so that had I not previously visited Long Island, and heard reports of other parts of the State, it would, I must confess, have given me but an indifferent opinion of farming in America.

With various stoppages and hindrances it was late before we arrived at the end of our journey. My companion had been frequently in this county before,

and seemed to have a general acquaintance both with
farmers and farming concerns. At length, at a short
distance from the main road, and about two miles
from Bloomingburgh, in Sullivan county, he ordered
the man to stop at the door of a Mr. ——, and not
having previously heard him make any allusion to re-
lationship, I was a little surprised on the old gentleman
approaching us, to find him address him by the familiar
appellation of " *uncle*," a mode of salutation, of youth
to age, it appears, nearly as much in vogue, throughout
this western, as that of " *father*" was in the eastern
world. Had we been a few minutes later, we should
have found the whole household in bed, the major
part, I believe, had been there some time, and the
arrival of a couple of guests one of the last things
thought of; but there was no talk about " *bringing
night with us*"—" *who'd have thought of any body
coming now,*"—" *hardly know where to put your horses,*"
&c. &c; but those who were up welcomed us with cor-
diality; and those who had retired were quickly summoned, and evinced any thing rather than dissatisfaction at such an untimely interruption of their slumbers;
all set about to entertain us in the best way the circumstances of the case permitted : " *Uncle*" was very
diffuse on *politics* and *religion,* (standing and consecutive topics I find, go where you will,) and we had
pretty much settled some abstruse points in both ere
we had been half an hour in the house. *Aunt* and
cousins were all alive for news, and plied us with interrogatories at an unmerciful rate, which, however,
had I known the destiny that awaited me, I would

have continued most patiently responding to, until the night had so far waned, as to have enabled me to decline, with a perfect good grace, the superfluous *accommodation* of a bed. " What, the bugs again ?" —Bear with me, reader, though I can hardly *bear with myself,*—'tis even so. It is now three o'clock on the morning of the————12*th of August,*————and for the last two hours, unable any longer to endure the *in*side of the house, I have been making trial of the *out,* and, in trans-Atlantic phraseology, have *located* myself in an adjoining shed, after disturbing half the family, and I know not what else, in effecting my escape, but which, after all, by the bye, is but a sorry sort of retreat, since, though I have cleared the bugs, I have been pounced upon by a fine corps of musquetoes,—light infantry to the others to be sure, but almost ' making up in numbers what they want in weight,' and thirsting for my blood with a like avidity : either are bad enough, but united they oppose one of the most formidable barriers to a *peaceable* existence in the country I have yet met with; and it is the more trying to be subject to the annoyance just at that season of the year when the heat of the weather renders you less able to bear it. An *American* may smile at these remarks, but, as I have said, an *Englishman* will not,—*upon trial.*—A pig has just risen from his *berth* and paid me a visit—the most agreeable living thing I have seen for hours,—and, thanks, the morning dawns.

Determining, after what I had seen of the county on the preceding day, and evidenced of its *produc-*

tions during the past night, not to prolong my stay in it, betimes this morning, partly on horseback, and partly on foot, I commenced a little further survey; availing myself wherever, and so far as I could, of the experience of practical residents, but without tending much to remove the unfavourable impressions previously recorded. That portions of rich and valuable land are to be found in some parts, I readily admit; but the general character of it is rocky and rugged in the extreme. I do not believe that a farm of *two hundred acres* could be any where selected in the county, of which the *majority* could be called *well cleared, good land.* Perhaps the best is to be found the neighbourhood of *Goshen,* where a great weight of butter is made and sent to New York market, at which it is in high repute. There is also some quantity of hemp grown in the county.

Farms, with a fair house and outbuildings, are to be purchased for about thirty dollars per acre; price, of course, varying a little with circumstances. Articles of produce much as in Long Island, though the yield is generally less, and prices lower, and little, if any, fruit, &c. is cultivated for the New York market. Plaster is much used as a manure, worth at Newburgh seven dollars a ton; considered a sufficient quantity for twelve acres. Cider is chiefly made for private use. The county is well supplied with water, and there is abundance of iron ore, marble, lime, sand-stone, &c.; but for an *English farmer* I should consider it any thing but desirable.

Soon after four o'clock, *p. m.* I made for the high

road, and got into the *Western Mail*, a ponderous, uncouth vehicle, drawn by four good horses, carrying nine inside, and one on the seat, or rail, with the driver—a gentleman in his shirt sleeves, and in good keeping with the whole concern. I may here notice a peculiarity in the tactics of American coachmanship, which not unfrequently brings English Jehu's in contact with the wheels of their carriages, namely, that of *turning out* upon the *right* instead of the *left* side; one would verily think by way of opposition, as all to whom I have noticed the custom admit its impropriety—know not how it has obtained, but that so it is, and they are compelled to observe it.

Our progress along a rugged, and, in some parts, dangerous road, was from three to six miles an hour, the dust, at times, nearly choking us: we managed, however, to reach Newburgh soon after nine in the evening. Here it had been my intention to have taken the night boat to Albany, which passed by from New York about an hour afterwards; but the day having been very warm, my exertion not trifling, and a night of *campaigning* into the bargain, after receiving very positive assurances at the most respectable hotel in the place (the Mansion House, kept by Evan Davis) that I should be lodged secure from all invasion, I determined upon quartering here until morning; and shortly requested an introduction to my apartment, which I found as apparently neat and clean as I could have desired; the bed and all the furniture in it excellent and nearly new. Well, thought I, this is some improvement

upon Bloomingburgh—no vermin here—sure of a
charming night now, at all events—and with such
like agreeable reflections and anticipations consigned
myself to bed; but, alas! alas! "man is born to
trouble;" whoso doubteth it, let him travel in a land
of bugs and musquetoes. "Kind nature's sweet re-
storer, balmy sleep," had not commenced her visit ere
my most persecuting assailants were again at me;
—bugs I mean; and I was soon up and in a state of
open warfare, killing and slaying in all directions.
Finding myself thus deceived, and suffering severely from injuries received, I sallied forth, and was
soon in close and no very peaceful contact with
both landlord and waiter, who, until they went and
examined for themselves, would not believe that such
an appearance as I presented could have proceeded
from such a cause, or even that the wretched vermin
could have found access to the apartment into which
they very politely told me (but I was in no mood to
be complimented) that they never put any but the
most respectable of their company. To dispute the
point, however, against the joint evidence of our
senses, was out of the question, and after expressing
the utmost concern at the occurrence, and lamenting,
in consequence of guests received by the steam-boats,
in which the pest, or *pestilence*, if you will, abounds,
the great difficulty they had in keeping, or, in fact,
knowing, when they were free from it, I could only
make the best of my bad bargain, and retiring into a
drawing-room, threw myself upon a sofa, and, over-

powered with fatigue and vexation, dropped, perforce,
to sleep.

August 13*th*.—A most fine morning, and having
taken a dip in the beautiful Hudson, with other refreshing operations, I feel my condition somewhat
improved, though truly in a poor plight, and half
ashamed to walk abroad, even in this *land of freedom*,
which, by the bye, at the rate I am proceeding, will
prove any thing else to me.   I scarcely think to
venture into a bed again at any public establishment
in the country : the consequences are too serious
for any patient endurance, and if this be a fair specimen of American *entertainment* of travellers,
though already I can bear ample testimony to good
fare and hospitality, I, for one, must be content to
say, " England, *with all thy faults*, I love thee still."

In consequence of the morning boat, which ought
to have arrived here at twelve o'clock, having broken
a part of her machinery, and come to a stand a few
miles below, I was detained until near five in the
afternoon, when the " Chief Justice Marshall" made
its appearance, a very fine boat, though smaller than
the Albany, from which, in addition to her own, she
had received about 250 passengers, so that we were
pretty thick upon the ground.   It was a splendid
moonlight evening, and the scenery which lined the
banks of the river, though less grand than that
which we passed through on the previous day, possessed almost equal claims to admiration ; the towns
and villages on either side we could discern but in-
distinctly,—shall probably have an opportunity of

noticing them on my return, and therefore only observe that, after passing *Milton, Poughkeepsie, Hyde-
park Landing, Catskill, the city of Hudson,* &c. we
reached *Albany,* at one o'clock this morning the
————14*th of August*————but being unable to get
my luggage from the boat before daylight, (an arrangement which the frequent thefts committed at all the
landing-places of these vessels has rendered necessary)
I did not quit it until after four o'clock; during which
interval I was visited again and again by the agents of
the two lines of western stages, each eloquent upon
the decided superiority of travelling by that for which
he was respectively interested. They are termed
the " *Old*" (which until lately was the only line) and
" *Pioneer*" line. As a stranger, I at length decided
upon the former, and engaged a place to *Utica,* in
Oneida county, ninety-four miles W. N. W. of Albany,
to start at nine o'clock; afterwards getting into the
bar of an indifferent inn, the only one I saw open, I
dozed for an hour or so on three most uneasy wooden
chairs, when, recollecting the brief interval allowed
me for observation,—not that I forsook my *couch* with
any extraordinary reluctance,—I rose and proceeded
to reconnoitre the city; with which, as the capital of
the state, I cannot but express myself rather disappointed. 'It is situated on the west side of the Hudson river, and near the head of tide water. It was
settled in 1612; and next to *Jamestown* in Virginia, is
the oldest settlement in the United States. In 1614,
a small fort and trading house were built by the Dutch
on an island half a mile below the site of the present

city; and soon afterwards, Fort Orange, where the city now stands. The place was first called *Aurania;* then *Beverwyck,* till 1625; then *Fort Orange,* till 1647; and *Williamstadt,* till 1664. For a long time after its foundation it was inclosed with palisadoes or pickets, as a defence against the Indians, who were then numerous and powerful in its vicinity. Its charter was granted in the year 1686, and embraced an area of 7160 acres. A great proportion of its soil is sandy and unproductive, and under no system of useful cultivation.'

Upon my going out soon after six o'clock, I found a great part of the stores open, and nearly as much appearance of business as there would have been at mid-day;—generally speaking, commercial men in America (by which I include a great majority) commence the day much earlier than the same class in England, and whereas a London or Liverpool merchant will reach his office by *ten* or *eleven,* those of New York will be found at their posts soon after, and very often before, *eight* o'clock. The same want of uniformity and neatness which I had noticed at New York, was here still more conspicuous. There are many good buildings in different parts of the town, but nothing like a *good street* from beginning to end, and some of them are very badly paved, and not wholly free from appearances of vegetation; the two principal, *Market-street* and *Pearl-street,* run parallel with the river, and *State-street* nearly E. and W. The public buildings most worthy of notice, are the *Capitol* and the *State-hall.*

'The Capitol, which contains the legislative halls, the
common council chamber of the corporation, the supreme and chancery court rooms of the state, the
county clerk's office, the state library, and other apartments for business, stands at the head of State-
street, on an elevation of 130 feet above the level of
the river. It is a substantial stone edifice, erected at an
expense of 120,000 dollars; of which sum 34,000 was
paid by the corporation of the city. It is 115 feet in
length, 90 feet in breadth, and 50 feet in height, consisting of two stories, and a basement of ten feet.
The east front is adorned with a portico of the Ionic
order. In the senate and assembly chambers, and
in the room used for holding the court of chancery,
are full-length portraits of Washington, of the various
executives who have administered the government of
the state, and of Abraham Van Vechten, Esq., an
eminent counsellor at law, residing in Albany. There
is also in the senate chamber a good bust of Dr.
Franklin.

'The *State Hall,* for the offices of the Secretary
of the State, Comptroller, Treasurer, Surveyor-General, Attorney-General, and Clerk of the Supreme
Court, is situated on the south side of State-street,
nearly equidistant from the Capitol and the Albany,
Farmers' and Mechanics' Banks; both of which stand
at the foot of State-street, and are elegant, white marble edifices. There are in this city four Banks, and
fourteen houses for public worship. Also a large
brick building for a Lancasterian School, a Theatre in
South Pearl-street, an Athenæum, and an Arsenal in

North Market-street. The Museum is in South Market-street, and is one of the best in the country. North of the Capitol, stands the *Academy*, the most elegantly constructed building in the city. It cost about 92,000 dollars, exclusive of the lot on which it is erected, and some donations. It is built of freestone, three stories in height, and ninety feet in front. It is one of the most flourishing institutions in the state; has five teachers and about one hundred and forty students.' The principal Hotels are the *American Hotel*, in State-street, a large and elegant establishment; the *Mansion House*, and *City Hotel*, in north Market-street; the *State-street House* in State-street, which, with others, no doubt, present every requisite comfort and convenience.

In point of trade, wealth, and resources, *Albany* is considered to rank next to New York. The Erie and Champlain Canals, those great works of the day, which I shall take an opportunity of noticing more particularly, unite at Watervliet, eight miles and a half north of the city, and flow into it in one channel; so that the produce of the north and the west, and an immense amount of merchandise from New York, &c. pass through it. No census has been taken since 1820, though one is now in progress;—its present population may be about 20,000, but I speak without data. There are a number of stages leaving daily, in different directions, and *extras*, or hired conveyances, to be had in abundance.

I much regretted that I had not an opportunity of visiting two objects of interest in the neighbourhood, namely, the *farm of J. Buell, Esq.*, and the *Shaker Settlement*, of which I extract the following notices:—

'The highly cultivated farm of J. Buell, Esq., is about two miles west of Albany on the *Cherry Valley* turnpike. This farm, consisting of eighty acres, has been wholly reclaimed from commons since 1818, and is now under profitable cultivation. Mr. Buell possessed the first requisite for improvement—*a consciousness of the want of knowledge in his new employment.* He diligently sought for this knowledge in the practice of the best farmers, and in the study of the sciences upon which agriculture is based; directing, and superintending himself the labours of his farm. His improvements consist in selecting the best implements adapted to his soil—in substituting fallow crops for naked fallows—in extensively and successfully cultivating the Swedish and common turnip, *as a second crop,* after clover and small grains—in introducing new and valuable grasses—in the cultivation of live fences, which he has growing of the white European thorn, of the native thorn of our woods, and of the three-thorned or honey locust—and in the economy and application of ordinary, and the use of new manures. His object has been to grow only good crops, and these at the least expense. In 1827 he sold from sixty-four acres in tillage and grass, under farm culture, produce to the amount of more than 1500 dollars, exclusive of the consumption of a large family. His kitchen and flower gardens, abounding in the finest native and foreign fruits, ornamental trees, shrubs, and flowers, will also be visited with interest.'

' *The Shaker Settlement* at Niskayuna is eight miles north-west of Albany. The Shakers are the followers of Ann Lee, called by them *Mother Ann,* a religious enthusiast, who was born in England some time antecedent to the revolutionary war, and while yet in her youth suffered much tribulation and deep exercises of spirit, in her conversion from the sins of this world to a state of greater perfection. She endured severe trials and much persecution, according to her own account, from her countrymen; but was afterwards favoured with visions and an exhibition of miracles in her favour. Although in early life herself the wife of a poor blacksmith, the principal tenet of her creed is absolute and entire celibacy, which is defended on various spiritual grounds, and fully set forth in a work recently published by the society. In consequence of the persecutions experienced by Mother Ann, in England, she came to this country, and established a small society, which has been followed by the establishment of others, of which this is one. Her followers regard her memory with pious veneration, and consider themselves as the only people in possession of the true light. Some of the oldest and most perfect members, it is said, pretend to "speak with tongues," heal diseases by the touch, &c. The marriage contract is dissolved on joining the society; their association is a perfect community of goods, all private property being thrown into the common stock, and they profess to banish the love of ambition, wealth, and luxury from their gloomy territories.

'They own at this place 2000 acres of excellent land,

laid out and kept in the order, neatness, and cleanliness, which always distinguish their sect.   This is divided into four farms, or families, as they are called,
occupied by about seventy-five persons each, of both
sexes and of all ages.   They cultivate garden stuffs,
seeds, &c. for sale, as well as every thing necessary for
their own support, and they manufacture various useful and ornamental articles.   These, as well as the
surplus produce of the farm, are sold, and the avails
deposited in one of the Albany banks until required.
The division of labour which they carry into practice,
every occupation being entrusted to separate members,
and their economical habits, render their gains very
considerable.   The men work as farmers, carpenters,
shoemakers, tailors, &c. ; the women at weaving, spin-
ning, washing, cooking, and in the duties of the farm ;
making and mending clothes,—the occupations of
each sex being performed in separate buildings. They
also eat separately, and neither of them will sit down
to a meal with what they call the " world's people."
The dress of the men is drab, perfectly plain ; that of
the women, grey, with white caps, all made as plain
and easy as possible.   They all have a peculiar walk,
but especially the females, in consequence of their
mode of worship, from which they derive the name of
Shakers, a strange and disagreeable mode of dancing,
accompanied with a monotonous song.   The young
members of the community are regularly taught the
steps of this dance by the older ones before they are
permitted to join in public worship. It is usual before
the admission of a member to all the privileges of the

society, to impose a noviciate of three months, when, if he so desires, he may leave them ; if not, he is regularly admitted a member, and throws his property into the common stock.

' Notwithstanding the severity of their discipline as to celibacy, it is said the harmony of their society was lately much disturbed in consequence of a "love affair." A young man and woman, both belonging to the society, in despite of the doctrines of their leader, fell from their estate of " single blessedness," and yielded to a worldly attachment. This heresy, as might be expected, produced considerable commotion. The members wrestled with the tempter, and the elders prayed for and with the victims to the dreaded enemy of the sect ; but all to no purpose. They left the society and were married. It is creditable, however, to the members, that after finding their efforts to prevent this result unavailing, they sent the happy pair sufficient furniture for comfortable house-keeping, assigning as a reason, that they had laboured for the society, and that it was no more than justice to reward them.'

Before nine o'clock, with seven persons, besides myself, in our vehicle, I was again in motion for Utica. The morning was very fine and warm, but the dust terrible. The first place we arrived at was the city of *Schenectady*, fifteen miles from Albany ; the road as bad and the country as uninteresting as I have often travelled over, and there appears but very little in the town itself to attract the notice of a stranger. It is situated on the Mohawk river, over which there is a bridge 330 yards in length, built of wood and roofed over. The *Erie Canal* also passes through it, but in consequence of the number of locks between and Albany, no *packet-boats* run farther than *Schenectady*, and the intervening distance must therefore be passed by the stages. ' By the present arrangement, boats leave Schenectady every morning and evening, reaching *Utica* in twenty-four hours, and *Buffalo*, at the foot of *Lake Erie*, in four days. The price of conveyance in the packet-boats is three cents per mile, meals extra.'* Spafford says that the present city ' is built on the site of a large Indian town, anciently called *Con-nugh-harie-gugh-harie*, literally *a-great-multitude-collected-together*. It was built by a band of the Mohocks, or Mohawks, and could at one time send 800 warriors to the field. At a very early period of our historical knowledge of this country, the Indian settlement at this town was abandoned, (for reasons never understood by the white people,) and those Indians settled among their red brethren in the west. A long time before the American revolution they had entirely abandoned it.' In 1819 it suffered severely by fire, 170 buildings being destroyed, and a large amount of other property. It may now contain 4000 inhabitants; has a college of some celebrity, called *Union College*, at which about 200 students are educated annually; there is also a Lancasterian and other schools,

* These boats are exclusively for the conveyance of passengers, comfortably and conveniently fitted up, and towed by two or three horses. They are generally preferred to the stages,—are no doubt much easier—but give me land, however bad, or if it *must* be water —the ocean—no " dull canal with locks and chains," &c.

three or four churches, or *meeting-houses*, (for the *body of professors* assembling, and not *the building*, is usually understood by the term *church* here,) a bank, one excellent hotel near the canal, and others elsewhere, besides tanneries, stores, &c. Sixteen miles further is *Amsterdam*, a very poor place, containing forty or fifty houses, where we dined indifferently. Passing on through *Caughnawaga, Fort Plain, East Canada Creek*, &c. there is little to interest the traveller until arriving at *Little Falls* in Herkimer county, when the scene becomes pleasingly romantic. 'The place takes its name from a cataract in the vicinity, which in size is much inferior to the celebrated *Cahoes*, and has, therefore, been denominated the *Little Falls* of the Mohawk. A continuation of the chain of Catsbergs crosses the river at this place, and forms a rough bed for the waters of the cataract, which pour over the rocky fragments in the wildest confusion. Approaching from the south-east, a lofty ridge of mountains, frowning in grandeur on either side, conceals the course of the river and the falls, whose vicinity is announced only by the distant din and foam of its waters. For a considerable distance, a narrow pass only is allowed for a road, with immense natural battlements of rock on either side, affording a most sublime and interesting spectacle. About half a mile from the village the road turns suddenly to the left, presenting a view of the falls tumbling with irresistible violence over a gradual rocky descent of about eighty rods. At the termination of the ascent is situated the village, containing about one hundred houses and eight hundred inhabitants. A little cluster of buildings, rising between the rushing waters of the Mohawk on the one hand, and the rugged cliffs and eminences on the other; the smooth current of the stream above gently gliding to the tumultuous scene below, and beyond the distant vale of the Mohawk, diversified with fields, orchards, meadows, and farm-houses,—all contribute to set off the romantic appearance for which this place is so justly celebrated. This village derives most of its importance from the facilities for trade and commerce afforded by means of the Mohawk river and the Erie canal. Boats were formerly transported around the falls by means of a canal on the north side of the river. This old canal contains eight locks, and is now connected with the Erie canal on the south side of the river by means of an aqueduct 184 feet in length. The descent of the Erie canal here, in the distance of one mile, is forty feet, which is passed by five locks.'

The road from this place continues to pursue the course of the river, and overlooks a rich alluvial vale known by the name of the *Herkimer and German Flats*, the latter on the opposite side of the Mohawk. Near the middle of these flats is situated the village of Herkimer, the capital of Herkimer county.—Let me here remark that the term *village*, in America, must be understood as synonymous with town in England, and *town* or *township* as *parish;* as this is the way they are uniformly applied, the Americans neither having nor needing any thing answering to our *parish;* an institution which no English farmer in the present day, and for *days to come,* will need de-fining.—Herkimer, like most on this day's route, is an insignificant place, consisting chiefly of two streets and contains about eight hundred inhabitants.

The remainder of the way to Utica, we travelled too late in the evening to discern any thing of the face of the country; it was, however, less hilly, and, from what I could learn, rather loosely cultivated and uninteresting. There is *some* excellent land in the county of Herkimer, and much of a very inferior description; the best is to be found in the southern part, along the banks of the Mohawk, where, as in Montgomery county, which preceded it, good farms, with buildings and improvements, are to be purchased at from 25 to 40 dollars per acre. Clover seed is here cultivated to a considerable extent, and, it is said, at a good profit to the grower. The northern part of the county is very mountainous, cold, and barren, with immense forests of various kinds of timber, every way ineligible for agriculture.—We reached *Utica* about twelve o'clock in the evening, having travelled during the day, though at grievous bodily expense, at the rate of six miles an hour, including stoppages; a feat which I will venture to say would never have been performed by an English coachman. The road, nearly the whole of the way, was very indifferent—rocky, and uneven, and, for the most part, unguarded. We had jolting enough not only to have broken our vehicle, but almost to have dislocated every bone in our bodies: those, however, who are unused to Mac-

adamized smoothness think nothing of it, and the
only emotion excited by the head being banged
against the top of the coach, or a violent concussion
with your opposite neighbour, (an oft-repeated occurrence in the course of the day,) was a smile, or a
hearty laugh, in proportion to the extent and magnitude of the jolt,—a proof, amongst the many, what
inconveniences and hardships may be tolerated,—
borne even with equanimity, when we have no ability
or idea of redressing them.

I noticed a peculiarity in the toll-gates as we passed
along, (which articles are much less frequent than in
England,) namely, their drawing up in portcullis
fashion, instead of opening as ours do; a custom
in eastern countries referred to by that beautiful and
sublime passage in the Psalms, "Lift up your heads,
O ye gates!" &c.

Another and a very convenient dissimilarity relates
to the coachman, who does not expect the slightest
fee or remuneration.   There is no eternal opening of
the door, and " Please, Sir, I stop here;"—"Please,
Sir, I don't go any further;"—" Please, Sir, remem-
ber the coachman," which is not always quite so
pleasing as they would kindly desire it to be.   Here,
the fare paid, generally without opposition, about
four cents a mile, you have done with all demands
relative to the coach.   At the end of every stage the
man retires with his horses, which he has to attend
upon himself, though this is a much less onerous
duty than in England, brushes, curry combs, &c.
being but little in request.   I do not, in any instance,

recollect seeing him at all assisted even in *taking out*
or *putting in.*   Pretty soon after he has cleared himself away, the driver, who is next to proceed, appears
with his team, and though this changing is not quite
so expeditious an affair as you may sometimes witness when running opposition with us—I think I
have known it performed in twenty seconds—you are
off again in as little time as under the circumstances
you would suppose possible.

There is a very striking difference, too, perceptible
at the inns :—look for no bowing landlord or obse-
quious waiter at the door to welcome your arrival ;
you may alight or not, as you please, and in some
instances be served as if *you,* and *not they,* were the
party obliged.   Neither expect to find any snug parlour or *Travellers,* or I suppose I must now say, *Commercial Room,* to retire to ; the bar seems the only inhabited apartment about the house, and there, upon
arrival, the company immediately proceed : within it are
always to be met with conveniences for washing—the
very first operation—and a comb and a brush attached
together by a string, suspended most likely from the
ceiling, *pro bono publico,* and used *sans ceremonie* by
by all comers and goers, though *I* took the liberty of
declining the accommodation.   You would suppose
that all the news and affairs of the commonwealth,
(as they most likely have) had gained access to this
place, or, at any rate, you feel perfectly assured of
being in a land where that valuable engine, the press,
suffers not the slightest embarrassment : papers, daily,
and weekly, local, and from different parts of the

Union, are strewed about in 'charming profusion,'—
the merits of all persons and all things are discussed
by all present,—the walls are covered with advertisements of elections—fares of stages and steam-boats,
when and where running—auctions—sales of land—
sales of stock—sales of merchandise—sales of every
thing that can be sold—quack medicines without end
—the most prominent 'specifics for *dyspepsia.*'—but
take *exempli gratia* the heads of half a dozen matters
which I saw succeeding each other:—" Real estate for
sale, at a low price and easy terms to the purchaser."
—" Gotham.—Chronicles of the city of Gotham, from
the papers of a retired common council-man; by the
author of John Bull, in America; just received and
for sale by E. Peck and Co."—" Lectures on Univer-
salism, by Joel Parker, pastor of the third Presbyterian
Church, Rochester."-—" Journal of Health, price
twenty-five dollars per annum."—" Canal transportation."—" Capital prize of 20,000 dollars! Fortune's
home."—" I want a *first-rate* miller, and am willing to
pay a first-rate price, for this fall. G. G. Kingman,"
—" Stage fare reduced ! ! ! !—-Pioneer stages from
Rochester and Utica, four dollars per seat and under;
and to intermediate places in proportion. *Caution to
the Public.*—A variety of methods having been resorted
to in order to impress the public mind with the belief
that the Pioneer stages are discontinued, the public
are respectfully informed that the proprietors of the
said line are running two daily lines of stages between
Rochester, Canandaigua, and Utica, and one daily
line from Utica to Albany, (sabbaths excepted;) and

that in point of *comfort, speed, and low rates of fare,* this line shall not be surpassed : office, &c.—R. Hunt, agent."—" Broken Banks ! Bills of the Bank of Columbia, Middle District, and Washington and Warren, purchased by the subscriber. C. W. Dundas, Clinton House."—" Wadsworth's cheese."—" New shad."— "Antibilous Pills."—" Cash for corn and rye."— " Cash for wheat."—" More new goods at the auction store, No. 1, Buffalo-street, near the market."—" Lake Ontario steam-boat."—" Ontario female seminary."— " Stray horse.—Came into the stable of the subscriber, on the 19th instant, a light bay horse, with white hind legs, and one white fore foot, supposed to be five or six years old—the owner is requested to identify his property, pay the charges, and take him away—Luman Ashley."—A trunk gone."—" American independence for ever,"—" Debilitated :" —but, perhaps, the foregoing may suffice.

I could notice a few other customs, peculiarities, &c., but scarcely thinking this day's travel furnishes a fair specimen, they may rest for future opportunity and confirmation.

I was set down in Utica, at *Bagg's Tavern,* a commodious Inn *located* at the corner of Main and Genesee-streets, and finding that the western stage, passing through New Hartford, where I was designing to tarry a week with a few ex-English friends, who had settled in the neighbourhood, did not leave till five in the morning, though pressed to make trial of a bed— a *luxury* I had not *enjoyed* since quitting Newburgh— I preferred rolling myself up in my cloak, on the floor where I was, and calling in the aid of my carpet bag for a pillow, after the fatigues of the day, thought but little of the lowliness of my resting-place, secure, at least, from evils I had endured in *more exalted* ones, and slept away till near the time of starting.

August 15th.—This morning, before five o'clock, our *concern* was all in readiness, and the driver most impatient for the appearance of my yesterday's companions, who, jaded like myself, seemed to prefer the carriage whereon they were reposing to the one which they were now summoned to enter, ' where hope of present slumber flies.' Jolt, jolt, jolt, however, we were soon at it again ; the morning was cheeringly fine, and the anticipated pleasure of meeting friends I had not seen for years, with the novelty of all around me, diverted my thoughts from what might not, otherwise, have furnished them with very agreeable occupation ; and the distance to New Hartford being little more than four miles, I was happily at the end of my journey ere I had time to become sensitive to injuries, grievous enough by repetition.

Alighting at the first public establishment the place afforded, after freeing myself from no trifling accumulation of dust and dirt, and partaking of an excellent breakfast, I set out, with some previous direction, to discover the retreat of my friends, which I found pleasantly situated, about two miles from the village, ' fast by a sheltering wood,' with a good road, as roads go here, passing by it, and in the midst of rich and well cultivated lands.

The wonted excitement of meeting subsided, we, of

course, fell into chat of persons, and things, and
many by-gone scenes of the ' Old Country.' which
time or distance had yet failed to obliterate, and
passed the day, much after the fashion of days of like
character, gratified with each other's society, and mu-
tually pained, pleased, or surprised, at our respective
communications and developments.

Some very refreshing rain fell during the afternoon,
but scarcely more than enough to lay the dust; the
sun broke out again in the evening, and the day closed
as fine as it commenced.

August 16*th*.—I have arisen this morning from the
first bed I have *passed an hour* in since leaving Brooklyn, and it is needless to add, after a night of most
welcome and refreshing repose.

After breakfast I rode with one of the family to
Whitesborough, a village about four miles distant,
situated on the *Sadaquada,* or Sauquait Creek, and
passed by the Erie canal, with which the main, and I
may say the only, street runs parallel.   It contains but
few good houses, though many are to be observed in the
neighbourhood.   It is said that the first *framed* house,
erected in the county of Oneida, still in existence, was
at this place.—We returned by way of the *York
Mills,* considered the most extensive cotton manufactories in the State of New York; and passed, besides,
several considerable manufacturing establishments of
different kinds, all indicating the rapid advances which
trade and population are making in these parts.

On subsequent days I visited other places and parts
of the country, committing *memoranda* and informa-

tion to my *Farming Journal* from which I extract the following :—

' The value and quality of land, as may be imagined, varies very much in different parts of this county, The best quality of soil is perhaps to be met with in the neighbourhood of Utica, which thriving and in-creasing town will soon furnish a market for a large amount of produce raised around it. Farms in the adjacent townships, say, of New Hartford, Clinton, Paris, Whitesborough, and Westmoreland, are worth from 25 to 50 dollars per acre, dependent upon cir-cumstances before alluded to. *Wood land* is fully as valuable as cleared. Much of the northern and western part of the county is unsettled, and about the *Oneida Lake* wild land is selling from 5 to 10 dollars per acre, the distance probably 25 or 30 miles from Utica, and 10 from the canal. The soil is for the most part of a strong loam, well calculated for grazing, and fully as productive in grass as grain, though good crops of all descriptions of the latter are raised. The best farms that can be purchased, and this remark may apply generally, I should think the most elegible, —particularly for an Englishman. But little land is rented, hardly enough to establish a rate of rental —I think, however, I shall not much err if I state it at from 1 to 1½ dollars per acre : when taken in this way it is almost invariably by the year, though there are instances of farms being held on lease.

The *share,* or *halving system,* as it is called, is not very extensively practiced. The terms of this contract are :——the tenant finding half the seed and the teams, doing the whole of the work, and dividing the produce with the landlord. If the farm be a good one, the landlord frequently finds teams and milch cows, which are valued to the tenant on coming on, and upon which value he pays about equal to 7½ per cent. per annum during the time he uses them.

The proportion which arable bears to grazing land, in this part of the county, is about one-third.

The usual produce of *wheat* may be given at from 12 to 35 bushels per acre; of *barley* from 20 to 40; of *oats* from 15 to 60; *Indian corn* from 15 to 50; *potatoes* from 150 to 300 bushels; *hay* from 20 to 60 cwt. The great variation in quantity much dependent upon management. Hops and apples are very uncertain; turnips do not succeed well. The present, and which are about the average prices, are, say of wheat, 1 dollar per 60 lbs. Barley, 45 cents per 48 lbs. Oats, 25 cents. Indian corn, 56 cents per 58 lbs. Potatoes, 20 cents per bushel. Hay, 5 dollars per ton. Hops, 12½ cents per lb. Cyder sells at from 1 to 3 dollars per barrel, (30 gallons, wine measure.) No clover seed is gathered, but a good deal of *timothy grass* seed, which brings from 1 to 2 dollars per bushel. Flour is worth about 5 dollars per barrel, of 196 lbs.

The value of horses is much as in Long Island; as also that of cows and sheep. For stall-fed cattle, 5 cents per lb. may be obtained. Fat lambs are worth 1 dollar. Store cattle, say two-year old steers, sell from 10 to 13 dollars; three-year old, from 20 to 25 dollars per head. Store pigs, 4 cents per lb. alive.

The native cattle are generally raised, and are considered full as well adapted to the country as the imported ones; the cows are small, but good milkers; the oxen grow large, weighing sometimes 1500 lbs. each. It is quite customary to sell fat stock by its weight when alive.

The horses, most in use for farming and other purposes, resemble the English *stager*: no heavy *cart horses* are used.

The sheep are mostly a cross with the native and merino, and cut about 3 lbs. of wool each, worth 37½ cents per lb.

Butter, taking the year round, sells for 12½ cents per lb. Cheese, from 6 to 8 cents. Apples, from 25 to 50 cents per bushel. Turkeys, from 6 to 8 cents per lb. Geese, 25 cents each. Fowls, 4 or 5 cents per lb. Beef is worth from 6 to 8 cents per lb. Veal, 3 to 4 cents. Mutton, 4 cents. Lamb, 30 cents per quarter. Fresh pork, 6 cents per lb.

Labourers' wages vary from 5 to 12 dollars per month—of course, exclusive of board—but few are hired by the day; about half a dollar the usual price when that is the case: they work from daylight to dark all the year round.

The land, as in Long Island, is tilled about equally by horses and oxen. Fallowing is much more in practice here than there.

The ploughs in use are all single, with cast-iron *mould boards* and *shares*, well adapted to the country: the cost about 8 or 10 dollars each.

Waggons are every where much lighter than in

England, calculated for a pair of American horses, weighing about 8 or 10 cwt., and worth from 50 to 60 dollars. But few *horse* carts are used; those drawn by oxen are a heavy stout vehicle, much as in Herefordshire, worth 40 dollars: other implements are very similar to those used in England.

Manure, in this part of the State, is not made a sufficient object of; oftentimes altogether neglected; but the farmers ere long will learn its value, if I mistake not. For years after land is cleared it does not require it: it is then too full of vegetable matter—in fact, nothing else; but I have seen some naturally excellent land exhausted with cropping, and beggared for want of manure. At Utica it may be plentifully obtained from 12½ to 18 cents per ton.

The usual description of fences are *worm*, or crooked rail fences, and post and rail: the cost of making them about 50 cents a rod.

The roads are mostly indifferent; they are repaired by a levy on the farmers, and a poll-tax of a day's work on every capable resident man in the parish: thus, *working on the roads* has a very different acceptation here to what it has with us, the most respectable farmers, &c. taking their turn quite as a matter of course.

The wild land is generally well, some of it *nobly* timbered; many *hemlock* and other trees I have observed from 70 to 90 feet in the but, without one intervening bough, and of a proportionate thickness: the cost of clearing it is about 10 dollars per acre.

There are a number of small streams, about the

centre of the county, which form the Mohawk river, rising in the N. E. and supply most valuable mill-seats; the quality of the water, however, obtained for domestic purposes, is often very bad, sometimes wholly unfit to drink.   Fever and ague, diseases which shake the constitution to pieces, prevail occasionally, and the winters are very protracted and severe; more so, it is said, than further either to the east or west, so as to suspend farming operations for five or six months in the year, but the county, I believe, is considered as healthy as most.'

I might add further, but these observations, very loosely thrown together, will probably more than suffice the generality of readers.   The contrast between Orange and Oneida counties, as regards the state of their agriculture, is greater than can well be conceived. Spafford, speaking of the latter, says, ' Its agriculture is of the first order, and twenty years hence there will not be an acre of waste land in the county.'   He also says, ' It has now probably more capital employed in manufactures than any county in this State.'   He gives its area at 1136 square miles.   Latitude between 42° 46', and 43° 33', N. and long. 1° 05' and 1° 55' W., from New York.

As I arrived at Utica from Albany very late in the evening, and left it at an early hour in the morning, only having visited it once since, and that not for any purpose of writing a description, I must be content to offer a much shorter notice than I could wish to have given.

'This flourishing village stands on the south bank

of Mohawk river. It occupies the site of old Fort Schuyler, where a garrison was kept previous to the revolution. Some remains of this fort are still to be seen between the eastern extremity of Main-street and the river. A few Germans were settled here previous to the revolutionary war; but a part were captured by the Indians, and the remnant sought a place of more security. The first permanent settler established himself about four miles west of Fort Schuyler, in 1784. Five years afterwards a few families established themselves on the site of the present *village*, and in 1798 a village charter was granted to the place; since which it has rapidly increased in population. In 1813, it contained 1700 inhabitants; in 1816, 2828; in 1820, 2972; in 1823, 4017; in 1826, 6040; in 1828, 7460; and in 1829, 9081. The village is regularly laid out, the streets of a good width, and mostly paved. Genesee-street, in particular, is peculiarly pleasant, and for the most part adorned with elegant stores and dwellings.

'There are numerous literary, benevolent, and religious institutions in this place. Among these, the *Oneida Institute of Science and Industry* is perhaps the most worthy of remark, from its uniting manual with mental labour on the part of the students. There is a farm attached to it, comprising 114 acres, upon which each student labours from three to four hours per day; and it is said that the experiment of two years proves that labour, from three to five hours per day, pays the board of the student in this plentiful region. It is principally intended for the education of those

designed for the ministry, but its privileges are common to all youth of unexceptionable character. There
are also a classical academy, a library, lyceum, and
nine churches, some of which are very elegant.'

Utica is, as stated, 94 miles from Albany, 142 from
Rochester, and from Buffalo 200.

Another place in the neighbourhood, which I have
seen with much interest, though in point of size insignificant to Utica, is Clinton. It is a very pretty
village, six miles from New Hartford, and contains a
number of respectable houses and buildings. Its
situation is at the foot of a hill of considerable ascent,
which is planted on each side with poplar trees, and
on the summit of which stands *Hamilton College,* or
colleges, for though the buildings are united there
have been three separate erections. The corner stone
of the first edifice was laid by that celebrated republican patriot, Baron Steuben. Until very lately it was
ranking high amongst institutions of the kind in the
State, but I regret to hear that in consequence of some
misunderstanding having arisen between the masters
and students, it has been altogether deserted. 'Tis
said, however, that a few of the latter are about to return, and perhaps eventually it may regain its former
pre-eminence : so vitally important are such institutions to the welfare of an infant republic that every
lover of freedom, every *good man,* must ardently desire
their prosperity.—From its elevated site, overlooking
the village, there is a fine view of the surrounding
plain, the fertile vale of the Mohawk, and the country,
for many miles in extent, in different directions.

Paris, Westmoreland, and other townships, though abounding with good land, and chiefly well cultivated, as villages are unimportant.

Previous to my arrival at New Hartford I had felt a little undecided as to my future route, but having no time for hesitation, and wishing to see what was considered the most interesting and fertile part of the State, I soon determined upon extending my journey westward as far as Buffalo, occasionally diverging through some of the counties as I passed along, and returning by Niagara, and either upon or along the shore of Lake Ontario.   Having so decided, this morning,—

August 23rd,—I engaged a place by the *Telegraph Stage,* from New Hartford to Auburn, in Cayuga county, distance about seventy miles ; and soon after eight o'clock had seated myself upon the most obdurate leathern seat of the vehicle, and was bounding and rebounding along as vigorously as ever, though well up to my travelling traces again, and prepared ' to dash through thick and thin.'

The first village we arrive at is *Manchester,* five miles from New Hartford; next, *Vernon,* eight miles further; neither requiring comment; the land good and seemingly well farmed nearly all the way.   Five miles from Vernon is *Oneida Castle,* a village situated upon the Oneida creek, and at which there is a settlement called here *a reservation* of the *Oneida and Tuscarora Indians,* several of whom I saw.   A *squaw (woman)* I particularly noticed, who came to solicit charity, with one of the most marked and disgusting

countenances I think I ever beheld. I was told, and
have no reason to doubt it, that she was one hundred
years old, more or less ; she appeared tolerably stout
and robust, and I suspect what was evinced to the
contrary was about as much feigned as real. Several
children also, nearly in a state of nudity, came to us
for a like purpose, and displayed their agility by keeping up with the stage, and we drove pretty fast, for
some distance, though I thought their performances,
notwithstanding the attention they appeared to excite,
very inferior to those of the urchins of our own country,
who will not only run parallel with the coach, but
with amazing rapidity turn over and over upon their
hands and feet into the bargain, and, alas ! I fear,
with quite as good a plea of necessity. The tribe
occupy about one-third of the township, and their
number is estimated at 1100. They still retain some
of the customs of their forefathers, and their usual
dress is nothing more than a blanket thrown across
the shoulders, and tied round the neck. They are
wretched agriculturists, as their lands fully demonstrate ; but I am told, for several months in the year,
they totally neglect them, and repair to the forests in
the northern part of country, on hunting excursions ;
—so hardly are we weaned from inbred habits and
propensities ! A correspondent of Spafford's states
that ' there are missionaries amongst them to teach
them letters and religion, and they pay one of them
near two hundred dollars a year, besides making him
a great many presents. These Indians are a harmless,
inoffensive set of beings, but have lost much of their

ancient spirit and energy. Several of them have become voluntary apprentices to different mechanics, placed amongst them by the Baptists, such as blacksmiths, wheelwrights, &c.; and many of the Indian women are becoming weavers and spinners, under the instruction of benevolent females of the missionary family.'—' Mr. Williams,' adds the Doctor, ' late a missionary here, now of Green Bay, is of mixed blood, lineally descended from the Rev. Mr. Williams, of Deerfield, whose captivity and sufferings we have all read when children. He is a man of very considerable education, and seems to lead in a plan for collecting all our Indians into one great band, but I know nothing of the success or prospects of the scheme.'

The road from this place, through the small villages of *Lenox* and *Quality Hill* to Chitteningo, eleven miles, is much elevated, commanding a fine view of the lofty mountains to the north: the soil is rich, but strangely overgrown with the *Canada thistle*, the down from which is wafted about in all directions, and has almost the appearance of falling snow.—Before reaching Chitteningo there is one of the finest specimens of *native forest* I have seen in the country—I ever saw —tree interwoven with tree—*a dense mass of forest*— seeming to bid defiance to the footsteps, ay, even the hands of man; and yet but a few years may elapse ere this wilderness becomes a fertile plain, ere the share of the husbandman passes over its surface, and the abodes of happy industry are raised upon it! So rapid are the strides of improvement and cultivation in this enterprising country.

The village Chitteningo, on the creek of the same name, and about two miles from the canal, to which a cut has been made, has little to attract the attention of a stranger; but on arriving at Syracuse, through Hartsville and Fayetteville, fifteen miles, you are agreeably surprised at seeing a handsome thriving village, quite a business-like place. The canal passes directly through it, on both sides of which there are a number of spacious stores and warehouses. The population I should estimate at something like 1,500. On alighting at the principal hotel, which is a very handsome and commodious brick building, I observed a thermometer hanging in the shade, and exposed to a current of air, standing at 88°; this was about four o'clock in the afternoon. No doubt, during the day, it had been as high as 90°.

My stay here did not admit of my visiting the valuable and very extensive salt springs which abound in the neighbourhood, and to which Syracuse is indebted for its growth and existence. The reader, however, in the subjoined information, will have little cause to regret *my* want of opportunity.

' A little west of Syracuse, a plain of 300 acres, (*a part of which we passed over,)* is nearly covered with vats for the manufacture of salt by solar evaporation. The water is brought in logs from the great spring at *Salina,* one mile distant, and supplies, with very little attention, the various ranges of vats. A light roof is constructed to each vat, which can be shoved off or on at pleasure, to permit the rays of the sun to act upon the water, or to prevent the dampness of the atmosphere from commingling therewith. The salt is taken out of these vats twice or three times during the warm season, and removed to store-houses, from whence it is conveyed in barrels to the canal for transportation.

'The spring at *Salina* was first discovered by the Indians, many years since, by being the resort of deer and other animals. The first white settlers were in the habit of boiling the water for domestic purposes. Since then the spring has been excavated to a considerable depth, and affords the strongest saline water yet discovered in the world, forty gallons yielding about a bushel of pure salt. The water is forced up to the top of an adjoining hill by a powerful hydraulian, driven by the surplus waters from the Oswego canal, which commences at this place. The salt water is in this way conveyed eighty-five feet above the canal to a large reservoir, into which it is discharged at the rate of three hundred gallons per minute. It is hence carried to the different factories in Salina and Syracuse. Of these there are about one hundred at Salina, and twenty-three at Syracuse; there are also twenty-six at Liverpool, about six miles N. W. of Salina, and twenty-five at Geddesburgh, two miles W. of Syracuse. The works and springs all belong to the State, to which imposts are payable to the amount of 63 cents per barrel of five bushels,* and every manufacturer pays 2 cents per bushel for the use of the water. The water is conveyed from the

* These duties are applied by the constitution of the State towards the extinguishment of the canal debt.

reservoir to the different manufactories and evapo-
rating fields by means of wooden pipes.   The salt
is manufactured generally by boiling and evaporation.   There are, however, two establishments in
which it is made in large wooden vats by means of
hot air passing through them in large metallic pipes.
The manufactories contain from fifteen to forty pot-
ash kettles, under each of which a constant fire is
kept up, so that the water may not cease to boil.
The first deposit of the water is thrown away.   The
pure salt soon after makes its appearance, and is re-
fined for the table by means of blood, milk, rosin, &c.
The springs are considered as inexhaustible.   In
1828, there were 1,160,888 bushels inspected ; and
in 1829, 1,291,820 bushels; showing an increase of
130,932 bushels.   Of this, 745,741 bushels were inspected at Salina, 229,317 at Syracuse, 187,540 at
Liverpool; and 129,222 at Geddes.

  ' Salina is a village of much less magnitude than
Syracuse, but it is not improbable that they will ere
long become a continuous town.   The Onondaga Lake
is about a mile distant from the place.   It is six miles
long, and two broad.   Gypsum and petrifactions are
found in great quantities in the vicinity of the lake.

  A la route, Marcellus is the next place, containing
perhaps fifty houses, and in the neighbourhood are
found great quantities of water lime or cement, and
some petrifactions.   It is thirteen miles from Syracuse.

  Six miles further brought us to Skaneateles, a much
larger and more interesting village, very pleasantly

situated just at the foot of the Skaneateles Lake, along
which you have a fine view for several miles. The
lake is about fifteen miles in length, and ½ to 1½ miles
wide. In its vicinity are several genteel residences,
as well as in the village, and also a *Friends'* boarding-
school. The population of the place is estimated at
3,000. The following stage of seven miles brought
us to *Auburn*, about half-past eight in the evening,
having been twelve hours and a half in accomplishing the seventy miles, which, taking into account the
state of the roads, the heat of the day, &c. is by no
means to be complained of. During the latter part
of the way the country was but partially cleared, but
wherever cultivated, it appeared rich and productive.
I did not find the price of land varying much from
30 dollars per acre; that is, for improved farms with
good buildings upon them. The average produce,
say of wheat, 25 bushels per acre, sold from 75 cents
to 1 dollar per bushel, chiefly at the stores in the
village nearest the farm.

I am here quartered at the *American Hotel,* an
establishment upon a very extended scale, kept by
—— *Noyes.* The building is of freestone, five stories
high, with piazzas, twenty feet or more in width, up
to the third story. Many of the apartments are large
and elegantly furnished, and I am informed they can,
if requisite, make up 250 or 300 beds. It has been
recently erected, and, excepting at New York, is quite
the best inn I have seen in the State; so much has it
pleased me, in fact, that I am tempted to forego my
half resolve, not to make trial of a public dormitory

again in the country.   I shall venture this once upon
the credit of fair promise, and will *report progress* in
the morning.

August 24*th.*—For *once* appearances *have not* been
deceitful.   I have slept undisturbed, excepting that I
was aroused at a pretty early hour this morning by
the loud pealing of thunder, without any disposition,
however, to complain either of cause or consequence,
the limited time I shall have to spend here not war-
ranting much indulgence in this way ; to which, when
most an idler, I'm not over prone.

As an object of first attraction I proceeded to visit
the *State Prison,* situated here, and considered one of
the first in the Union.   ' It was commenced in 1816,
and is constructed upon the plan of a hollow square,
inclosed by a wall 2000 feet in extent, being 500 feet
on each side.   The front of the prison, including the
keeper's dwelling, is about 300 feet, and the two wings,
extending west, are 240 feet each.   The north wing
contains the solitary cells and hospital, and the south
wing is divided principally into two large rooms.   Between the two wings is a grass plat with gravel walks ;
to the west of which is the interior yard, covered with
gravel, containing reservoirs of water, and surrounded
with workshops.   These shops, besides the paint shop,
form a continued range of 900 feet, and are well
lighted by windows in the sides and from the roof.
They are built of brick, and are well secured against
fire.   The outer walls, against which the shops are
built, are thirty-five feet high in the inside, and the
other walls about twenty.   They are four feet thick,

and the walls of the prison three feet thick. The expense of the whole, without including the labour of convicts employed, was above 300,000 dollars. The prison being erected on the bank of the *Owasco*, water-power is applied, in many cases to great advantage, in propelling machinery."

About six o'clock I applied at the door for admittance, which was granted on my paying twenty-five cents, and one of the keepers commissioned to conduct me over the establishment. We first visited the cells, which the convicts leave at half-past five in the morning. These gloomy abodes are about seven or eight feet long, by four feet wide, and perhaps about seven feet in height. They are lighted from windows in the roof of the passage into which they open through ponderous iron doors. All the furniture they contain is a hammock, which is let down in the day-time, a stool, and a Bible upon a shelf in one of the corners.—From these we passed on to the workshops, where the convicts were busily employed in their different avocations; tailoring, shoemaking, weaving; machine, button, cabinet making, &c.; coopering, and smiths' work in general. These various manufactures, besides what are requisite for the prison, are furnished to all the principal stores in Auburn, and sent to different parts of the State. My guide afterwards conducted me to the cooking apartment, where some of the convicts were engaged in preparing the morning's repast for the rest, and which I presently saw arranged with great neatness in the general eating-room: it consisted of coffee, Indian corn bread, and boiled fish. At half-past six they were summoned by a bell to partake of it, upon which occasion I had a good opportunity of observing some of the most striking characteristics of the system. The convicts were arranged in separate corps, " moving in single file, with a slow lock step, and erect posture, keeping exact time, with their faces inclined towards their keepers, (that they may detect conversation, of which none is ever permitted,) all giving to the spectator somewhat similar feelings to those excited by a military funeral." In a short time all were seated at the different tables, in the most orderly and regular manner, and, upon a signal being given by the keepers, with one simultaneous movement commenced their meal. Had I not witnessed the scene, I should have supposed it morally impossible for such a number of individuals to be assembled together,* for such a purpose, with so little noise and confusion. It was a very interesting, though at the same time a very painful and humiliating spectacle; and various were the reflections which hurried across my mind whilst looking round upon these imprisoned victims of crime, of almost every grade and malignancy. Some appeared calm and resigned, or sensible of the guilt and degradation of their situation; others displayed an entire indifference to their fate; whilst in a few I noticed the black expressions of obdurate cruelty, ferocity, and revenge, demonstrating but too plainly the justice of the doom which had overtaken them.

---

* There are at this time 635 persons in confinement, twenty-two only of whom are women.

Breakfast concluded (and there did not appear, on the part of the keepers, the smallest disposition to hurry over the ceremony; all were allowed sufficient time, and materials too, even for a hearty repast,) the prisoners rose again in like order, and were forthwith marched back to their different workshops and employments;—here, the guide informed me, they were kept until twelve o'clock, when they were again summoned to dinner, after which they resume their labour till six, when their daily toil is done: they are then marched off to their separate cells, each carrying his supper with him, and eating alone, if not in darkness, his last cheerless meal. There is a chapel within the prison, which the prisoners attend regularly every sabbath; a Sunday school has also been established; and in the hospital every attention is paid to such as require it.

The severity of the punishment here exercised consists in preventing every kind of intercourse of one convict with another: whether at their work, or at their meals, they are compelled to observe the most absolute and uniform silence; not the slightest attempt at communication would escape notice; and every offender against this tenacious and positive requirement is punished by flogging,—an alternative, however, rarely needed. I observed the young and the old, and every description of character, mixed indiscriminately together, but from which, with the restrictions imposed, no evil consequence can possibly arise. A decided majority, upon leaving the prison, have become reformed and useful members of society. It is

altogether conducted upon an admirable principle,
and reflects the highest credit upon the projectors and
the country; affording, at the same time, an exalted
contrast, when compared with *our* miserable recep-
tacles for this class of society : *in them,* if *reformation*
take place, it is by miracle; *here,* frequent, and *the
end and object of the institution.*

On returning to the hotel again, soon after seven
o'clock, I found a pretty large company collected for
breakfast, a very excellent one, and of which, after the
ordinary fashion, we all partook at one common table.
This ceremony over I sallied forth to take a hasty view
of the town, (*village,* I should say,) ere the stage arrived which was to convey me onward.—Auburn is
situated on the Owasco creek; it consists principally
of one street, running east and west, which contains a
number of good stores and private dwellings, a court-
house, and a large hotel, independent of the one I am
quartered at, called the *Western Exchange.* There are
also, at the eastern end of the village, some extensive
mills and manufactories.   Its population is called
more than 4,000, with every appearance of increasing,
as buildings are springing up all around.   The adjacent country is very level, and of no particular interest : the land is loosely cultivated, and, without
reflection, you would be ready to say that the town
had pitched itself here before it was well prepared to
receive it.   The canal is distant about seven miles to
the south; but it is intended, either by a cut or railroad, to form a communication with it, which will
greatly add to the importance and facilities of the place.

Leaving Auburn, we next came to Cayuga, (eight miles,) a small village standing on the eastern side, and near the extremity of the lake of that name, and over which we passed by a wooden bridge, one mile and eight rods in length,—a most barbarous structure, built upon piles, and conveying the idea, if not the reality, of great insecurity; as the planks, or logs, upon which you pass, uncovered with gravel, soil, or other material, are of all shapes and sizes, heedlessly laid across from side to side, without nails or any kind of fastening whatever. In many instances I observed them scarcely resting upon the supports on each side, and the waters of the lake every where visible below: of course, as they were acted upon by the weight and motion of the coach and horses, they were perpetually jolting up and down, so that it was a matter of astonishment to me how the animals could pass over at the rate they did, a good brisk trot, without getting their feet between them; the accompanying noise and clatter, too, was any thing but agreeable. An English traveller, however, must leave all his fears and prejudices at home, and be here content to dash on, over, under, or through whatever it may please the driver and his steeds to convey him. The lake is about thirty-eight miles long, and of very various breadth, from one to four miles. "A steamboat is plying daily between the Bridge and *Ithica*, a beautiful and thriving village at the head of the lake, thirty-six miles distant," and near to which I understand are several falls well worth notice.

Some good farms are to be met with in the neigh-

bourhood of the lake, as well as in other parts of the
county.

The next village is *Seneca Falls,* (three miles.)   It
is said to contain upwards of 2,000 inhabitants, though
I should have rated the population at much less; has
several mills, a tannery, distillery, and a few stores.
" A canal, twenty miles long, has been constructed
from this place to the Erie canal at Montezuma,
which, connected with a branch of the Seneca river,
gives an uninterrupted water communication from
Geneva to the lakes and the ocean."

Four miles further is *Waterloo;* but I am no great
admirer of Waterloos, nor can I, in its present state,
bestow the inordinate praise upon this place which
some have done.   It is a half shire town, considerably
larger than *Seneca Falls;* contains a court-house, jail,
and several stores, but it is altogether a most irregu-
larly-built and unfinished place, and whatever importance or interest time may add to its character, I
have spoken of it as it *now is,* and without much of
either.   I observed several mills upon the Seneca
river, or *outlet,* on which the village stands.

Passing on to Geneva, seven miles from Waterloo,
I am pleased to be able to make a much more favourable report.   For the last two miles, as we approached,
the road became highly interesting, winding along
the northern end of the *Seneca Lake;* just to the west
of which, at a considerable elevation, the village is
situated; one of the principal streets running immediately down to the lake, and the other along the
summit of the bank and parallel with it; extending be-

yond which are many elegant private residences, the
gardens and grounds overhanging the lake, and which,
whilst they add to the beauty, command a fine prospect of the charming scenery around. The public
buildings consist of a college, recently erected, but
which is handsomely endowed, and promises to arrive
at eminence; three or four churches, a bank, and two
pretty comfortable inns. Many of the stores are
commodious and well furnished: one I noticed advertised as follows:—" A Heimpus, *variety store ;*"—
a tolerably correct definition of stores in general,
especially in the country towns, which not unfrequently display the most heterogeneous collection of
articles that can be well conceived, and embrace in
their individual capacity what with us would occupy
a score of different professors.

I should think the present population of *Geneva*
might be estimated at 3,000. It is twelve miles from
the Erie canal, but has a water communication with
it, which has much increased its trade and importance.
From hence a delightful excursion is frequently taken
down the lake, in a steam-boat plying daily, to
Jeffersonville at the head of it. The lake is thirty-
five miles long, and three or four miles wide, and is
esteemed one of the purest and most beautiful sheets
of water of the kind in America.

After spending the chief part of the day at Geneva
and its delightful environs, I took my departure for
Canandaigua, fifteen miles distant,—in travelling to
which I passed over one of the finest farming districts
I have yet seen in the State of New York. The land

is agreeably undulated, of excellent quality, well fenced, in smaller inclosures than I have noticed in other parts, and in a superior state of cultivation. The grain was mostly housed, but, independent of *report*, the stubbles themselves were ample evidence of the plentiful crops which had been taken off them, and the grass and seeds were looking remarkably healthy and well. Farms in this part, with good houses and buildings upon them, and chiefly they are so, are to be bought at from 30 to 45 dollars per acre. Wheat is selling for 70 or 80 cents a bushel, and meat from three to six cents per pound, which may be given as about the general average prices of those articles; and labourers' wages are usually from ten to twelve dollars per month. In the immediate neighbourhood of *Canandaigua village* the land, I am told, is chiefly held by two or three large proprietors, whose farms are from 1,000 to 1,500 acres each.

What a contrast, delightful contrast, does this state of things present to the situation in which Dr. Spafford reports that he found them in 1797! "The settlement of this township," observes the Doctor, "commenced in 1790, and in 1797 I found it but feeble, contending with innumerable embarrassments and difficulties. The spring of that year was uncommonly wet and cold. Besides a good deal of sickness, mud knee deep, musquetoes and gnats so thick that you could hardly breathe without swallowing them, rattlesnakes and ten thousand discouragements, every where incident to new settlements; surrounded by all these, in June of that year, I saw, with wonder, that these people, all Yankees, from Massachusetts, Connecticut, and Vermont, were perfectly undismayed, 'looking forward in hope,' 'sure and stedfast.' They talked to me of what the country would be, by-and-by, as if it were *history,* and I received it as all *fable.* In order to see the whole 'power of the county,' a military muster of all men bearing arms, I waited a day or two, and attended 'the training.' Major Wadsworth was the commanding officer, and including the men who *had guns,* and the men who *had not,* the boys, women, and children, it was supposed that near two hundred persons were collected. This training, one of the first, was held at Captain Pitts', on the Honeoye, and lasted all day and all night. The early settlers of every new country are sanguine in hopes and expectations, and it is well they should be. Lands were selling, in 1797, in the very heart of this fine region, at 25 cents an acre."—"I like," continues the Doctor, "to trace the progress of affairs from their small beginnings, never 'despising the day of small things.' The reader will indulge me in this digression, so out of the way with most people, but perfectly in character with the pursuits of a general gleaner." Like him, I beg pardon, if necessary; the comparison of past and present was too pleasing to allow me to forego it.

It was between eight and nine in the evening when we arrived at *Canadaigua:* the day had been remarkably fine, though 20° or 30° cooler than yesterday, changes which are rather trying to weakly constitutions. We were driven up to *Blossoms Hotel,* a building little inferior in size to the *American Hotel*, in Auburn, but much older, and not so clean. The landlord, a jolly sort of fellow, had just returned from an excursion to the Western Lakes and Ohio, and being visited by numerous congratulatory friends and acquaintance, the house was in a tolerable state of confusion for the remainder of the evening,—the bar, of course, being the only general room of resort. After some few ineffectual attempts at *journalizing*, I inquired of the waiter as to the probable security with which I might make my advances to a chamber, and replete with most satisfactory assurances, was glad to effect my escape, and leave them to feast on their *wit and wine*, which, though abundant, were neither of first rate quality, as much and as long as they liked.

August 25th.—Foolishly presuming upon the waiter's recommendation, and the comfortable night passed at Auburn, I have not escaped without a scar, though in a far less woful plight than heretofore, and happy to think I am getting more out of the way of the nuisance.

Before breakfast I made my first, and almost only, survey of Canandaigua, which I admire even more than Geneva. Its situation is on the north-western extremity of the Canadaigua Lake,* where the main street, nearly two miles in length, commences, rising gradually to its termination. It is planted on each side with trees, and expands about the middle of the

---

* The Lake is fourteen miles long, and from one to two in breadth, and has a steam-boat daily plying upon it.

village into a fine open square, where the court-
house, clerks' office, episcopal church, and other handsome public buildings are situated. The private residences, both in the village and vicinity, are uncommonly elegant, laid out with courts and gardens, and
every way worthy of the affluence and respectability
of their occupants; many of them commanding a
beautiful view of the lake and its surrounding
scenery. The population amounts to 5000, more or
less—*not less,* I think, certainly—and in 1790, Spafford says, *there was but a single human habitation
in it.*

A short time previous to my visit, a large steam
flour mill, belonging to Messrs. Pomeroy and Bull,
of New York, standing just at the entrance of the
village, had been entirely destroyed by fire. The
occurrence is supposed to have originated in the
contents of a pipe, falling on a cloth, or some combustible substance in an adjoining room;—one of
the many evils arising from the use of that worthless
weed—tobacco; and not the first or second of the kind
that has come under my immediate knowledge:—
would that it were for ever banished from the abodes
of civilization ! The inconvenience produced by
the calamity, I see thus adverted to in a Canandaigua paper:—" The destruction of this flouring
establishment, which was built in the best manner,
and at a ruinous expense, by its original enterprising
proprietors, is not only a severe loss to those directly
interested, but to our village, and to our neighbours
in towns adjacent. This mill created, as it were, a

ready and convenient market for large quantities of
wheat; imparted animation to business round about,
and gave employment to numbers of our citizens.
Its importance to the community, like the blessing
of health, is mostly severely felt, by sudden depriva-
tion. The property was insured by the Etna Company to the amount of 8000 dollars."

Canandaigua stands upon the great western stage
route to Buffalo and Niagara; is distant from the
former place 89, and from the latter 109 miles, and
208 from Albany: it is also 12 miles south of the
Erie canal, with which it has a water communication.

In the neighbourhood are several springs charged
with inflammable gas, or, as they are called, *burning
springs,* well worth the attention of the virtuoso.

From hence to Rochester, (only 27 miles in a direct
line,) I performed a very circuitous route, travelling
partly by stage, partly by waggon, and partly on
foot, through *Victor, Minden, Pittsford, Henrietta
Corners,* &c. The road is very bad nearly the whole
of the way, and there is a good deal of land un-
cleared; but, at the same time, there is much in a
fine state of cultivation, and I passed over some very
eligible farms; the prices, products, expenses, &c.,
much as those quoted in Oneida county. About a
mile to the south of Pittsford, a small village ten miles
from Rochester, a farm was pointed out to me, now
offering for sale by a gentleman whose family are settling in *Michigan,* where population is much on the
increase. It consists of three hundred acres of land,
the quality of the soil varying between sand and loam;

is well timbered, well fenced, and has a good house and outbuildings upon it. The price *asked* is thirty-five dollars per acre, but I have no idea that ten dollars less would be *refused*. I also called upon a gentleman, by the request of a friend, who has recently emigrated from England into this neighbourhood, and is farming upon a small scale. He complains of a want of society, and many deprivations and inconveniences, *a great deal to put up with;* and I give him full credit for all. I sincerely hope he may ultimately find himself rewarded for the sacrifices he has made; but, in my opinion, for one ignorant of farming, and wholly unused to a country life, *he has retreated sadly too far from New York;* and little would it surprise me to hear, before any remote period, that he had arrived at a like conclusion. I left him some English newspapers, which I *guess* he would not put by unread.

It was late this evening before I gained a footing in Rochester; too late, and I am too much tired, to explore further. The day has been very fine; temperature quite agreeable.

August 26th.—Before seven o'clock this morning I had perambulated the streets, as well as a part of the suburbs of this remarkable village, which has fully answered every representation I had heard of it. It is, indeed, scarcely credible that in the period of eighteen short years a place of the present extent and importance of Rochester should have arisen from the wilds of a forest; and, if such evidence were needed, it would alone speak volumes as to the energy and enterprise of a people who, with the obstacles and impediments which they must have had to contend against, have produced such splendid results. There are not only spacious and well-arranged streets, with corresponding stores and warehouses, and private residences of elegance and respectability; but, besides a court-house, gaol, and eleven churches, two markets, two banks, and several very excellent hotels, there is a museum, institute, an athenæum, an arcade, a Vauxhall, public baths, reading-rooms, &c. &c., and a population of more than 13,000 souls! and, in the face of all this, there are even now the stumps of trees standing in some of the streets. Surely, as Spafford well observes, " it must be admitted that the growth of this place has been rapid, almost beyond example in any country, even in our own, the best supplied with such examples."

I found *mine host* here a respectable and obliging man, and under his auspices I visited objects of most interest in and about the *village ;* amongst others, the Falls, where *Sam Patch,* that notorious *fall jumper,* finished his mad career in the autumn of 1829. There are two falls within a short distance of each other, the one descending twelve, the other ninety-seven feet. Upon a projecting rock about the centre of these he erected a scaffold twenty-five feet in height, making together 122 feet, from which he fearlessly leaped into the gulph beneath. " He did not rise at that time to the surface, nor was his body found until the following spring, when it was discovered at the mouth of the Genesee river, six miles below. His arms were probably dislocated at the first shock, as he carried them horizontally; and the depth of the water being only fifteen feet, it is supposed that he was killed by striking on the rocky bottom. He was a little less than three seconds in falling, and struck the surface with a force of about 8000lbs." My attendant, however, tells me that he was pretty generally known to have been intoxicated at the time; and to that circumstance, more than any other, is to be attributed the fatal result, as, independent of his performances at Niagara, he had once or twice before, when sober, jumped from that very spot, without the slightest injury or inconvenience. All that can be said of it is, that any where and every where they were the acts of a madman, and sooner or later were likely to incur a destiny, I had almost said, due to such presumptuous, absurd temerity.

I afterwards visited the market, which I saw well supplied with meat, fish, fruits, and vegetables, all of various kinds. The first named article was selling at from 4 to 6 cents per lb., others equally moderate. Eggs 10 cents a dozen. Butter 10 to 12 cents a lb. Cheese 6 cents a lb. Flour (retail) $4\frac{1}{2}$ dollars a barrel, wholesale $4\frac{1}{4}$. Wheat $87\frac{1}{2}$ cents to 1 dollar a bushel. Oats 25 cents a bushel; considered a low price. Hay 5 dollars per ton.

Wheat is now eagerly bought, and brings a better price than at any other season of the year, as the canal being open the millers are making every effort to get their flour to New York, &c., ere the frosts commence. —At this, as at most of the villages, as I have passed

along I have observed advertisements at the stores, in
the public papers, and the bars of inns, offering *the
utmost cash price for any quantity of wheat*, &c.

The weight of flour made here annually is prodigious. " Within the limits of the village are eleven
flouring mills, containing fifty-three run of stones,
capable of manufacturing 2,500 bushels of flour, and
consuming more than 12,000 bushels of wheat every
twenty-four hours. Some of the mills are on a scale
of magnitude perhaps not equalled in the world, and
all are considered unrivalled in the perfection of their
machinery." The charge for freight of flour from Rochester to New York is 90 cents a barrel.

Besides flour, there are various other mills and
manufactories, distilleries, breweries, &c. &c., every
thing bespeaking the rising wealth and importance of
the place.

The canal runs directly through the village, and is
carried across the Genesee river, which also flows
through it, by an aqueduct. The river, at the distance
of seven miles, empties itself into Lake Ontario;
thus affording an easy and valuable navigation to the
Canadas. During the summer a steam-boat is plying
upon the Lake, between Niagara and Ogdensburgh,
on the river St. Lawrence.

Canal packets and stages are leaving Rochester
every morning and evening, east and west; and stages
in different directions frequently during the day. I
have omitted to mention—but I have omitted a great
deal, for which want of time must be my apology—
that there are two daily, and, I think, three weekly

newspapers now in publication at this busy, spirited place.

From Rochester, instead of proceeding direct to Buffalo, I took the stage to Geneseo, (31 miles S.) wishing to see the country along the banks of the Genesee river. Two miles out of the town I noticed a thrashing machine in operation, a *wooden* one to be sure ; but still a thrashing machine. It is the first I have seen in the country, was worked by two horses, and appeared to be rather an object of curiosity in its neighbourhood. A few miles further we had the misfortune to get capsized, the linchpin of the hind-wheel falling out, if (as I very much query) there was one in at starting. The road, however, was tolerably good in the part where the accident oc-curred, and all escaped without injury; though not without the grievous discomfiture of a few fair nymphs, my companions in peril. Had it happened at any of the bridges or unguarded passes, with which this country abounds, it is more than pro-bable there would have been a full and final end to coach, horses, and cargo. It was further fortunate that a village was near at hand, from which we pro-cured help, righted the carriage, stuck in a wooden linchpin, and in the course of twenty minutes were rattling along as if no disaster had befallen us, or could by possibility occur again.

We got to Geneseo about five in the afternoon. The land, the whole of the way, presented the ap-pearance of extreme fertility, though not better than in the township of Canandaigua, and the cultivation

I thought far inferior; a considerable portion of it
seemed to want good drainage, and some of the arable
lands were in a most foul state, admitting, however,
many exceptions.

The township of *Geneseo* was settled in 1790, by a
family of the name of *Wadsworth*, from Connecticut,
who own an immense tract of land between and Rochester, and are farmers themselves upon a very
extensive scale.

Evening.—I am just returned from a walk over a part
of their flats, which extend for miles along the banks of
the river, and more beautiful or luxuriant meadows and
fields I never beheld. They were engaged in getting
their hay, (as said, the last crop in America, except
Indian corn,) which was an immense bulk, nor had
their crops of grain been less abundant; thirty-five
bushels of wheat to the acre being considered below
the average. Hemp is also cultivated to some extent. The country, however, in the neighbourhood
of the flats has the character of not being very
healthy; instances of the fever and ague are frequently occurring, and were I to choose a *location*,
I should greatly prefer other parts of the State.

The village of Geneseo has nothing particular to
recommend it. It is small and has but few good
houses or buildings of any kind in it. There are
three hotels, (and by chance I have been at them
all,) which, though tolerably large, are sad dirty,
comfortless places. I have no wish to quarter in
them again.—The day has been very fine, but rather
to be called cool, than warm, for the season.

August 27th.—We have had a night cold enough for November, and this morning the flats are all enveloped in fog, as dense as ever rested on *English fen.*

The water at breakfast was so intolerably bad, that even in coffee I could not take it, and was obliged to call for milk;—I mention this because I think it *important to be noticed:*—excepting at Brooklyn, I do not recollect to have tasted really pure, good water in any part of the country where I have been; frequently it has been almost undrinkable, and, *whereever worst, there* has been most of the fever and ague prevailing.

Having seen quite as much of Geneseo as I desired, I should have taken a private conveyance this morning to Avon, (ten miles distant,) in order to meet the Buffalo stages, which usually pass through that place about nine o'clock, had I not been assured by the agents of the regular coach here that I should reach by their vehicle in abundant time; in which they most completely deceived me. As usual, we had to drive round to the different inns, and several private houses to pick up passengers, who were not in readiness, and with one hindrance and another were near two hours behind the stated time of starting; and, when off, went dreaming along at the rate of three miles and a half per hour—there is no opposition on this road—I, therefore, only arrived at Avon in time to know that I could proceed no further for the day, all the western stages having passed. Remonstrance was in vain; the parties here disclaimed all participation in the imposition, regretting it like myself; my fare was paid, and there was an end of it.

As an object of attraction in the neighbourhood, a recently discovered mineral spring was mentioned, and the landlord proposing a route by which we might connect a little sporting with it, and his son, a fine, intelligent youth, to accompany me, I began to feel my chagrin rapidly abating, and slipping on a shooting dress, we were shortly in the woods with our guns, attended by a pretty good pointer dog. We found a few woodcocks and squirrels, but, upon the whole, had indifferent success. As to what *we* denominate *game*, it is by no means abundant in the country, except *quail,* which are *generally* plentiful. Hares and pheasants there are none ; and partridges, (in some places *called* pheasants) are scarce. Woodcock and snipe are uncertain both as to season and situation. 'Tis true that great quantities of *other* birds may sometimes be killed ; for instance, *wild ducks* and *pigeons,* which are occasionally seen in flocks of many miles in extent; but after all, and much as I have heard American shooting extolled, in my opinion it is a poor, insipid diversion, compared with the English, pursued without any kind of system or science, and reminding me more of the onsets of our mechanics and shopmen, let loose at Christmas and on holidays, to range the fields, *no matter where,* and pounce upon *all, no matter what,* than of any thing worthy the name of *shooting.* Let no English sportsman think to better himself by emigration in this respect; I'll answer, upon trial, for his total disappointment.

There is not, there cannot be, an individual living who holds our *game laws* in greater abhorrence than I do, considering them as barbarous and absurd as they are wantonly tyrannical and unjust, —the very *fag end* of the old *feudal system* when barons could lord it over their debased vassals at their pleasure, and when in the *humane* diction of the day, if one of them " did course or hunt, either *casually* or wilfully a beast of the forest, so that by the swiftness of the course, the beast did pant, or was put out of breath," he was authorized *to flay him alive.** These days, thank Heaven, have passed away, and the doctrine of *equal rights* and *equal privileges* is becoming rather more fashionable—somewhat better understood, and I hope yet to live to see this bloodthirsty code altogether expunged from a statute book it has so long disgraced; but if I *must* sport, I confess I should prefer meeting every unpleasantness still attendant upon these odious enactments, and *shooting* at English game, in *English style,* to *going a gunning,* with the most unbridled license, after the *American* fashion. Perhaps Long Island, and a few other parts, might prove *some* exception to these remarks; but, generally speaking, American shooting will be found much of the character I have described it.† In ranging the woods I was particularly struck

* Vide " Manwood's Forest Laws."

† Understand me as speaking of shooting in the State of New York, and with what the Americans call *shot guns;* in the other States, or with the *rifle,* I know but little of it.

with their desolate and trackless appearance, as well
as the death-like silence which reigned around : there
is nothing of the delightful harmony so often heard
in ours, but you might almost fancy yourself the only
object that had life within them, excepting that you
are now and then aroused by the hoarse *barking* of a
crow, just resembling that of a dog; the screaming of
the buzzard hawk, or the tapping of the wood-pecker.
Notwithstanding the infinite variety of American
birds, (upwards of 130 different kinds have been
enumerated,) I believe there is only the *mocking bird,*
which can imitate nearly all others, that has any note
to be termed *singing.* Their plumage, however, far
surpasses those of Europe, and many of them are, in
this respect, in the highest degree splendid and beautiful. I saw not a single snake in my day's ramble,
or any other venomous reptile.

We visited the *Springs,* but there is at present
merely a single house upon the spot, and nothing
to interest any one about them, except a person
desirous of analyzing the waters, or making trial of
their efficacy; neither of which motives had induced
my visit. They are said to be strongly impregnated
with alum and sulphur. The quality of land, &c.
offered no exception to my yesterday's notice of them.

For the benefit of future travellers I shall here put
on record my *bill of fare* and charges at Avon. There
are two inns, and I think not more than a dozen other
houses ; but the one I have to do with is kept by a
person of the name of Douglas, and stands on the
left side of the road from Geneseo to Rochester.——It

was about eleven in the morning when I arrived, and, previous to commencing our sporting, I took a slight lunch. At a late hour I returned to dinner, which was introduced, with many apologies, as being past its best, &c.; but, without particularizing, I wish it may never be my lot to sit down to a worse. To this I was supplied with a pint of tolerable port wine, half of which I might drink; and before retiring I took a glass of negus. My lodging, to be sure, was not superb, since the house being rather unexpectedly filled with company at a late hour, and it being inconvenient to accommodate me with a single bedded apartment, I preferred my cloak and the parlour floor to occupying a room with strangers, according to custom here, careless who or what. This morning—*August 28th*—I am just risen from a breakfast which, if I say was a good one, is but giving it very moderate praise. The whole and entire charge for the entertainment from beginning to end, amounts to 81 cents, (3s. 4¼d. English). Waiter, 0; chambermaid and boots, ditto ; and civility and thanks into the bargain. Will this be credited in England ? It will be some time before it is *practised*, at all events. We should dub ourselves not a little favoured, after such accommodation, sleeping excepted, to be let off with five or six times the sum I have paid.

I must also notice here a very novel contrivance, which has attracted my attention, for serving up a repast;—a sort of cupboard, containing a number of shelves, is let down into the kitchen below, the top of it fitting and corresponding exactly with the boards of

the dining-room floor, so that, in that position, you
cannot distinguish it from any other part.   When
a meal is in a state of readiness to be served, the
various dishes, &c. are placed upon these shelves, and
as soon as the freightage is complete, you see the
whole, put in motion from below, tier after tier, gently
rising into the apartment, where attendants are in
readiness to transfer it to the table, upon which it is
all smoking in the space of a few seconds, subject to
the equally prompt attacks of its vigorous assailants.
I was a good deal amused with the performance,
doubtless a most convenient one, in a country where
the saving of labour is so great a desideratum, and
waiters are a class of men liking about as much ease
and indulgence as their masters.

From Avon to Buffalo is 67 miles; through Caledonia, 10; Le Roy, 7; Stafford, 4; Batavia, 6; Alexander, 8; Pembroke, 5; Alden, 7; Clarence, 10; and
thence to Buffalo, 10 miles.

The only places worthy of notice are *Le Roy* and
Batavia, the others being more like straggling *houses
by the way side,* than villages; a few years, however,
sometimes do wonders in this country, and I therefore give the names, about all I can do, that I may
not be accused by the next traveller of overlooking a
populous and thriving town.

Le Roy is situated on *Allan's Creek.* It is a very
pleasant village, and contains a number of good
houses and stores, and, I should think, nearly 4,000
inhabitants. The Erie canal runs seventeen miles
to the north of it, and, in the words of my friend

Spafford, it appears to be "thriving as fast as any thing can thrive, which is not on the ' *Grand Canawl*,' towards which every body is looking and running."

The village of Batavia stands on the north side of the Tonnewanta Creek. It is the capital of Genesee county, rather larger than Le Roy, containing 4,200 inhabitants, and it appears a place of considerably more business. It is built in very compact style, and the stores and private residences have a neat and elegant appearance; many of the latter would not disgrace any town or city in the State. There are two or three good inns, and the " *Holland* Company"* have an office here. A court-house and its attendant jail I may add, of course.

A little before entering the village, I was pleased to observe a pretty extensive brewing establishment, which, I was informed, was answering well to the proprietors. Great good has been effected in various parts of the State, and I believe I may say *States*, though much still remains to be done, by the very laudable exertions of what are called *Temperance Societies*, notwithstanding the unmeaning ridicule and ill-judged sarcasm which some have been disposed to direct towards them. They have been expressly formed to correct what had become a serious and even alarming national evil and disgrace; more or less pervading all ranks, and sapping the moral as well as the civil usefulness and respectability of

---

* So called from being residents of that country: they own extensive tracts of land in Genesee, and other counties in the State of New York.

thousands,—*the too free use of ardent spirits.* Since
they were first established, the consumption of these
deleterious articles, which, from their extreme cheapness, are within the reach of almost every one wishing to purchase them, has been greatly diminished.
One or two respectable innkeepers have assured me
that they have found it less by one half, and almost
in an inverse ratio has the demand for *malt liquor*
increased, and I trust there is fair reason to hope
that this more natural and wholesome beverage, with
cider and light wines, will so far supersede the use
of the other as to become the common drink of the
country.

Batavia has been further conspicuous as the residence
of the notorious *William Morgan*, the great *masonic*
apostate, and whose revelation of the secrets of that
would-be all mystic fraternity not long ago threw the
whole neighbourhood into a most violent and disgraceful state of excitement, which even yet has not
wholly subsided.   What a theme to distract the
mind of a rational being, much more to disturb the
harmony of any portion of an enlightened republic!
I heard the relation with sorrow and disgust.

Between Le Roy and Batavia, and, indeed, as far
as Alexander, as a fine agricultural district, I much
admired the face of the country. The land is of
excellent quality, and appeared to me as well farmed
as any I have seen in the State, not even excepting
the beautiful township of Canandaigua. The farm
houses and outbuildings are generally good, and
such as bespeak the comfort and respectability of

their proprietors. *Improved farms* are to be purchased here for rather less than at Canandaigua;
say, from twenty to thirty dollars per acre, and the
prices of most kinds of produce are also a trifle
lower: wages and other expenses much the same.

We stopped to dine about two miles to the west
of Pembroke, at an odd house, answering the twofold purpose of farm-house and hotel, not unfrequently the case in thinly-populated districts, where
a very comfortable repast was served up to us, unac-
companied with that breathless expedition I have
noticed elsewhere. I had really time to lay my
knife and fork upon my plate ere every chair had
started back to its respective situation in the apartment,—a feat by no means to be lightly spoken of.

The landlord told me of a good farm for sale near
this spot, the owner wishing *to retire from business.*
The size of it is 250 acres, with a corresponding
house and outbuildings, well fenced, &c.;—thought
it might be bought for twenty dollars per acre.

On approaching Alden, and westward of that
place, the country assumed a very different appearance, being yet but little cultivated, and the road
wooded on both sides; here and there patches of
cleared land intervened, sufficient to demonstrate
the latent fertility of the soil.

Before arriving at Buffalo, travelling became, indeed, no sinecure, it being our hard destiny to pass
over what the Americans call a *"corduroy road,"*
than which nothing can be conceived more direfully
hostile to the comfort of either man or beast, or the

safety of the vehicle. It is, in fact, *a road of logs,*
of trees felled on the spot, and placed in contact
with each other from side to side; the genuine corduroy rib, to be sure ; coarse enough for horse jockey
taste, however extravagant : but the thing mentioned,
no farther delineation is needful—the cause is ade-
quate to any thing, and the effect does no discredit
to the cause. Poor Peter's pilgrims with their peas
were well off, by comparison, even when the driver,
in pure tenderness of heart towards us, condescended
to limit his speed to two miles per hour; but when
that speed was accelerated to five and six, why, then,
good bye to description, and to *seats of honour,* and
all other seats; 'twas rather too much for a joke :
the reader's imagination, if tolerably fertile, will best
help me out. Finally, however, we escaped without loss of life or limb, which is saying as much as
will be received without suspicion, and I gladly wave
the *traveller's license* of adding more;—would that
I could even dismiss the recollection !

But after all, sad as the confession, if the road
is to be passed, I know not how it could be
otherwise accomplished. The soil of these woods
has no consistency beyond that of decomposed, or
half decomposed, vegetable matter, wholly inade-
quate to sustain the weight of carriages at any time,
and, in the wet season, mere bog. Still you are
strangely tempted to think, or, at least, to wish that
these said logs had some earthly covering or other
upon them ; but then again, you are told of a newly
settled country, and the value of labour; the latter,

according to Dr. Smith, a poser for every thing, so
I may as well hold my tongue, and patiently "endure
what can't be mended;"—be the name of *corduroy*,
however, for ever infamous !

The day was fast wearing away when we entered
the village of Buffalo. It had been remarkably fine,
and the wind happening to meet, instead of to follow
us, rendered agreeable what would, otherwise, have
proved a choking affair indeed. Throughout nearly
the whole of the way, the log road excepted, whenever we were in motion, there was nothing to be discerned in our rear but one dense cloud of dust ; trees,
houses, and even villages, as soon as we had passed
them, were lost to our view, and woe betide those who
chanced on this day to be shaping their course in an
opposite direction : it would require very familiar acquaintance to pronounce upon their identity with
any thing like certainty, when landed at their respective destinations.

We were driven up to a splendid hotel at the south
end of the village, called the *Buffalo House*, kept by
E. Powell, jun.: it is less than a mile from the Lake,
which in twenty minutes after my quitting the stage
I had found my way into, and enjoyed the luxury of a
moonlight dip in its refreshing waters. On returning
to the inn I learnt that the last *general* meal of the day
had been long ago despatched, and I had, therefore,
hard fate, to put up with a quiet repast by myself
In the few instances of my *delinquency* in this
way, I have thought my hosts, for the time being,

would have been quite as well pleased had I omitted to give them so much additional trouble.

I amused myself for some time afterwards in a reading-room belonging to the establishment, and on retiring was shown into an apartment which for neatness, and even elegance, I have not seen surpassed on my route, only equalled at Auburn.

August 29*th.*—After such fair promise it is almost needless to say that I have arisen this morning free from a *vermin visitation*, or other nightly annoyance; and, as if by contrast to the *solitude* attendant upon my last evening's meal, have breakfasted with some thirty or forty sitting down to the table, and *mine host* and *hostess* presiding.

By this time I have seen something more of the *routine of affairs* at inns, &c., than at the close of my first day's stage travelling, which has but tended to confirm the observations I was then about to have made. They are not the comfortable, do-as-you-like public or private sort of places which the English hotels are ; and though the fare may be quite as good, oftentimes in greater profusion, few Englishmen, with the system pursued, would relish it half so well.—Suppose a roomy bar, as heretofore described, full of strangers, and residents of the town, who half live at the hotels, standing about, ten minutes before dinner, as impatient as a throng at a theatre, until the ringing of a bell announces the repast ready to be pounced upon. Forthwith one simultaneous rush takes place to the dining, or *general*, or *only eating room*, and each, as near as may be, seating himself in the vicinity of his favourite dish, the dire attack commences. A novice would be apt to conclude that all had a heavy bet depending upon the quantity devoured in a given space of time; 'tis an affair in which each one is concerned exclusively for himself, carving, or *cutting*, and cramming down whatever he pleases, leaving his neighbour at liberty to do the same, or to do nothing at all,—all alike to him,—except, as I am pleased to do the Americans the justice to say upon these, as all other occasions, the utmost deference and most respectful attention is ever paid to the ladies. But few words, perhaps, are spoken by the whole company; as each individual clears, or rather *dismisses* his plate, for it is rarely half *cleared*, " another, and another, *and another*" succeeds, until he has gone the whole round of soup, fish, flesh, pudding, pastry, and dessert,—all frequently upon the table together,—and brought the performance to a close; which is no sooner effected than up he starts, as if some contagion were spreading round the table, or there were a greater merit in bolting than in properly masticating a meal; in devouring with precipitancy than in eating with decent deliberation; and, hurrying off to the bar, addresses himself to smoking, chewing, &c.—spitting every where, of course, with most perfect freedom :—who would suffer restraint in a land of liberty! In the intervals between meals there is usually as much taken in the way of drams, tossed down with equal expedition, as would serve an Englishman, *at* his meals, twice over. The difference is, that the one enjoys it, relishes it;

the other takes it because it is habitual to him ; and, without a moment's reflection in any way about it, is satisfied, *for the time,* if the act be only performed.   I do not give this merely as a specimen of coach travelling; there haste and helter-skelter are often unavoidable ; but I consider it a fair outline of these proceedings at hotels, in any part of the country where I have been, as much upon one occasion as another.   At private houses, and in good society, there is no want of courtesy, and the most genuine good-breeding and hospitality ; but even here I think I have noticed a system of despatch neither necessary nor quite agreeable ; a confusing and intermixing of courses, &c., for instance ; ever understanding that it is heresy itself not to vanish with the cloth, and what to an Englishman would very much give the idea of hurrying over a meal to start a journey.

Let no one charge me with advocating any of those after-dinner excesses so common with us ; none can more despise and condemn them ; but some pause, at least, before retiring, and a friendly glass or two, if you will, I must think not only a social and agreeable, but a decent and proper custom.   I can see no reasonable objection to it.   The plea of the *abuse* of any practice is but a poor argument to constrain us to forego its *use* or *propriety,* neither of which appear to me unconnected with this.   For myself, however, I shall retain my prejudices, let others think as they will.—I may be asked whether at an hotel a gentleman would not be furnished with a private room and table, if he desired it ?   With the first no doubt he might; but as to the latter, if it were not refused altogether, it would be esteemed a most out-of-the-way request, and in all probability be made so unpleasant to him that he would be most easy, in a short time, to dispense with it, and take his chance, *pell-mell*, with the rest.

What is done with the parlours, I know not. At every good inn there are mostly several, and those on the first floor are to be seen carpeted, about half furnished, the door standing wide open, and no one in them. The drawing-rooms above are often elegant, and these I have occasionally seen occupied, but more commonly empty. As to lodging, when not intruded upon by *company* of one sort or other, it is all that can be wished :—you are generally waited upon by black servants, who are civil and attentive, and expect *not money*, but *fair words*.

But to speak of Buffalo,—upon my first view of which, after the route I had pursued to it, I was filled with admiration and astonishment; and could I for a moment have suffered myself to lose all recollection of the *canal*, and retain only the idea of its *land* approach, I should have been almost tempted to believe that such an appearance as it presents, at the termination of a forest, had been rather produced by magic or supernatural than by human means. In point of size it only yields to New York, Brooklyn, Albany, Utica, and Rochester, and how long any of these places, but the two first, may be able to boast even such superiority, is, in my opinion, a matter of great uncertainty. The situation of Buffalo, however con-

sidered, is commanding and important beyond most.
Standing at the foot of Lake Erie—now connected
with Lake Ontario by he *Welland Canal*—it has a
direct communication with the Canadas; is open to
the mighty lakes Huron, Michigan, and Superior, and
an almost limitless extent of western continent; and,
on the other hand, at the head of what is justly termed
the *Grand Canal*, it is equally connected with the
Hudson River, New York, as well as all intermediate
places, the Eastern States, and, in fine, with the
shores of the Atlantic. It is, as it were, the rallying
point for the agricultural produce of the west, and
the migratory population, the commerce and manufactures of the east, the connecting link of the varied
interests of a great portion of this vast empire, and
embracing within itself most of the advantages which,
separately, may attach both to inland towns and sea-
ports, but which are rarely united as in Buffalo.
Spafford, alluding to Rochester, has well, if I mistake
not, portrayed the future prospects and destiny of
this place:—"Looking forward," says he, "a few
centuries, or half centuries, weighing all the balances
of probabilities, the changes likely to be produced by
steam navigation, by canals, and the march of population, and capital, and business westward,—not to
Florida and the shores of the Mexican Gulf, but to
the shores of the great lakes of the west, extending a
line of navigation through Michigan to the Missis-
sippi, and pushing it through the Missouri, and across
the Rocky Mountains to the Pacific Ocean,—I see a
line of perspective so extended, so wide-spread in the

sphere of its action, that it seems bou dless, almos
as the fields of imagination into whica the contemplation conducts me."

Leaving general for particular;—Buffalo stands on
a fine plain at the mouth of the *Buffalo Creek*, an
outlet of Lake Erie, and at the head of the Niagara
river. The canal commences near this outlet, and
from it lateral canals are cut in various directions,
upon which numerous and extensive stores and warehouses are already erected, and many more in progress. Like Canandaigua, it consists principally of
one fine broad street, called *Main-street*, having besides three public squares; and much that I have
observed of the character and appearauce of the
buildings, public and private, there, and at Rochester,
may apply to Buffalo. I think there are fewer erections of wood than at either of those places, whilst
they are equally spacious and elegant. It has two
handsome churches, and a court-house, built in very
good style, an academy, of which report speaks
highly, and where there are 100 students; with
printing establishments, libraries, public baths, &c.;
and in the bar of the inn I am at, and *at* that inn,
I see the play of *"Is he Jealous?"* advertised for
performance to-morrow evening;—so soon the refinements, luxuries, and dissipations of life succeed to its
comforts and conveniences. The present population
amounts to more than 6,000.—And this is *the* Buffalo
which has arisen from *that* Buffalo, the British with
the horrid brand of war reduced to ashes, *leaving
but one house standing,* in 1814!—Never may that

execrable, that self-inflicted scourge of the human
race, with all its long train of evils and calamities,
revisit its borders more, but, with the blessings of
peace, and the industry and enterprise of her sons,
may Buffalo become all that they can desire, or I
anticipate—a great and highly distinguished commercial town, the honour and ornament of their
august republic!

Being here, as stated, at the *fountain head* of that
splendid national work, the Erie canal, to which I
have so frequently alluded, the following notice will
not perhaps be deemed uninteresting :—

" This magnificent structure," says the writer,
" was commenced under the patronage of the State,
on the 4th of July, 1817, and was completed in 1825,
uniting the waters of the Erie and Hudson, at an
expense of less than seven millions of dollars, a sum
trivial in comparison with the immense advantage
derived to the State from such communication. The
canal, beginning at Albany on the Hudson, passes
up the west bank of that river nearly to the mouth
of the Mohawk; thence along the bank of the Mohawk to Schenectady, crossing the river twice by two
aqueducts. From Schenectady it follows the south
bank of the Mohawk until it reaches Rome. In
some places it encroaches so near as to require
embankments made up from the river to support it.
An embankment of this description, at Amsterdam
village, is five or six miles in extent. What is called
the long level, being a distance of 69½ miles, without an intervening lock, commences in the town of

Frankfort, about eight miles east of Utica, and terminates three-fourths of a mile east from Syracuse; from thence the route proceeds thirty-five miles to Montezuma, situated on the east border of the Cayuga marshes, three miles in extent, over which to the great embankment, seventy-two feet in height, and near two miles in length, is a distance of fifty-two miles; thence eight and a half miles to the commencement of the Genesee level, extending westward to Lockport, nearly parallel with the ridge road, sixty-five miles. Seven miles from thence, to Pendleton village, the canal enters Tonnewanta Creek, which it follows twelve miles, and thence following the east side of the Niagara river, communicates with Lake Erie at Buffalo. The whole line of the canal, from Albany to Buffalo, is 363 miles in length. It is forty feet wide at the top, and twenty-eight feet wide at the bottom. The water flows at the depth of four feet in a moderate descent of half an inch in a mile. The tow-path is elevated about four feet from the surface of the water, and is ten feet wide. The whole length of the canal includes eighty-three locks and eighteen aqueducts of various extent. The locks are constructed in the most durable manner of stone laid in water lime, and are ninety feet in length and fifteen feet in width. The whole rise and fall of lockage is 688 feet; and the height of Lake Erie, above the Hudson, 568 feet. The principal aqueducts are, one crossing the Genesee river at Rochester, 804 feet in length; one crossing the Mohawk at Little Falls, supported by three arches, the centre of seventy feet, and those on each side of fifty feet chord ; and two crossing the Mohawk river near Alexander's bridge, one of which is 748 feet, and the other 1188 feet in length. The whole workmanship evinces a degree of beauty and proportion consistent with the greatest strength. In many places the sides of the canal are either paved with small stone, or covered with thick grass, designed to prevent the crumbling of the soil by the motion of the water. To the main canal are a number of side cuts or lateral canals: one opposite Troy, connecting with the Hudson; one at Syracuse, a mile and a half in length, to Salina; one from Syracuse to Oswego, thirty-eight miles in length; one at Orville; one at Chitteningo; one at Montezuma, extending to the Cayuga lake, five miles, and from thence to the Seneca lake at Geneva, a distance of fifteen miles; and one at Rochester of two miles in length, which serves the double purpose of a navigable feeder, and a mean of communication for boats between the canal and the Genesee river. It is highly probable that these lateral cuts will increase in ratio with the enterprise of the numerous adjacent villages scattered along the line of the main canal. From these and various other improvements, which public enterprise has already suggested, the State of New York is destined to reap a full harvest of prosperity. If her national glory has already dawned with so much lustre, what will be its meridian splendour, when her magnificent improvements, uniting with her own the navigable waters of her sister States, shall serve as so many ligaments to bind the confederacy in the indissoluble bonds of friendship and interest?"

" The debt contracted for the Champlain and Erie canals amounted, on the 1st of January, 1826, to 9,108,269 dollars, including 1,621,274 dollars expended in the construction of feeders, lateral canals, dams, &c., and in the payment of salaries of the commissioners and other officers engaged in the work. The revenue from the tolls of both canals, in 1822, amounted to 64,071 dollars; in 1823, to 151,099 dollars; in 1824, to 289,320 dollars; in 1825, to 500,000 dollars; in 1826, to 675,190 dollars; in 1827, to 859,058 dollars; and in 1828, to 883,000 dollars. On the 1st of January, 1830, the canal debt, including the expenses of constructing the Oswego, Cayuga, and Seneca canals, and exclusive of the extinguishments which had been made, amounted to 7,706,013 dollars; and the tolls received for the preceding year, to the sum of 816,302 dollars,— the Oswego and Seneca canals not having furnished a revenue equal to the interest of their cost and the expense of their repairs. To the payment of the interest and principal of the canal debt, is appropriated not only the tolls, but also the duties on salt and auctions, with other sources of income, which amounted, in 1829, to 377,677 dollars, making the total receipts of that year, including tolls, 1,193,979 dollars."

The day has been overcast, temperature agreeable, and closes with rain.

August 30*th.*——

> " The morn is up again, the dewy morn,
>   With breath all incense, and with cheek all bloom ;
>   Laughing the clouds away with playful scorn,
>   And living as if earth contained no tomb."

Swimming in Lake Erie at five o'clock.——

I was diverted in passing along *Main-street* at observing the extreme singularity of the names over the shop doors, &c. ; a circumstance, indeed, I have often noticed elsewhere; and, in addition, you will mostly see portrayed upon a sign suspended over, or at the side of the door, some *touch* of the profession practised within ; for instance, at a *doctor's*, I saw a *mortar and pestle;* at a *bookseller's*, two large *folio volumes;* at a *Miss Jeremiah's,* a most exquisitely trimmed *bonnet;* and at a *fancy dyer's,* a board, upon which was announced the character of their establishment, had every letter painted with *different coloured* paint ;—so much for customs.

Near Buffalo there is a *reservation* of the Seneca Indians; but their numbers do not now amount to more than a few hundreds, and even these are annually diminishing, and retain but little of their original character, habits, and customs; a few years, comparatively, will sweep this race of inhabitants altogether from the face of this wide continent, of which they were once the sole and undisputed possessors; and I leave it to the philosopher, the moralist, the philanthropist, the Christian to say, whether, if the good of mankind, and not the mere aggrandizement of territory, had led to their extirpation— for whatever virtues or brilliancy of character they might possess in some respects, they were the mere children of the forest, averse to all but the savage and uncivilized states of life—looking upon America *now,* and comparing her with what she *then was,* and under such a people *ever would have been,* whether, in all the varied, vast, and important advantages which have followed their subjugation, *the result would not have justified the act?* As it is, we can only say that the *result* has been *greatly glorious—* would that we could add, the *means* and the *motives* were as *greatly good!*

And now, having lingered a whole day at Buffalo, only twenty-two miles from Niagara, and within the sound of that mighty cataract,* I felt this morning an overpowering excitement in anticipating the august spectacle which, in a few hours, would be presented to my view. Every description I had heard or read, and every conception I had formed of that stupenduous work of nature, was this day to be disappointed or realized. I was to behold a scene which is pronounced by all who have witnessed it, to stand unrivalled in any country, and to be able to answer in the affirmative that first and all-important interrogatory which meets a stranger on returning from the western world, " *Have you seen Niagara?"* Such were the impressions with which I

* In reference to the distance at which the falls are audible, Dr. Spafford observes, " The sound is heard at various distances; extending five, eight, ten, twenty, and even thirty miles, when wafted by a gentle breeze. I have once heard it thirty miles in a direct line; and I think that in 1797 I approached within five miles, without hearing any of that roar, which soon became tremendous from a change of wind."

recommenced this most interesting portion of my journey. And here let me remark, that, in attempting to convey to others, who do not happen to have been as much favoured as myself, not an idea of the scene—that were impossible—but something of the feelings with which I surveyed it; and considering the limited interval arrangements allowed me for observation, I shall not fastidiously and wholly reject the sentiments of those who have preceded me, when I consider them strikingly appropriate, or so nearly resembling my own, that I might either appear, however unintentionally, to have availed myself of, or studiously evaded them, to be, perhaps, less pointed and accurate;—with this acknowledgement, then, I proceed.

I have before said that the Niagara river, which forms the communication of Lake Erie with Lake Ontario, commences at Buffalo, receiving into it not only the waters of Lake Erie, but those of Huron, Michigan, and Superior, well denominated the *inland seas of the west*.* The elevation of Lake Erie above

* " *Lake Huron* is 218 miles from east to west, and 180 broad.

" *Michigan* is 300 miles long and 50 wide.

" *Superior*, the most westerly, is 459 miles long, and about 109 wide. About forty small and three large rivers enter this lake, on one of which, just before its entrance, are perpendicular falls of more than 600 feet. The water of the lake is remarkably transparent, so much so, that a canoe over the depth of six fathoms seems rather suspended in air than resting on the water.

" *Lake Erie* is on the boundary line between the United States and Upper Canada. It is 290 miles long from south-west to north-east, and in the widest part 63 broad.

Lake Ontario, nearly half in the State of New York, " is in length 171 miles, and in circumference 467. In the middle, a line of 350 fathoms has been let down without finding a bottom."

that of Ontario is upwards of 330 feet. The river is
about thirty-five miles long, and from half a mile to
six or seven in width, and nearly equidistant from
each lake is crossed by a branch of the Alleghany
mountains, which intersect almost the whole continent of America, and to which circumstance we
are indebted for the falls of Niagara. From Buffalo,
the approach may be made either on the American
or Canadian side of the river. I preferred the latter,
and getting into a stage about eight o'clock, was
conveyed three miles to *Black Rock*, a small, but
increasing village on the east bank of the river, and
upon the line of the canal; like Buffalo destroyed by
the British in 1814. The river here is about a mile
in width, running with a very moderate current, and
twenty-five feet deep. Over this we were ferried in
a boat, with paddles worked by horses. On the
Canada side, just as you land, are a few houses,
christened "Waterloo,"* very near the site of old
Fort Erie,† the scene of desperate engagements be-

* As if one must be reminded, wherever one goes, of that bloody
struggle for the suppression of *one* tyrant, that *five* or *six* might
form a *vile league*, which, with horrid blasphemy, they dared to designate "*holy*," against all that was dear and sacred to man. But,
"every dog has its day," and they, thank Heaven! have had theirs,
and are fallen and falling, amidst the scorn and execration of "free
millions."—So perish all and every thing opposing the cause of civil
and religious liberty, on its broadest basis, the world over!

† "Fort Erie was rendered memorable as the theatre of several
severe engagements during the last war. The last and most decisive battle fought at this place was on the night of the 15th of August, 1814. The fort was occupied by the Americans, and its possession was considered an object of importance to the British.
Taking advantage of the darkness of the night, they made repeated
and furious assaults, and were as often repulsed; until, at length,
they succeeded by superior force in gaining a bastion. After main-

tween the Americans and the British, during the last
war, as was, in fact, nearly the whole extent of the
river from lake to lake.

Continuing along the banks of the stream, we
shortly came opposite *Grand Island,* which is twelve
miles long, and from two to seven broad, and was
ceded to the State of New York by the Seneca
Indians in 1815. We were about twelve miles distant, when looking in the direction of the falls, I
saw the spray, which I at first mistook for smoke,
rising in columns to a very considerable height, and
the whole horizon around skirted with light clouds;
I also began to hear the sound of them very distinctly. Besides Grand Island, the river contains a
number of other small islands,* and independent of
the influence of that excitement by which, at every
progressive step, the mind and feelings become more
deeply aroused, the ride itself, the whole distance,
is one of singular beauty and interest. Until we
reached Chippewa,† the stream had been gliding

taining it for a short time, at the expense of many lives, accident
placed it again in the hands of the Americans. Several cartridges
which had been placed in a stone building adjoining exploded, producing tremendous slaughter and death among the British. They
soon retreated, leaving on the field 221 killed, among whom were
Cols. Scott and Drummond, 174 wounded, and 186 prisoners. The
American loss was 17 killed, 56 wounded, and 11 missing. This
action was followed by a splendid *sortie,* near the Fort, on the 17th
of the following month, which resulted in a loss to the British of
nearly 1000, including 385 prisoners, and to the Americans of 511
killed, wounded, and missing."

* The largest of these is *Geneva Island,* about a mile long, and
nearly the same in width. It belongs to the British.

† " The *battle of Chippewa* was fought on the 5th of July, 1814,
and has been described as one of the most brilliant spectacles that

along with a smoothness which left you wholly un-
prepared for the ruffled and tumultuous scene it was

could be well conceived. The day was clear and bright, and the
plain such as might have been selected for a parade or a tourna-
ment; the troops on both sides, though not numerous, admirably
disciplined ; the generals leading on their columns in person ; the
glitter of the arms in the sun, and the precision and distinctness of
every movement, were all calculated to carry the mind back to the
scenes of ancient story or poetry, to the plains of Latium or of Troy,
and all those recollections which fill the imagination with images
of personal heroism and romantic valour.

" After some skirmishing, the British Indians were discovered in the
rear of the American camp. Gen. Porter, with his volunteers and
Indians, were directed to scour in the adjoining forest. This force
had nearly *debouched* from the woods opposite Chippewa, when it
was ascertained that the whole British force, under Gen. Riall, had
crossed the Chippewa-bridge. Gen. Brown gave immediate orders
to Gen. Scott to advance with his brigade, and to Gen. Ripley to be
in readiness to support. In a few minutes the British line was discovered formed and rapidly advancing, their right on the woods,
and their left on the river. Their object was to gain the bridge
across a small creek in front of the American encampment, which,
if done, would have compelled the Americans to retire. This bridge,
however, was soon gained by Gen. Scott, and crossed, under a tremendous fire of British artillery, and his line formed. The British
orders were to give one volley at a distance and immediately charge.
But such was the warmth of the American musketry that they
could not withstand it, and were obliged to retreat before the appearance of Ripley's brigade, which had been directed to make a
movement through the woods upon the enemy's right flank. The
British recrossed the Chippewa bridge, which they broke down in
their retreat, having suffered a loss in killed and missing of 514.
The American loss was 328."

" One mile farther is *Lundy's Lane*, celebrated as the ground on
which an important battle was fought, twenty days after the battle
of Chippewa. The scene of action was near the mighty cataract of
Niagara, and within the sound of its thunders, and was, in proportion to the number engaged, the most sanguinary, and decidedly
the best fought action which ever took place on the American continent. The following letter, written by a surgeon of one of the
(American) regiments, the day after the engagement, contains
many interesting particulars :—

' In the afternoon the enemy advanced towards Chippewa with

so soon to present; but "here," in the words of an
eminent traveller, "the grand spectacle begins"—

a powerful force. At six o'clock Gen. Scott was ordered to advance
with his brigade and attack them. He was soon reinforced by Gen.
Ripley's brigade; they met the enemy below the falls. They had
selected their ground for the night, intending to attack our camp
before daylight. The action began just before seven, and an uninterrupted stream of musketry continued till half-past eight, when
there was some cessation, the British falling back. It soon began
again with some artillery, which, with slight interruptions, continued
till half-past ten, when there was a charge, and a tremendous stream
of fire closed the conflict. Both armies fought with a desperation
bordering on madness; neither would yield the palm, but each retired a short distance, wearied out with fatigue. Such a constant
and destructive fire was never before sustained by American troops
without falling back.
 ' The enemy had collected their whole force in the peninsula,
and were reinforced by troops from Lord Wellington's army, just
landed from Kingston. For two hours the two hostile lines were
within twenty yards of each other, and so frequently intermingled,
that often an officer would order an enemy's platoon. The moon
shone bright; but part of our men being dressed like the Glenga-
rian regiment caused the deception. They frequently charged, and
were as often driven back. Our regiment, under Col. Miller, was
ordered to storm the British battery. We charged, and took every
piece of the enemy's cannon. We kept possession of the ground
and cannon until twelve o'clock at night, when we fell back more
than two miles. This was done to secure our camp, which might
otherwise have been attacked in the rear. Our horses being most
of them killed, and there being no ropes to the pieces, we got off but
two or three. The men were so excessively fatigued they could not
drag them. We lost one howitzer; the horses being in full gallop
towards the enemy to attack them, the riders were shot off, and the
horses ran through the enemy's line. We lost one piece of cannon,
which was too much advanced, every man being shot that had
charge of it, but two. Several of our caissons were blown up by
their rockets, which did some injury, and deprived our cannon of
ammunition. The lines were so near that cannon could not be used
with advantage.
 ' The British loss in killed and wounded and prisoners was 878,
and the American loss 860 '
 " The road to the falls passes directly over the hill where the British artillery were posted at the time Scott's brigade commenced

here the *rapids** commence; and leaving *stages* and such like material vehicles, let us suffer ourselves for a short time, in fancy's airy car, to follow the impetuous current. There is a gradual expanding of the river from Waterloo to this place, and here it attains the width of nearly two miles; but on a sudden it is narrowed, and its rapidity is redoubled by the declivity of the ground on which it flows, estimated by some at sixty, by others at ninety feet, as well as by the sudden contraction of its bed. The channel is rocky, and the interspersed fragments of rock increase the violence of the stream. As it proceeds, it becomes more closely hemmed in by rocks on the right encroaching upon its channel, and sweeps along with prodigious velocity. Before

the action ; and the houses in the village of Bridgewater, the trees and fences in the vicinity, still retain marks of the combat. Many graves are seen upon the hill; among others that of Capt. Hull, son of the late Gen. Hull, who distinguished himself and fell in this action. Most of the slain were collected and burned upon the battle ground ; on which spot it is in contemplation to *erect a church.*"
—[A pretty sort of ground for a *reverend Christian* to *consecrate!*]

* An American term for a broken and rapid current.

" Falling into the current, within a mile of the falls, is considered fatal. Several accidents of this kind have happened, and only one per- son has ever been known to reach the shore. Many bodies have been found below the falls; those that have fallen in the centre of the stream, without any external marks of injury ; and those that have fallen near the shore, much lacerated and disfigured. The latter has probably been occasioned by coming in contact with the rocks in shallow water, before reaching the cataract. A few years since an Indian, partially intoxicated, in attempting to cross the river near Chippewa, was forced near the rapids, when finding all his efforts to regain the shore unavailing, he laid down in his canoe, and was soon plunged into the tremendous vortex below. He was never seen afterwards."

arriving at the *great pitch* it is intersected by two
small islands, namely, *Bath* and *Goat Island*, which
divide the current into two arms, thus creating a
fall both on the American and Canadian sides; "and
resting on their rocky basis, seem, as it were, to
swim between the streams, which here rush down at
once into the dread chasm below."* The main, or
Horse Shoe Fall, is on the Canada side; its circumference is estimated at 600 or 700 yards, and its
height at 158 feet. The sheet in falling does not
pitch immediately downward, but, as may be in-
ferred from its rapid motion, it advances about fifty
feet from the perpendicular of the cataract, and descends in the form of a curve.

To describe my sensations when from the *Terrapin
Rocks* the mighty scene opened upon me, is utterly
beyond my power;—many another has had to make
a like confession, and as a talented and intelligent
writer, whom I have repeatedly quoted, remarks,—"The
immense volume of water that forms a river of a mile
wide can only be conceived by those who have seen large
rivers, and have indulged in some habitual reflection.
I had (says he) enjoyed these advantages, and had
read many good descriptions of Niagara Falls, before
I had an opportunity to consult the impressions
derived from personal observation, and still the scene
was altogether new to me when I stood, and gazed,
and wondered at the sight:—a broad, rapid river
poured at once down a precipice of more than 150

* " Dr. Dwight has estimated that more than one hundred millions of tons of water pass over the falls every hour."

feet into an awful chasm of about three-quarters of a mile wide, and near 300 feet deep, reckoning from the surface of the river bank ! The first effect of this sight is absolutely indescribable. My head became giddy, and it seemed to me that every nerve was affected in the same way with those of the head : nor was it till after some minutes that I dare crawl to the brink of the precipice to take a nearer view."

The *Terrapin Rocks* are approached by a rudely-constructed bridge from Goat Island. They extend about 300 feet from the shore to the Horse Shoe Fall, and, at their farthest verge, absolutely overhang the vast abyss into which the torrent rolls with all its thrilling and majestic grandeur.

" No one," says another, " can witness this at first without involuntary shrinking back." He must allow, however, of one exception : I had noticed the remark, and to give every possible effect to the scene which I was about to survey, when I advanced upon the bridge, I closed my eyes, and, as far as I could, kept them in that state until I found myself as it were suspended over the cataract.

I confess the impression was awful, but to me, if I may so say, it was *awfully enchanting;* my excitement was raised to a pitch which seemed to dispel the idea of danger, and I verily believe if, at that moment, I had known it to be imminent, I should have retreated from the position with some hesitation and reluctance. I was dumb with high and enthralling amazement.

"There was a mass of many images
Crowded like waves upon me."
"The tablet of unutterable thoughts was traced."

My feelings asked for words, and in the same instant mocked the power of language. I felt the weakness—the littleness—the nothingness of man, and the immensity of that Being whose almighty fiat had called into existence the magnificent scenes which surrounded me, and poured along the cataract which foamed and thundered at my feet. I was as if commingled with the very elements—living in the tumult: the world seemed annihilated and dead: every faculty and power of the soul was taken captive—riveted to this spot. The creations of fancy had fled away; imagination was beggared by reality; and I felt at once that Niagara—the mighty Niagara!—was all, and more than all, it had ever been represented to be —what no pencil could paint, or pen portray—great beyond every conception of grandeur—sublime beyond all idea of sublimity!

How long I continued in this reverie of rapture I know not; 'twas too overpowering for endurance. The spell was at length broken: I was recalled to the vapidness of life, and, like one just aroused from a trance, retraced my steps to the shore; but the impression remains fixed, and permanent, and vivid, as when stamped upon the mind, and when I lose the recollection of that hour, and that scene, time must have drawn its veil over all that I would cherish, and thought and memory become extinct:—I must cease to live.

The reader will forgive me this digression—rhapsody, or whatsoever he is pleased to term it: the feelings of the moment were ardent and irresistible, inspired by the majesty of the scene: they can never recur again but upon a like occasion—at the same spot.

We will now commence on the Canada side, and make the entire circuit.

My first point of observation was upon the Table Rock,* a little lower down the river bank than the great fall, and although the view from this is indeed superlatively grand, it did not, in my mind, produce all those overpowering emotions which I experienced in the situation alluded to, and I surveyed the particular features of the scene perhaps with more attention.

Viewed from the point, this falling sheet sometimes resembled an immense avalanche of snow, as during its descent amongst the rocks of the rapids it acquires a foaming whiteness before it reaches the *great pitch*, but much depends upon the position of the sun, the state of the atmosphere, force of the wind, &c. Its colour was occasionally a dark green, and not unfrequently it exhibited every brilliance of hue and shade that can be imagined. The surface below presented the wildest confusion: the water, after its

---

" * A large crack in the Table Rock, which has increased annually for some years, renders it very certain that a considerable proportion will ere long fall into the abyss below. The part thus cracked is nearly fifty feet in width, and might be blasted off without difficulty. The height of the rock has been ascertained to be 163 feet."
It is highly disgraceful to those who have the power to remove it to suffer this rock to remain in its present state. It *may* fall any moment—it *must* fall before long, and whenever it does, it will be remarkable if lives are not sacrificed. Is there no one who will interfere to prevent it?

descent, partly rising again in thick columns of mist, towering above the falls, and mixing with the clouds; thus producing—for the sun was bright throughout the day—perpetual and most splendid rainbows; the remainder breaking upon the masses of rock, in the bed of the river, filled the whole chasm with spray, and which, the wind meeting me on my approach, I perceived, like small rain, at a considerable distance off.

From the Table Rock I next passed under the fall. The descent is by means of a spiral stair-way which is inclosed, and on arriving at the bottom of which I had to doff every vestige of clothing, and was furnished by the guide, who was about to accompany me, with a waterproof garment in lieu of it: the necessity of this exchange I full soon discovered, being completely enveloped in a cloud of spray. The path is a very rugged one, under awfully overhanging rocks, and as we approached nearer and nearer, the roar, the tumult, and the agitation which encompassed us, " around, above, below," was appallingly, grandly terrific. The violence and density of the spray, too, increased at every step, so that we were obliged to carry our heads down to respire at all; and in one part, where there is a considerable projection, it was driven against us with such almost incredible vehemence that it required no trifling effort to keep on our feet. I can compare it to nothing better than the most violent of thunder rain, which, instead of falling vertically, is propelled horizontally, with the fury of a tornado. The walking, too, is rendered more difficult by the number of small eels, which are twisting

about under your feet in all directions. At length,
however, staggering and stumbling on, we reached
what is called *Termination Rock*, 153 feet from the
commencement of the volume of water, and beyond
which there is no proceeding, the descent being nearly
perpendicular. Few, I believe, evince any inclination
to explore thus far, though *tales are told* of persons
taking a meal underneath, and so on; which, for the
mere *say-so*, certainly *might* be done, as any one, if
so disposed, might treat himself to dinner in a shower-
bath, nor fear having to complain of a *dry morsel;*
but be assured the inconvenience of such a ceremony
under the Falls of Niagara would, if possible, be an
hundred-fold greater. After remaining some time
seated on the farthest projection of rock, contemplating
the wildly majestic and novel character of the scene
around, I returned to the stair-way, and on reaching the
little building which has been erected at the top of it,
and casting off my drenched surtout, I was presented by
my guide with a printed form of certificate, in testimony
of the performance, in the following words: To wit,—
" This may certify that Mr. John Fowler has passed
with me behind the Great Falling Sheet, under the
Falls of Niagara, to 'Termination Rock.' Given
under my hand, at the office of the General Register
of Visitors, at the Table Rock, this 30th day of August, 1830.—(Signed) W. D. WRIGHT, G. N. F."

Continuing from this along the bank, about a
quarter of a mile lower down, is a man in attendance
with a small boat to ferry across the river. To a
stranger it would appear altogether impossible for a

boat to *live* in such a water, and certainly the impetuosity and strength of the current, together with its
numerous eddies, are not quite pleasant; but I had
every confidence in my ferryman, apparently grown
gray in the service, and was right little disposed to
indulge in any groundless apprehensions of danger.
He even told me, but this *he* esteemed a *feat*, that his
son, a boy of twelve years of age, had, more than once,
swam across.

" The bed of the river here is formed by two ridges
of rock, which extend a great way further down,* and
it is still more narrowed, as if a part of this mighty
stream had.vanished during the fall, or were swallowed
up by the earth."—We landed within about eighty
yards of the fall on the American side. This is much
smaller than the *Horse Shoe Fall,* not being more than
300 yards wide; the sheet is also greatly thinner, and
it descends almost perpendicularly, so that there is
no possibility of passing behind it, but in consequence of a rocky barrier in front it can be approached
to within a few feet, making up your mind to return with a wet jacket. It is rather higher than the

* " The great northern terrace of high plain meets the Niagara
river of Lewiston, seven miles below the falls, which is just at the
foot of it; and here must have been originally the Falls of Niagara.
The corresponding strata of rocks and earths, with every geological
feature, carry irresistible evidence of this prodigious excavation.
" In the autumn of 1795, it is said a shock of an earthquake was
felt here, when a large piece of the rock that formed the cataract
fell, and perceptibly changed the form of its curvature.
" Indeed it is altogether incredible to suppose this immense body
of water should descend thus, and not be constantly wearing away
the rocks that lie in its way. How long it may have taken to cut
this vast chasm is of no importance."

Horse Shoe Fall, being 164, whilst that is only 158
feet, and I thought the roar quite as tremendous, indeed it struck me as being louder. I ascended from
this place by a long flight of stairs, which has been
constructed to the top of the bank, and passing along
the shore about a quarter of a mile, came to a bridge
which has actually been carried across the rapids to
Bath Island,* and upon which, (will it be believed ?)
there is a large paper mill, as well as other mills, in
operation : there is also a house where the weary traveller may find most comfortable refreshment, and
where I partook of all the dinner—it was a very slight
and hasty one, to be sure—I either had or needed
during the day. My feasting was of another character,
but the richest, the noblest, the most sumptuous ban-
quet I ever did, I ever can enjoy. At this place there
is a tolerable collection of shells, petrifactions, and

* " Gen. P. B. Porter, of Black Rock, to whom the public are indebted for the construction of this bridge, informed me that its erection was not effected without considerable danger. Two large trees,
hewed to correspond with their shape, were first constructed into a
temporary bridge, the buts fastened to the shore, with the lightest
ends projecting over the rapids. At the extremity of the projection,
a small butment of stone was first placed in the river, and when this
became secure, logs were sunk around it, locked in such a manner
as to form a frame, which was filled with stone. A bridge was then
made to this butment, the temporary bridge shoved forward, and
another butment formed, until the whole was completed.   One man
fell into the rapids during the work. At first, owing to the velocity
with which he was carried forward, he was unable to hold upon the
projecting rocks ; but through great bodily exertions to lessen the
motion by swimming against the current, he was enabled to seize
upon a rock, from which he was taken by means of ropes.
" The sensation in crossing this bridge over the tremendous rapids
beneath, is calculated to alarm the traveller for his safety, and
hasten him in his excursion to the island."—*Traveller's Guide.*

various curiosities, the produce of this interesting
neighbourhood. I also saw a large stuffed swan,
which venturing too near the fall had the misfortune
to be carried over, and was picked up dead below by
the man who ferried me across.

From Bath Island I passed by another bridge on
to Goat Island, which is perhaps about a mile in circumference, overgrown with trees and shrubs of different kinds, some of which I made pretty free with
on behalf of friends in England : but here, in my opinion, is obtained decidedly the finest view of the
rapids, and the principal fall, which is to be had from
any situation around them. I allude, of course, to the
Terrapin Rocks ; but these I have already spoken of,
and let me not trust myself upon enchanted ground
again. There is another very small island adjoining
Goat Island, called *Iris Island,* from which a stair-way
has been constructed to the foot of the falls, affording
an excellent position for contemplating them from
that part. " It was from ladders erected near this
place that the celebrated *Sam Patch* made a descent of
118 feet into the water below, a short time previous
to his fatal jump at Rochester, in the autumn of 1829."

Here I completed my tour of the falls, recrossed the
rapids, and was again ferried over the river to the
Canada side, where I retired to the Pavilion,* and enjoyed a most splendid *coup d'œil* of the whole scene,

* " The Pavilion, kept by Mr. Forsyth, is a lofty eminence above
the falls, on the Canada side, affording from its piazzas and roof a
beautiful prospect of the surrounding scenery. It is a handsomely
constructed building, and can accommodate from 100 to 150 guests."

regretting that I had only been able to devote hours
where I could willingly have lingered months, and
should realise new beauties, fresh sources of interest,
with every succeeding day. I did not feel, however,
as if taking a last adieu! I could not force myself to
believe it: the moment will be hailed with rapture
whenever these impressions are verified. I have seen
Niagara in all the splendour of summer; I would
again behold it in the icy array of a Canadian winter.

And now, reader, thou has followed me—I would
hope not quite impatiently—around this mighty
scene, which, instead of being compressed in a few
pages, might well furnish matter for a volume. To
the little *I* have said, add all thy loftiest conceptions
—the most vivid colourings of thy fancy—give wings
to thy imagination, and soar to any height thou wilt
—I still tell thee, *thou hast no idea of Niagara;* believe *this* thyself, and thou art then, perhaps, as
familiar with it, as any multiplication of words could
make thee, and to the testimony which I have given
let me add that of the celebrated Duke de la Roche-
focault Laincourt, who visited the falls in 1795. "I
must repeat it again and again," says he, "that
nothing can stand the test of comparison with the
Falls of Niagara. Let no one expect to find here
something pleasing, wildly beautiful, or romantic;
all is wonderfully grand, awful, and sublime. Every
power of the soul is arrested: the impression strikes
deeper and deeper the longer you contemplate, and
you feel more strongly the impossibility of doing
justice to your perceptions and feelings."

From Niagara I had wished to return by the Lake
Ontario, landing either at *Oswego* or *Sacket's Harbour;* but the steam-boat in which I thought to have
taken a passage, being a few days too late for me,
I was compelled to alter my plans, and proceed
by stage along the *Alluvial Way,* upon the lake
border, which is considered one of the great natural
curiosities of the country.* Took a conveyance
along the Canada side of the Niagara river to *Queens-*

* " This is called the *Ridge Road,* or the *Alluvial Way.* It lies
along the south shore of the Lake Ontario, and is composed of
common beach sand and gravel stones, apparently worn smooth by
the action of water; and the whole intermixed with small shells.
Its general width is from four to eight rods, and it is raised in
the middle with a handsome crowning arch from six to ten feet.
Its general surface preserves a uniform level, being raised to meet
the unevenness of the ground through which it lies. At the Genesee
and Niagara rivers, it is found to be elevated about 120 or 130 feet;
and this, of course, determines its elevation from Lake Ontario, from
which it is distant from six to ten miles, and towards which there is
a pretty uniform, though gradual descent. That this stupendous
work of nature was formed by the action of water is very evident,
and that water must have been no other than the Lake Ontario,
now settled away 130 feet below its ancient boundary; and the
whole intermediate space is said to be good land, exhibiting strong
evidences of alluvial origin. It could hardly escape the observation
of the enterprising inhabitants of the west, that on the surface of
this ancient work of the waters of Ontario, a very excellent road
might easily be made through its whole extent. At an early period
one was opened with little labour, extending from Lewistown, on the
the Niagara river, to the Genesee, terminating at the spot now occupied by Rochester, a distance of eighty-seven miles. The circumstance deserves notice, that between this *Alluvial Way* and the shore
of Lake Ontario, there are few of those ancient works, the mounds,
tumuli, &c. of a race of people about whom we know nothing but by
such like monuments; pretty good evidence that their era preceded
that of the present level of the waters of that lake, or of their retire-
ment below the *Alluvial Way.*"

town, seven miles, where I crossed to *Lewistown*, The river at this place has a very strong current, and is sometimes considerably ruffled. The banks are three hundred feet high; but they soon decrease to about twenty or thirty feet, at which elevation they continue to Lake Ontario, seven miles below. *Lewistown* shared the fate of most of the frontier villages during the war; but it is now rebuilding in neat and respectable style, though 1 should imagine it will never arrive at equal commercial importance with the villages along the line of the canal. Besides a church, custom-house, &c., it has to boast of a very excellent hotel, much such a one as a person in want of every kind of comfortable refreshment would desire to fall in with. I have noticed generally that there is no difference in the charges at these places for breakfast, dinner, and *tea*, or *supper*—call it what you will; both meals are here comprised in one;—the customary demand for each is 37½ cents, and, as before hinted, there are no addendas, as with us, to half the amount of the bill. I recollect not long ago, when travelling in England, my expenses at a certain inn were 10s., and the servants' fees, in the usual way of remunerating them, and as I did upon the occasion, amounted exactly to 5s. I have no doubt, however, before any distant day, it will be found that the American servants, (I beg their pardon, I ought to have said " *helps*,") will consent to accept of a little remembrance from a parting guest without any manifest embarrassment.

I have seen one effort of the kind made, *and only one,* which was received very graciously.

August 31*st.*—After a few hours' repose, which restored me to all the transporting scenes of the day, at half-past three o'clock this morning, I was in, or on the stage for Rochester.

In the distance we pass through some eight or nine villages, none of which are worthy of mention, excepting Lockport, and that I was too much straitened for time to reconnoitre as I could have wished. I see it thus noticed in the *Traveller's Guide :*—" By far the most gigantic works on the whole line of the canal, are at this place. After passing along the canal between sixty or seventy miles on a perfect level, the traveller here strikes the foot of the ' *Mountain Ridge,*' which is surmounted by five magnificent locks of twelve feet each, connected with five more of equal dimensions for descending; so that while one boat is raised to an elevation of sixty feet, another is seen sinking into the broad basin below. The locks are of the finest imaginable workmanship, with stone steps in the centre and on either side, guarded with iron railings, for the convenience and safety of passengers. Added to this stupenduous work, an excavation is continued through the *Mountain Ridge,* composed of rock, a distance of three miles, at an average depth of twenty feet. When viewing this part of the canal, we are amazed with the consideration of what may be accomplished by human means.

"'The village of Lockport is mostly located on the mountain ridge, immediately above the locks; and though "founded on a rock," surrounded with rocks, and with little or no soil, it has already become a place of importance. In 1821, there were but two houses in the place; now there are between three and four hundred. The canal here being on the highest summit level, and supplied with water from Lake Erie, (distant about thirty miles,) an abundance is obtained for hydraulic purposes, and the surplus at Lockport has been sold for 20,000 dollars. In the excavation through the mountain, several minerals were discovered, among which some of the finest specimens of the *dog-tooth spar* ever found in the United States. At first they were easily obtained; but latterly they have become an object of profit, and are sold at prices corresponding with their beauty."

As to the *Alluvial Way*, I am any thing but pleased with it, to *travel along*, and so far from recommending it to tourists, as some have done, I recommend all, but the mere geologist, to keep off it; I consider it beyond comparison the most uninterresting eighty miles of ground I have passed over in the country, and whatever thanks may be due to *nature* for the effort she has made to open a pathway through a wilderness, her handmaiden *art* must at all events be excluded from the least possible participation therein. For the first thirty or forty miles it is pretty closely wooded on each side, occasionally, perhaps, *relieved* by a rib of *corduroy*; of which distinguished mention has been previously made; and now and then a hut or two, and a few acres of half-cleared land, will be observed. It passes over, or is intersected by several small creeks and streams, at which parts it is wholly unguarded, and might be offering a very premium upon *capsizing*, or other equally *agreeable* occurrence to break in upon the wearying sameness of its character; indeed, an accident of the kind had happened a few days previously; but, fortunately, the stage at the time was without a single passenger, and the driver escaped unhurt, though both himself and horses had a most *hair-breadth escape* of being dashed to pieces.

As we *neared* Rochester, the road became leveller, and the country more cleared and cultivated; but the land appeared of indifferent quality, and agricultural affairs at a very low ebb. The dust was all but insupportable, and much as I have had occasion to complain of it elsewhere, it has been nothing like so bad as on this road. I have had to ride with my handkerchief tied over my head the greater part of the way; but notwithstanding that, and every other experiment, at times I was half suffocated.

Having frequently alluded to the inconvenience which a traveller sustains from the dust of an American road, perhaps a better idea of the justness of my complaint may be entertained if I mention the principle upon which they are usually repaired. When a road—now I am not including *all*, I say *usually*—has become in a state in which the wheels of carriages, in place of running upon its surface, have to perform their revolutions some eighteen inches or more below; and when we should unhesitatingly begin to prefer our indictments and so forth, the neighbouring farmers are very civilly applied to for a loan of their services, and as civilly and promptly repair to the defective part with oxen, ploughs, &c., and commence breaking up the sides of the road just as they would one of their own fallows: this done, the oxen are released from the ploughs, and yoked to a large shovel, or scope, with two handles, held by the driver: this is pressed down into the ground which has been previously loosened, and when as much is upon it as it will retain, the cattle, with admirable docility, and almost without a bidding, start with it at once into the centre of the road, where their driver tosses it over, and returns for further supplies; thus on till the repairs are completed. " Completed !—but when are the stones laid upon it?" Reader, thou art asking a very rational question, which I answer by informing thee that whenever any adjacent field abounds with these substances to the injury of its vegetation, and it is not too much trouble to remove them, they are gratuitously bestowed upon the road, where no hammer of *M'Adam* or *any other* Adam ever molests them, but in all their original shapes and sizes they are suffered to remain, occupying just those positions which chance, the laws of gravity, stage wheels, &c. may determine. And thus, with much *republican simplicity,* is an operation performed in a day or two, which would cost us as many months, and employ one or more overseers, surveyors,

and half the poor of the parish.*   Do not marvel,
however, after this, independent of now and then a
jolt, that in a dry season there should be 'something
too much' of dust, and, in a wet one, a little super-
abundance of mud and mire; though, taking the run
of times and seasons, travelling is really more tolerable
than under such a state of things could be well supposed, and, except in newly settled districts, not to be
greatly complained of—as good, no doubt, as England
afforded in equally juvenile years—and every year im-
proving.   The Americans, I imagine, would have had
better roads but for their admirable *water conveyances*,
in which they so far surpass us, that it were becoming to be pretty modest in *our* animadversions
upon the *other*.   I have spoken of the matter, *en pas-
sant*, with that perfect good will which I have noticed
other things, and feel towards them upon all occasions.
They are a great people—have done great things—are
doing great things—and, ere long, *we* shall not have
to tell them to *do more — I guess*.

Of Rochester I can only confirm what I have previously stated.   It is decidedly the first place upon
the line of canal, and of all, excepting Buffalo, is
likely to take the lead, but I shall be much deceived,
if, in the course of—may I say—a few years, Buffalo
does not leave every other in the rear.

My route from Rochester to New Hartford, and in-

---

* This latter term may almost need explaining to an American,
but the mass of *enlightened* people in England are so well acquainted
with it that I will not do him the injustice to infer his disability to
comprehend it.

deed to Albany, was so nearly the same as the one by which I travelled westward that it would be as tedious as unnecessary to dwell upon it. Omitting dates, I will take incidents and objects in hasty rotation :— And first, about two miles to the south of Pittsford, the *grand* (canal) *embankment,* as it is termed, over the *Irondequoit* Creek*, had given way and caused a most serious inundation in the neighbourhood : at the principal breach it had swept a course, for some distance, from sixty to a hundred yards wide, and five or six feet deep, depositing immense quantities of sand in the surrounding fields and woods. An orchard I noticed which presented a singular appearance, the trees being all buried as high as their buts, and the boughs full of fruit resting upon the sand, as if growing immediately out of it. The occurrence had taken place a week or two prior to my passing the spot, and all had been put to rights again, but from the loose and sandy nature of the soil in the vicinity 1 should fear there is but little security against a repetition of it. It seems the most imperfect part along the whole

---

* This ought to be called " *Teoronto.*"

Dr. Spafford, speaking of the *Bay*, observes,—" The Indians call it Teoronto, a sonorous and purely Indian name, too good to be supplanted by such vulgarisms as ' Gerundegut, or ' lrondequoit !' The Bay is about five miles long and one wide, communicating with the Lake [Ontario] by a very narrow opening, or such it used to have ; and Teoronto, or Tche-o-ron-tok, perhaps rather nearer the Indian pronunciation, is the place where the *waves breathe and die,* or *gasp and expire.* Let a person of as much discernment as these ' Savages' watch the motion of the waters in this Bay, facing the north, after a storm on the Lake, or a violent gale, and he will admire the aptitude of its name, and never again pronounce *Gerun.degut,* Irondequot, or Irondequoit."

line of the canal.—Might not the canal have been carried farther to the south and have avoided this creek and the necessity of an embankment altogether ? I am suggesting, however, with professed ignorance of attendant circumstances; my map may be incorrect, or what not—I only wish that an execution so great, and so complete in most parts, may not remain defective in any.

One of the next things that caught my eye, though seemingly insignificant by comparison, was scarcely more agreeable, namely, a handbill offering a reward of twenty-five dollars for the apprehension of a *shop lifter* at Canandaigua, and not the only one I have noticed. A few years ago such an advertisement would have been no trifling novelty, but whoever will take the trouble to observe the specimen of society daily teeming in from the ' old country,'* and diffusing itself particularly in the State of New York, will be at no loss to account for the occasional appearance of such things now—the cause and effect are at once, and equally self-evident.

From Canandaigua to Geneva we varied the route a little by taking the Castleton road; along which the land was chiefly in a superior state of cultivation, and in quality, and all respects, fully supported the very favourable opinion before expressed of the agriculture of this fine district. About a mile to the west of Geneva, I saw the only *quick hedge* I have

* The emigrations from Great Britain and Ireland to the State of New York, during the last twelve months, amount I believe to more than 20,000.

noticed in my travels, which appeared to be thriving remarkably well; much, indeed, would it contribute to beautify the country were this description of fence to become general. I begin almost to tire of their everlasting wood and stone.

Since leaving *Albany,* I had been frequently told, I suppose by those interested in supporting the old line of stages, that the *new,* or *Pioneer* line, had sold out their stock, and discontinued running. I had my suspicions as to the accuracy of the information, and at Geneva I found them fully confirmed, there being a meeting of the proprietors at the inn where we dined, at which it was resolved to carry on the most vigorous opposition. I am no friend to illiberal or uncalled-for opposition, but I hate monopolies of all kinds; and as regards these stages, before there was a choice of conveyances, I have heard enough of the inconvenience which persons sustained in travelling just upon the terms which might be dictated to them; and once myself, when upon a cross road, where the old line had it all to themselves, besides breaking down, which, to be sure, might have occurred to either party, I had such a sample of their proceedings as I should not wish to experience again. We scarcely averaged more than three and a half miles an hour; and in urging the drivers even to that speed, had to submit to no little insolence into the bargain. When upon the main roads, where both lines have been *plying,* the state of things has been widely different,—the fare moderate—speed nearly doubled, and a spirit of accommodation evinced by drivers and all connected with the establishment. I hope and trust the public will so far support the new line, as to warrant them in keeping the field. There is travelling enough for both, and the disposition to travel will keep pace with the facilities afforded. Where two concerns may thrive, and the public at the same time be much better accommodated, there can be no reason why one should engross its exclusive patronage, to confer upon it a smaller amount of benefit. *"Live and let live,"* is a good old-fashioned maxim, notwithstanding being somewhat *outre* in the present day :—I wish both parties success, and a fair competition and understanding between them; but neither merely to oppose or subvert the other.

We reached Auburn late on the evening of a very fine and warm day, but it was succeeded by a night which set us all a shivering, and I remarked that the natives seemed to feel it quite as much as myself. We were eight inside, with the leathern curtains of the carriage closely buckled down, and well wrapped up in cloaks, &c.; but all would not do; at the end of every stage we were glad to run to a fire, where there happened to be one, or up and down the street to warm ourselves. In the morning, by nine or ten o'clock, it was as hot as it had been on the preceding day; the curtains were rolled up, and our clothing again made as light as possible. These great variations in the temperature between day and night, between one day and another, and oftentimes between different parts of the same day, are much complained of. A good deal of the "*fever and ague*" is generally prevalent at this season of the year—perhaps, in part, attributable to this cause.

Upon arriving at New Hartford, I was met by a general complaining of the want of rain, and the herbage appeared to me to be more burnt up than I had seen it farther westward. My friends informed me that they had scarcely had even a shower since my leaving, and there had been none of any consequence for some time before. Farmers here must "make hay while the sun shines," for what with the heat and draught of summer, the frost and snow of winter, and the *puddly* state of the land in the spring, there is much less time allowed for the cultivation of it than in England; and farmers, I think, are more on the alert, and eager to embrace every opportunity which presents itself. There are somewhat fewer "gentleman farmers" than with us,—or, I should rather say, than there *had used to be* with us, the race having been pretty well plucked and thinned of late; —and, with few exceptions here and there, masters and men take the field together, and continue their operations, with but little interruption, from morning till night. One of the first settlers at New Hartford, ere such luxurious conveniences as houses were in fashion, resided for some time in a hollow tree, and hence is frequently distinguished by the appellation of "*the hollow tree man;*" he is now, however, a respectable freeholder, has built himself a very comfortable habitation, where he may securely repose *under his own vine,* if not under *his own fig tree,* and

close a life of labour and privation in peace and
independence. He is not, perhaps, in affluent circumstances, as we esteem affluence, but he has more
than enough to bound every want, and, therefore,
he is a rich man. Could any of our aristocratic
lordlings say as much?

During the little pause I made at New Hartford, I
availed myself of an opportunity of visiting *Trenton
Falls,* fourteen miles north of Utica. They are situated
on the *West Canada Creek,* the largest northern branch
of the Mohawk ;—but here is a much better description than my hurried view enabled me to concoct:—

"These renowned falls," says the writer,* " are on
West Canada Creek, between 22 and 24 miles above its
confluence with the Mohawk. The West Canada
Creek is a powerful stream, and constitutes almost one
half of the rivers at their coalescence. The falls are
six in number, and occupy an extent of rather over
two miles. The West Canada Creek in its way
from the summit of the highlands of Black river to
its lower valley, lying between the latter and Has-
senclever mountain, crosses a ridge of lime-stone
four or five miles in breadth, stretching through the
country from the Mohawk to the St. Lawrence. Its
course over this ridge by its tortuous bed is six or
seven miles, two and a half of which are above the
falls. The waters of the creek, soon after they have
reached the lime-stone, move with accelerated strides
over the naked rocks, to the head of the Upper Fall,

* James Macauley, Esq.

where they are precipitated eighteen or twenty feet down an abrupt ledge into a spacious basin. The whole descent to the head of this fall in the last two miles is computed at sixty feet. Here a deep and winding ravine begins, which extends down the stream more than two miles. Its average depth is estimated at 100 feet, and its average breadth at the top, 200 feet. The sides and bottom consist of lime-stone, deposited in horizontal layers, varying in thickness from some inches to a foot and upwards, and abound with organic remains. The sides of the ravine are shelving, perpendicular, and overhanging; and some of the trees that have taken root in the fissures of the rocks are now pendant over the abyss, where they form the most fanciful appearances ima-ginable. The country along, and neighbouring the ravine, descends to the south, and is mostly covered with woods, which exclude every appearance till you arrive upon the very verge.

"The water at the *Upper Fall* descends eighteen or twenty feet perpendicularly. Below there is a capa-cious basin, out of which the stream issues in a diminished bed into the ravine, the entrance of which is between lofty barriers of rocks. This fall, when viewed from the bridge, or from the high ground west of the creek, has a fine appearance.

"At the *Cascades,* consisting of two pitches, with intervening rapids, the water falls eighteen feet. The bed of the stream is here contracted, and the sides serrated; the banks of the ravine rising with abruptness almost directly in the rear.

"The *Mill-dam Fall,* a little lower down, has an abrupt descent of fourteen feet, the stream being about sixty yards broad at the break.

"The *High Falls* are forty rods below the latter, and consist of three distinct falls, with intervening slopes and some small pitches. The first has a perpendicular descent of forty-eight feet; in floods and rises the water covers the whole break and descends in one sheet; but at other times, mostly in two grooves at the west side of the fall. The second has a descent of about eleven feet; the third, thirty-seven feet; and the three, including slopes and pitches, 109 feet. In freshets and floods, the entire bed at the High Falls is covered with water of a milk-white colour; and the spray, which at such times ascends in pillars towards the sky, when acted upon by the rays of the sun, exhibits the rainbow in all its brilliant colours.

"The fourth fall is called *Sherman's,* and is distant nearly seventy rods from the *High Falls.* The descent is thirty-three feet, when the stream is low, and thirty-seven when high.

"The last fall is at *Conrad's Mills,* at the very foot of the ravine, and is six feet.

"Besides the falls, there are several raceways or chutes, from ten to twenty rods long, through which the waters pass with great rapidity. The whole depression of the stream, from the top of the *Upper Fall,* to the foot of *Conrad's* is 312 feet; and if we add the descent above the Upper Fall, which is computed to be sixty feet, and that below Conrad's Fall in half a mile, which is estimated at fifteen feet, we shall find that the entire depression in less than five miles, is 387 feet.

" The falls, raceways, and rapids, and, in truth, the whole bed within the ravine, exhibit very different appearances at different times. In floods the whole is one tremendous rapid, with four cataracts, and several chutes.

" The best time to visit these falls is when the stream is low, because then there is no inconvenience or difficulty in ascending the ravine from the foot of *Sherman's Stairway* to the head of the upper raceway. Few persons who visit them have resolution to ascend the ravine from the Stairway to the basin at the Upper Fall. This, however, is not to be wondered at, because the lofty rocky barriers which constitute the sides of the ravine advance to the water's edge in many places, and terminate in frightful projections, which cannot be passed without the most imminent danger. Some of these difficulties, however, have been obviated by blasting away portions of the rocks and putting up chains;* and persons now go to the upper raceway without hazard.

" The ravine, with some few exceptions, is still bordered by woods, and persons desirous of visiting the falls are obliged to go to what is called *Sherman's*

* Several persons were so employed on the day I visited the falls, and loud and continued were the reverberations along the ravine at the time of the explosions. One fragment of rock of, I should think, near 2 cwt. blasted a few yards from the spot on which I was standing, was hurled across the ravine, and struck the rocks on the opposite side with great violence.

House, from whence they proceed through the woods by some rude paths. One of these leads to the Stairway, which descends to the bottom of the ravine, and the other leads up to the High Falls. The former is usually preferred. On reaching the strand at the foot of the Stairway, you proceed up the stream at first upon the strand, and then by a narrow winding footpath to Sherman's Fall. From hence you advance to the High Falls, a part of the way being overhung by large jutting rocks which menace you with destruction. From the head of the High Falls to the upper end of the raceway above the Cascades, the way is easy when the stream is low, but from thence, upwards, it is difficult and dangerous.

" While you are passing along the narrow and sinuous paths leading to the projections, and by the brinks of headlong precipices, you tremble with reverential awe, when you consider that one false step might precipitate you into the resistless torrent below, and in an instant consign you to a watery grave.*

* A most distressing accident very lately occurred here. The victim was a young man of the name of Bill, son of Dr. Bill, of Remsen. He was engaged at the time in conducting some female friends around the first point of a rock, a short distance above the lower fall, when, the water being high, he incautiously stepped into the edge of the current, slipped into the river, passed over the falls about forty feet, and was seen no more until two days afterwards. The *Utica Intelligencer* gives the following particulars :—" We learn that Mr. Bill made a number of attempts to gain the shore, as he was borne along by the current, which was too strong for him to resist. He was only immersed in water to his middle when he went over the first fall, and his friends were so much shocked that they were unable to render him any assistance. The party was composed of his sister, uncle, and two cousins, the former of whom immediately ran towards the public-house for assistance, but she

"Along the bottom and lower parts of the ravine, numerous organic remains are found enveloped in the rocks which are easily divisible. The remains lie flat in or between the laminæ, their contours and component parts being little distorted from their original shape and dimensions. Sometimes there is defect, occasioned in the transition from the animal to the stony or fossil state; but, in most instances, all the parts are so completely defined, that not only the order, but the genera and species may be recognised. These remains are easily separated from the layers in which they are inclosed. Their exteriors are commonly glossy, often very smooth, and ordinarily of a dark colour, being transformed into stone, and constituting integral parts of the rocks which envelop them. From a careful examination of certain of these remains, and their positions, we are led to believe that their prototypes lived and died on the spot, and that the rocks in which they are entombed are of posterior formation."

was so hurried when she arrived that it was some time before the bystanders were able to learn what she wanted to make known to them. Her appearance was distressing to every one; she had lost her hat, and in running for help, her hair had fallen over her shoulders, and she was in a state of mind little short of distraction. A number of persons went to the falls, and on arriving found the rest of the party almost overcome with grief, but no traces of the deceased could be found. The body was found two days afterwards below the lowest fall. The young man, it is said, completed his twentieth year on Sunday, the day before this dreadful event, and was full of hope and joy at the prospect before him in life. His look, as he was carried over the fall, is represented by the uncle as heartrending in the extreme, and the more so as they were unable, from their position, to assist him, which he seemed by that look to request they would do."

There is a very comfortable hotel on the spot, where every accommodation and refreshment is afforded to visiters.

Before my setting out for these interesting falls I was cautioned not to raise my expectations too high —told that I should think nothing of them after Niagara—that I should have seen them previously, and so forth—observations of no weight whatever. I contemplated the scene with an exquisite delight, as who would not? but if I am asked whether it bears any resemblance to Niagara, one short monosyllable will suffice me,—*No*—none at all,—no more than a river resembles the ocean, or a pigmy a giant. It is perfectly immaterial which you see first or last—they are totally distinct and different scenes, and the interest and emotions which they excite are as widely separate and dissimilar. One would charm and engage, whilst the other fixed you in rapturous and awful amazement; the one is grandeur and sublimity, the other in the highest degree romantic and beautiful.

It is natural to wish to realize by comparison; to impress upon the mind by what we have seen, some image or idea of what we have not; but every attempt of the kind must be abandoned here. Niagara must thunder on in peerless majesty, and Trenton bound along through its enchanting ravine, but they remain Niagara and Trenton still :—

> " When thy light bark to summer streams is given,
>   What deemest thou of the vessel on the deep,
> When mutiny within all law has riven,
>   And round it billows in dread thunder sweep ?"

To suppose a parallel is doing injustice to both.

Let each be viewed through its own medium of attraction, and each will be found deserving of all the
admiration that can be lavished upon it—and much
more.

The country between New Hartford and Trenton
is rather flat than hilly. The land, more or less cultivated, of good quality and well watered. Near
Whitesborough, on our return, we overtook one of
the largest droves of sheep I have seen on any public road in the State; there must have been some
thousands : they were a description of travellers,
however, we would most gladly have given the way
to, had an opportunity offered of making our escape :
—the very recollection of the atmosphere of dust
we had to respire through, sets me a coughing and
sneezing even now. I would scarcely have driven
the flock twenty miles to have been installed proprietor, without other fee or reward.

Two days before I left New Hartford, there had
been a considerable fall of rain, which set the
farmers busily to work getting their wheat into the
ground, and imparted to the herbage almost the
green and freshness of spring: the dust was laid as
if never again to rise, but in its place, on my
journey to Albany, we had to contend with a depth
of mud scarcely more agreeable ; though I was thus
furnished with a specimen of both kinds of travelling
here, the dry and the wet, neither of which you can
pronounce just to your mind,—like most other things,
best in the medium. Except in parts where the
road inclined to rock, and afforded the wheels some

support, I know not to what depth they were sunken in; at times it was about as much as the horses could manage to drag us along, and to relieve them by walking ourselves was utterly out of the question. We were twenty hours and a half in getting over our ninety-six miles, leaving Utica at half-past eight, on one morning, and reaching Albany at five on the following: for the last fifteen miles, namely, from Schenectady, the horses walked nearly every step of the way. Altogether, however, I fared far better than a much esteemed friend of mine in New York once did, in travelling between the same places, three entire days and two nights having stolen away ere they had completed the distance.

Albany had so few attractions for me, and the *Catskill Mountains*, to which I had determined to devote the day, so many, that notwithstanding my previous day and night of travel, I felt impatient for the departure of the steam-boat, on this morning, the *North America,* and before seven o'clock I was pacing the deck of that magnificent vessel. We were, I suppose, about 300 on board, with one half of whom I sat down to a breakfast, only too profusely good, and in an apartment which, for size and elegance, would have done no discredit to a palace.

The morning was brilliant, the rain had all passed over, and the sky as cloudless as ever. What a contrast to my yesterday! dragging through mud knee deep, along a dull road, at little more than four miles an hour, and now cutting the waters of the majestic Hudson at nearly three times that speed, and every moment fresh beauties and attractions opening upon the enraptured view. Well, our pleasures are made up of variety. It is sometimes worth enduring extremes for the sake of their opposites. Not that I would willingly have bartered the sunshine and smiles of to-day, for the darkness and gloom which preceded it.

By ten o'clock I had landed at Catskill. The only place of importance between and Albany is the city of Hudson, which stands on the east bank of the Hudson, twenty-seven miles from Albany. It is very finely situated, and contains about 5000 inhabitants; but we merely stopped for a few seconds to discharge and take in passengers.

Catskill is on the west bank, five miles lower down, and is a very pretty village. There are a number of houses bordering the river, but the principal part of the village is full half a mile from it. The *Catskill Creek,* on which are several mills and manufactories, flows through it, and here unites its waters with those of the Hudson. It has two or three churches, as many banks and hotels, and a number of neat and well-furnished stores. Its population is estimated at 4000. From the village to *Pine Orchard,* on which stands what is called the *Mountain House,* at an elevation of 2,200 feet from the level of the Hudson, is about twelve miles ; and having procured a car and a pair of good horses at the hotel, with one or two more of my steam-boat companions, I was soon making my way towards it. For the first seven miles the road is very good, and tolerably level, and we bowled along

in admirable style : I had not had better travelling in
the country.   At this distance we came to a little inn,
called *Lawrence's Tavern,* where *tourists* may pause
and refresh themselves, *if they will,* but which *horses
never ought to pass without,* unless it be the design of
the parties to accommodate them with an empty vehicle for the remainder of the distance, quite enough
for any animals to drag up that precipitous ascent.
The humanity of one of my fellow-travellers was
aroused a few moments earlier than mine, and elated
with his progress for the first few hundred yards, when
I alighted, with much self-complacency and importance he ventured to *suppose*—all his hurried respiration
would permit him to articulate—*that this was a new
sort of work to me ;* before reaching the top, however,
he found me not quite so much in my novitiate as he
had imagined, and evinced the least possible disposition to put my experience to the test.   I saw him but
once again throughout the day, and am inclined to
believe that he was honouring Catskill with his presence for the first and last time.   No matter ;—in
three hours and a half we had gained the summit,
and little should I have thought of ten times the
labour to have witnessed such a scene as there burst
upon us.   The day continued, as it commenced, most
propitious for the excursion, without the least of that
haze in the distance so often attendant upon the finest
days ; and I could distinctly see the far off *Green
Mountains* of *Vermont* to the north, the Highlands of
the Hudson to the south, and the range of the Tagh-
kanic to the east : the outlines of the latter towards

evening, when the sun was casting his expiring beams upon them, and bordering them with a golden radiance, were uncommonly fine. Through the whole extent of the valley, the "Silver Hudson," edged by well-cultivated lands, and elegant mansions, with numerous towns and villages, was gracefully flowing along; its surface often diversified by "some fair isle," the whitened sail, or the rising smoke from a steamboat; the only situation in which I ever thought the latter had any tendency to improve a prospect.

The face of the mountain below was finely wooded, and forests of trackless extent, appearing from this elevation to be only partially thinned by the advance of agriculture, were spreading all around. It was a scene altogether so beautiful, so boundless, so all-attractive to the "nature-loving eye," that I could have dwelt upon it with a heightening rapture the longer I had surveyed it; but time was stealing on, however imperceptibly, and having engaged to descend to the village, in order to proceed by the evening steamboat, which passed at eight o'clock, to Poughkeepsie, the rest of the party intending to remain at the *Mountain House*, to witness the rising of the sun, I inquired of the driver how soon he could run me down, and set off all alone to the *Kaaterskill Falls*, about two miles distant. —The approach is by a narrow road through a wood, and I had cause to regret the very imperfect direction I received at starting, as long before reaching the falls the principal path terminates, and several small and obscure ones branch off in different directions. I knew not which to pursue, and after some hesitation contrived to make choice of the wrong, which, with many windings and turnings, becoming more and more indistinct at every progressive step, led me at length into a thicket, and there disappeared altogether, leaving me to steer myself out as I could. I felt convinced, from the distance I had come, that I could not be very far from the falls, and listened attentively to catch the sound of them, but all around was silent.   Not to tire others, however, as much as I tired myself in getting clear of the labyrinth,—after beating about for some time, in no very enviable state of uncertainty, I at length found the falls, but almost without water, which at once unravelled the mystery of their having been so completely inaudible to me when not more than a quarter of a mile off.   " The stream takes its rise from two small lakes, half a mile in the rear of the hotel; and after a westerly course of a mile and a half, the waters fall perpendicularly 175 feet; and pausing a moment on a projection of rock, plunge again down a precipice of 85 feet more, making the whole descent of the falls 260 feet;" but the smallness of the body of water which is usually passing over them seems almost lost in the vast chasm into which it descends; scarcely entitling them, indeed, to the name of a *cataract;* the spot, however, is well worth visiting, if it were only for the view above the falls, where the eye roves over the finest and most extensive dell I ever beheld, wooded throughout, and the varied hues of autumn now adding to the foliage an almost more than vernal richness and beauty.

There is a small wooden hut at the place, where per-

sons are in attendance, during the summer season, to
lend any aid to visitors which they may require. I
have no doubt but it will become a place of much
resort. I would only recommend any one designing
to visit it—and they will find themselves well rewarded—either to set out more liberally directed than
I did, or to take a guide from the hotel; but the way,
ere long, may be made intelligible to the capacity of
any blunderer that can travel it.

On my return to the Mountain House,* I discovered that the limits which my charioteer prescribed to me had so nearly expired, that I had only
time to cast a parting glance over the scene of my
morning's enchantment, and obey the unwelcome
summons. Our descent was a most rapid one, occupying but little more than two hours, a performance
only fit for a driver and horses well accustomed to
it, the road being very much unguarded, and presenting quite enough of ravine and precipice to
accord with the tastes of the generality of travellers. My object, however, in meeting the boat was
effected, though we had run the matter so fine as
to prevent my taking the slightest refreshment before
starting; the necessity of which my somewhat subsid-
ing excitement had induced me to feel with no slight

---

* "This building is owned by the *Catskill Mountain Association*,
an incorporated company, with a capital of 10,000 dollars. It is
140 feet in length, 24 in width, and four stories high, and has piazzas
in front the whole length, and a wing extending in the rear for
lodging rooms. It is well furnished, and possesses every convenience
and accommodation requisite to the comfort and good cheer of its
numerous guests."

degree of urgency; nor did my situation seem much improved when transferred to the steam-boat, the *established* repasts of the day being at an end, and I had to make out a most moving case ere I could soften the caterer general to order the needful compliance with my wishes. From Catskill, or *Kaatskill*,* to Poughkeepsie is about thirty-five miles, a three hours' trip, as we left the former place at eight, and arrived at the latter at eleven o'clock:— And here have I found an hotel, excellent of its kind, the fatigues of the day only rendering me the more apt at appreciating its various accommodations.

September 11th.—I occupied the early part of this morning in strolling over Poughkeepsie. It stands on the east side of the river, from whence to the village is a pretty steep ascent of about three-quarters of a mile. It was first settled by some Dutch families, nearly 100 years ago, and "the Convention that met to deliberate on the federal constitution, and voted for its adoption, met in this place in 1788." It now contains about 5,000 inhabitants. The streets are well laid out, the two principal ones crossing each other at right angles, and the stores and private residences have a very neat and respectable appearance. There are several churches, or meeting-houses, banks —a very handsome one is now in erection—schools,

---

* We ought to write *Kaatskill* for the creek, *Kaatsbergs* for the mountains, and let the people have *Catskill* for the name of their township and village, to which they seem so wedded."—*Dr. Spaf-ford.*

hotels, breweries, factories, printing establishments, &c. &c. The post road from New York to Albany passes through it, and its trade and intercourse with both those places, particularly the former, since the admirable facilities afforded by steam navigation, are very considerable; it has also an extensive and frequent communication with the Eastern States. In the neighbourhood are some very elegant mansions, situated either upon the bank of the Hudson, with a verdant lawn extending to the water's edge, or upon the heights around, and commanding a fine view of the river and the adjacent country. It is a place which few could see without admiring;—" taken for all in all," I have scarcely met with one, to my taste, worthy of a precedence. The name, *Poughkeepsie*, is of Indian origin, from *apokeepsing—safe harbour*.

From hence I had engaged to pay a visit to a friend, residing near *Hartsville*, distant about eighteen miles in a north-easterly direction, to whom I had received no other address—a very customary and certainly a very comprehensive one—than " —— —— *Nine Partners;*" it would be as well at once to say *Dutchess County*, since *Nine Partners*, as the term may imply, is a tract of land originally granted to nine proprietors, comprising several townships, and extending from the Hudson to Connecticut. Fortunately, the family were extensively known; but, *un*fortunately, I missed the morning and only regular coach passing by Hartsville, having been deceived as to the time of its starting, and was conveyed as far as *Pleasant Valley*, seven miles on the road, in a very neat one-horse

car, by a person who carried the mail to *Pine Plains*,
&c., at the northern extremity of the county. The
road was excellent, and the country on either side
had a rich and fertile appearance, reminding me much
of Herefordshire, and some other counties in England,
—but of this anon.

At *Pleasant Valley*, a small village of no particular
interest, not meeting with any conveyance to my mind,
I determined to walk the remaining eleven miles; a
mode of travelling which, notwithstanding my partiality for it, the heat of the day rendered much more
fatiguing than agreeable, obliging me to raise my
umbrella to protect me *from the rays of the sun;* a
thing I have only had occasion to do *once for rain*
since I landed. Under these circumstances I was
well pleased to gain the door of my friends, where I
was received with all the sincerity of an American
welcome.

With this kind and hospitable family I spent nearly
a week, variously but always agreeably engaged, and
each member of it solicitous to add to my pleasures,
and promote to the utmost the objects I had in view
in visiting the county.

One of our excursions was to *Dover Falls*, east about
fifteen miles from Hartsville, which though not of the
magnitude of some I have seen, are well worthy of
notice; but I mention the circumstance the more from
a little feat which on this day it fell to my lot to perform, viz. the slaying of a *rattle-snake*. We were at
the time in a very thick part of a wood, and I was
just in the act of stepping over a log, on the opposite

side of which the creature was lying, coiled up. I had
so nearly set my foot upon it, that had it not been a
young one I suppose I should not have escaped its
envenomed fang; as it was, it was probably large
enough to have inflicted a fatal wound, but its dispo
sition seemed to be to retreat with all possible despatch. I had not pursued it far when I was so fortunate as to strike it, and thus capture the prize. It
had one rattle perfectly formed, by which I supposed
it was two years old, as I believe they have none
before that age, and one annually afterwards. When
I exhibited it at Dover, on our return, it appeared to
excite almost as much curiosity as if such reptiles had
never existed in the country; and it was generally
determined that one had not been seen in those parts
for twenty years or more. I know not how it chanced
to me to stumble upon such a prodigy; no one could
less have troubled themselves, either before or since,
on behalf of the serpent tribe than I have done, and
with the exception of a few harmless *garter-snakes*, I
have scarcely seen one in the country; but so it was,
and I have not failed to accord it due preservation,
for the inspection and satisfaction of my curious, as
well, perhaps, as for the conviction of my incredulous
friends.

Dover is quite a small village: the township six or
seven miles long, and nearly the same in width: its
eastern boundary is the State of Connecticut, where
it is hilly, as also to the west; but the centre is a remarkably fine and fertile plain, watered by several
streams, and well rewarding the labour of the agricul-

turist. In the course of the day we found a number of choice plants, flowers, and minerals, and some of the finest and most curious specimens of moss I ever met with.

The shades of evening were drawing on ere we took our departure for Hartsville, and I may almost say that we travelled by *starlight,* such was the irradiating brilliancy with which they shone: nothing can surpass the purity of the atmosphere in this county : I have seen skies and sunsets of the richest beauty and splendour, such as England never knows; such as the favoured land of Italy *may equal,* but not outvie; the concurrent testimony of those who have seen both.

On several other days, or parts of days, one of our party and myself were occupied in perambulating the neighbouring country with our guns. We met with little other game than woodcock, which, had we been provided with a brace of good English pointers or setters, would have afforded us excellent diversion : as it was, we killed a considerable number. My friend was more successful than myself, owing in part, perhaps, to the situations in which we found the birds, chiefly amongst Indian corn, and to which he had learned better to accommodate himself. It frequently grew so high, and so far out-topped me, that I often heard the rise of a bird within ten yards of me, without seeing any thing of it, and could only get *snap shots* at best. The few quail which we saw were uncommonly wild: in fact, between buck-wheat, which is a very favourite resort, and Indian corn, it was almost impossible to get them on the wing. The best month for shooting here is November: it is usually very fine: the corn is all gathered, and the game has nearly attained its full growth, so as to be strong enough, whether on wing or foot, to *give it a chance for its life*, and the *battu system* has no attractions for me. All the diversion which I could ever discover attaching to shooting, consists in anticipation, in pursuit, in the excitement of seeking and finding the game: there can be none in the mere *killing*, except as undeniable evidence of a good shot, an attainment few ambitious of such distinction, with moderate self-possession and practice, need despair of; but the *exercise*, which persons in general would never take without the accompanying stimulus of dog and gun, is worth all the rest put together. Whoever designs to sport here, though as I have said it will bear no comparison with English shooting, should take care to provide himself with good dogs; they are scarce, and frequently sell for extravagant prices. I should think a cargo of them would answer better than many another shipment. I know not what amount of commissions in this way I was *favoured* to receive; certainly more than I either promised or should find it very convenient to execute.

Upon these and other occasions during my visit at Hartsville, or ——— *Cottage*, I had an opportunity of seeing a good deal of the soil, agriculture, &c. of the county, and of any part of the State in which I have been—and I think I have been in the best—upon the whole, as a farmimg situation, I must now say I should give a decided preference to this.

It has been long settled, and to a considerable extent is well cleared and drained—the roads are good—the climate remarkably fine—rather more temperate than any other on the Hudson—and, not a trifling recommendation, the water is excellent, which cannot be said of that of any of the Western Counties, as I have but too frequently had occasion to notice.—I might mention other inducements—or which so appear to me—but opinions differ, and some, I have no doubt, would think the western part of the State greatly preferable.

The county of Dutchess, or Duchess, extends about thirty-eight miles along the Hudson. Its area is 725 square miles, or 464,000 acres. To the east and north-east it is mountainous, but for the most part the land is very finely diversified with hill and dale. Its quality is various, between sand, sand and loam, and some clay. It is watered chiefly by small springs and streams, which are very numerous, and there is abundance of good timber for all necessary purposes.

There is but a small proportion of land in the county that may not be converted to the raising of grain, though, perhaps, in general, not more than one-sixth is under the plough at a time. The produce of all the different kinds of grain is much as in Long Island, and the prices very little lower; and, though fruit is not grown, as there, for the New York market, it is the opinion of those to whom I have mentioned the subject, that it might be, to a very good account. Apples, for cider, are extensively cultivated.

[*Mem.*—From eight to ten bushels of apples will

yield thirty gallons of juice. The value of good sweet cider in New York, in the summer months, is from 3 to 5 dollars per barrel. The barrel (new) costs 87½ cents; freight to New York, 20 cents. The cartage from the different parts of the county to the river varies, of course, with distance, from 6 cents to 40 cents.—When the fruit is purchased, what is called *grafted cider* fruit (in contradistinction to the natural or indigenous) is from 15 to 40 cents a bushel. *Table fruit,* from 25 to 50 cents, and the *natural fruit* from 6 to 12 cents.]

Wool is considered as the staple produce of the county, and there has been grown this year about 400,000 lbs.: the price from 50 to 60 cents a pound. The quality is generally fine, averaging about 3lbs. to the fleece.

Some flax is raised in the county: price of the seed 125 cents. per bushel; of the flax, cleaned, 12½ cents a pound. Both yard manure and plaster are much used; the latter article in the quantity of 200 pounds to the acre; cost on the land 50 cents per acre. Some quantity of manure is also obtained from the swamps, &c.

Fallowing is but little practised, though, by good farmers, the system is quite approved of.

Wheat is generally sown after a summer crop of oats or barley.

Farms, in Dutchess County, are to be purchased at from 30 to 60 dollars per acre; much, as elsewhere, depending upon situation, &c.

But little land is rented.

The *halving system* is practised to a limited extent, as in Oneida County.

Labourers' wages the same as in Long Island.

The fences consist of stone and wood: the expense of raising them estimated at from 50 to 70 cents a rod.

Excepting two or three turnpikes, which are not here " the King's highways," but belong to private companies, the roads are repaired by the inhabitants: cost to the farmer about 5 dollars per 100 acres per annum.

Dutchess County is well and respectably populated; the inhabitants chiefly of English and Dutch extraction. Its trade and manufactures are considerable, and in a very thriving state. No mines are in working; but iron, and lime-stone, and marble are found in the county.

The usual times of *seed time* and *harvest*, throughout the State (varying, as in England, a week or two in different parts) are as follow, namely:—Wheat is sown the latter end of September, and cut in July:—Barley the latter end of April, and cut in July:—Oats the latter end of April, and cut in August:—Indian Corn is planted about the middle of May, in the quantity of one peck to the acre, or four grains to the *hill*, in hills three and a half feet apart, and gathered in October.

The *Farm Houses* in general are smaller than in England, and built of wood; the cost of a good one, to erect it, would be from 1,500 dollars to 2,500 dollars. To English taste there is a sad want of

neatness observable about them, and even where the
establishment is upon an extensive scale, they will
be found, in this respect, to fall many degrees below
what we are accustomed to see, the *occupier* being
merely a *tenant*, and not, as is nearly always the
case here, the *proprietor :*—as to gardening, laying
out ground, &c., with the idea of embellishment,
'tis out of the question. "Here," say the Americans,
"the English miss it when they come to this country
—these things *don't pay.*"

The *State taxes* are levied agreeable to the real
and personal estate of individuals by officers appointed for the purpose, any one having the privilege of correcting the amount, by affidavit made
at a seasonable time after assessment :—the rate is
usually in the proportion of one dollar upon one
thousand dollars. It is paid annually to one common collector, and includes all that is ever required
in this way, except a military charge or service,
which does not apply to foreigners, and a general
tax in time of war. As to *tithe,* I dare hardly allow
the word to be seen in my journal.

Upon the very important subject of *emigration*—
referring to farmers—so much depends upon situation, and circumstances in life, previous habits, character, disposition, constitution, and numberless other
things, that I would rather be excused giving an
opinion either *pro* or *con.* Thousands who come
over, return, to my knowledge, dissatisfied, but more
remain, and the majority, after a few years' residence,
appear to prefer this country to England. I would

by no means represent farming, in the State of
New York, as a lucrative undertaking; in the ordinary way of following the pursuit, and taking the
State generally, it will not return more than *seven*
or *eight* per cent.; but there is a wide difference
between *even that* and *sinking the capital*, as the
mass of farmers with us have latterly been doing.

Upon coming, however, one thing I would especially
recommend to all—to see different parts of the State,
and make due investigation before settling any where.
The common error of *disappointed* emigrants, next
to that of raising their expectations too high before
starting, seems to have been that of deciding too
soon after arrival.

I have endeavoured, as opportunity has admitted,
to collect, and state facts ; let parties form their own
judgment.

September 18*th*.—On this morning I left —— *Cottage* for Poughkeepsie, to which place I was accompanied by several of my kind friends, and from
thence by some of them down the Hudson to New
York.   We had a delightful ride ; but the *river*
named, every thing that can enchant in scene and
scenery at once presents itself to the mind; I think
it even charmed me more than on the first day I
witnessed it, and I envy not the taste of those who
can ever survey it without feelings of the highest
gratification ; still less of any (and those there are)
who can exist in a land, and almost on the spot where
such beauties are to be contemplated, and yet have
to acknowledge that they *have never gazed upon*

them! I should have thought myself repaid for crossing the Atlantic to have passed once up and down this river, in the *North America* steam-boat. How well I have been repaid by all I have seen, I can much more readily feel than express. We landed at New York at eight in the evening, having been just six hours in accomplishing the seventy-five or eighty miles.

NEW YORK——*General allusions, &c.*

AND here, having arrived again, as it were, at my starting-post, and completed (or with but little variation) the tour I designed to myself on setting out, let me indulge in a few general allusions to the country through which I have travelled, gathered, where time has forbid me the research, from sources on which I can rely, with such further consecutive remarks and observations as may chance to occur to me.

And first, to speak of the *size, boundaries,* &c., of the State of New York, I may observe :—Its greatest extent from north to south is 304 miles, and from east to west 316, exclusive of Long Island. It is bounded on the north by latitude 45, or Canadian line, the river St. Lawrence, and Lake Ontario; on the west by the Niagara river and part of Lake Erie; on the the south by the States of Pennsylvania and New Jersey, and the Atlantic Ocean; and on the east by Connecticut, Massachusetts, and Vermont. The area, exclusive of all large waters, is computed to be 43,214 square miles, or 27,656,960 acres. It is divided into fifty-six counties, and contained at the last census of 1825, a population of 1,617,488, but at the present time there can be little doubt that it equals 2,000,000, exclusive of foreigners, not naturalized.

The *Capital* of the State is *Albany*, although greatly inferior in consequence to New York; and many of the towns which are now springing up along the line of the Erie Canal, bid fair soon to surpass it in point of size and population—of these I may particularly notice Buffalo, Rochester, and Utica.

As may be supposed, the *Face of the Country* varies much, but I would make this general remark, that, though in extent not quite so large as England, it must be borne in mind that it forms the part of a mighty continent, where every thing appears upon a scale of correspondent greatness, and although none of its loftiest mountains are situated in this State, yet there are many that vie with our highest hills, and, excepting some counties, in place of the gentle undulations which the surface of England chiefly presents, are bold swells, and extensive plains and flats, vast forests and swamps, and in various districts much rugged and rocky land.—Its rivers, its lakes, and its cataracts are numerous, and several of them of the most grand and gigantic character.

The *principal Mountains* are the *Kaatsbergs* or *Catskill* mountains—generally considered a branch of the Alleghany or Apallachian range, which extend from Maine to Georgia; these, in Greene County, rise boldly to an elevation of near 4,000 feet. " Next are the *Mattewan* mountains, or *Highlands of the Hudson,* the *Helderbergs*, the *Shawangunk* mountain, and the *Taghkanick* mountain, in some sort of connexion. The great primitive region of the north, embracing the mountainous ranges west of Lake Champlain, comprises the *Kayaderosseras* mountain, *Palmertown* mountain, and the *Sacandaga* range of Saratoga county; the mountains about Lake George and Champlain, known, in part, by many local names. It embraces also the *Royal Grants*, the *Little Falls*, and *Anthony's Nose*, of the Mohawk country; the *Klipse*, and many others. The *Chautauque Ridge* is a strong feature of the south-west angle of this State, in the Lake country, as is the *Grand Plateau*, or great table land of the south-west of New York, and the north-west of Pennsylvania."

The *chief Rivers* are the Hudson, the Niagara, the Mohawk, the Black and Genesee rivers. Of these the Hudson takes the precedence. It rises in the high mountainous region on the W. of Lake Champlain, in numerous branches that spread over the S.W. of Essex and the N. of Hamilton county, and pursues a course almost due south for 300 miles, receiving in its way various tributary streams, and emptying itself into the Bay of New York. From its mouth to the city of Hudson, a distance of about 120 miles, it is navigable for the largest ships, and for sloops to Albany. "The combined action of the tides, arriving in the Hudson by the East River and the Narrows, at different periods, carries the swell upward at the rate of fifteen to near twenty-five miles an hour; and this circumstance clearly evinces a high superiority of oceanic

influence in the Hudson.   Swift sailing vessels, leaving New York at young flood, have repeatedly run
through to Albany with the same flood tide."   There
is no brackish taste in the water, that I could discover,
and I bathed in it, as high up as Newburgh, (sixty
miles,) though it is said to be sometimes perceptible
at Poughkeepsie.   In addition to the splendour of its
scenery, already noticed, the facilities which this
river affords for the navigation of steam-boats and
other vessels, are of paramount importance, and have
greatly contributed to the prosperity of the State.

The *Niagara River*, connecting Lake Erie with
Ontario, I have had previous occasion to speak
of.

The *Mohawk*, a large western branch of the Hudson
river, rises in the north-east of Oneida county, flows
through Herkimer, Montgomery, and Schenectady
counties, and enters the Hudson in different streams
between Troy and Waterford; the whole length of
its course is 130 to 135 miles.   " The stream of Mohawk is unequal, with many breaks and rapids, and
there are two falls of forty-two and near seventy feet ;
the *Little Falls* and *Cahoes*, (the latter near its confluence with the Hudson,) besides another small one
at the *German Flats.*"   A great proportion of land
along the Mohawk is very fine and productive.

The *Black River*, so called from the colour of its
water, rises near the centre of Herkimer county, and
pursues a northerly course of about 120 miles, when
it falls into the Lake Ontario.

The *Genesee River* rises on the great *table land* of

Western Pennsylvania, and flows northerly through
the counties of Alleghany, a small part of Genesee,
and through Livingston and Monroe counties, entering Lake Ontario a few miles below Rochester. Its
course in the State of New York is about 125 miles.
It has several considerable falls, amounting, together,
to no less than 476 feet. The flats bordering this
river are justly celebrated for their great fertility,
though, as I have said, I think they are equalled in all
respects by those of some other parts of the State.
Besides these there are a multitude of creeks and other
rivers: several very important streams have also their
sources in this State, as the *Delaware,* the *Susquehanna,*
the *Alleghany,* &c. It may be superfluous to add that
most of them abound with excellent fish of different
kinds—shad, salmon trout, sturgeon, bass, &c.

The *Lakes* are little less numerous than the rivers—
Lake Erie and Ontario I have sufficiently noticed,
though only a small part of the former and about half
of the latter is in the State of New York. Lake
Champlain, to the north-east, is also about half in the
State. Lake George is an arm of Champlain, and
wholly within the State. There are besides, Seneca,
Cayuga, Oneida, Onondaga, Ostego, and Chautauqua,
in counties of the same name.—Canandaigua, in
Ontario county.; Crooked Lake, in Yates county;
and Skaneateles, in Onondaga county; with many
others.

In addition to the *Erie,* there is the *Champlain
canal,* opening a water communication between the
Hudson and the St. Lawrence, through the Lake

Champlain, and also with the Erie canal, near its junction with the Hudson. Its entire length is sixty-three miles. It was commenced in June, 1818, and finished in September, 1825.

The *principal Islands* are Long Island, New York or Manhatten Island, Staten Island, and many small ones in the bay of New York, of which Governor's is the largest; and the islands of the East river. The Hudson has several small islands, but too trifling to require notice.

Under the head of the *Mineral Productions* of the State, " may be classed, iron ores, gypsum, salt, water lime, common limestone, the mineral waters of Saratoga, roof slate, marble, marl, peat, and a great variety of clays. The iron ores of Lake Champlain and the Highlands are very rich and abundant. Gypsum and water limestone are mostly in the western part of the State. The salt springs, principally in Onondaga county, are also diffused over a wide extent in the western counties. Limestone is found in almost every part of the State." Roof slate and marble chiefly in counties east of the Hudson, and marl in various parts.

Some indications of coal have been observed, but no considerable bed has yet been discovered. This deficiency, however, is pretty well supplied by the mines of other States, though the quality is greatly inferior to the English coal.

With respect to *Soil* and *Agriculture*, having frequently referred to them, I shall not enlarge here.

The subject to which I shall next advert is the *Climate*, and as Europeans generally are apt to attach considerable importance to it, perhaps I may be allowed to speak of it rather more particularly.

Between the New and the Old World there are several striking differences; but the most remarkable is the general predominance of cold throughout the whole extent of America: various reasons have been assigned for this, and much ingenious speculation indulged in. The following hypothesis of the learned Dr. Robertson appears to me as probable as any;—he observes, "Although the utmost extent of America towards the north be not yet discovered, we know that it advances nearer to the Pole than either Europe or Asia. The latter have large seas to the north, which are open during part of the year, and even when covered with ice, the wind that blows over them is less intensely cold than that which blows over land in the same latitude. But in America the land stretches from the River St. Lawrence to the Pole, and spreads out immensely to the west. A chain of enormous mountains covered with snow and ice runs through all this dreary region. The wind, passing over such an extent of high and frozen land, becomes so impregnated with cold, that it acquires a piercing keenness, which it retains in its progress through warmer climates, and is not entirely mitigated until it reach the Gulf of Mexico. Over all the continent of North America, a north-westerly wind and excessive cold are synonymous terms. Even in the most sultry weather, the moment that the wind veers to that

quarter, its penetrating influence is felt in a transition from heat to cold, no less violent than sudden."

The State of New York partakes of this general
feature, but has still its local characteristics, and the
climate varies considerably in different counties.
Thus, for a distance of 100 miles immediately up
the banks of the Hudson, where the tide and sea
air have an influence, vegetation is commonly ten
days to a fortnight earlier than in other parts of
the State, excepting the west. "In the northern
part, the weather is less variable; the winters longer
and more severe, with a clear and settled sky. This
region extends from the southern extremity of Lake
George, westward to the St. Lawrence and Lake
Ontario, as well as the counties bordering its southern
shore, and may be distinguished as the *northern climate*. The *western climate* comprises the country
extending from Oneida lake to Lake Erie. Here
south-westerly winds prevail a large portion of the
year: smaller showers collect more frequently, and
gales of wind are much less common. A gentle
current of air sets almost constantly from the south-
west, and north-easterly winds are almost unknown.
In this region the average temperature is about three
degrees higher than in similar latitudes in the
eastern climate."

In order to convey a better idea of the weather
and temperature prevalent in this country, as contrasted with our own, I have endeavoured to ascer-
tain its character throughout the different months
and seasons of the year; thus, *Spring*—(including

March, April, and May)—the commencement of March similar to January in England—raw and disagreeable—first appearance of vegetation about the latter end of March. April, chilly and damp; towards the end becoming more pleasant. May, much like June in England.—*Summer*—(including June, July, and August)—the temperature ranges say from the 1st of June, from 60° to 80° Fahrenheit through the month, then varying from 75° to 85°, perhaps for a few days 90°, or more, in the shade, through July and August, with occasional violent thunder-storms. —*Autumn*—(including September, October, and November)—September, fine, excepting one or two severe storms about the Equinox. October and November, fine, dry, clear weather, with cool mornings and evenings ; slight frosts, and, perhaps, towards the end of November, a little snow.—*Winter*—(including December, January, and February)—December commences cool, gradually increasing to cold, with heavy falls of snow, often lying several feet deep. January —the middle—extremely cold—thermometer sometimes standing at 12° Fahrenheit, or 20° below freezing point. The cold continues excessive until the latter end of February, when it generally moderates, and thaws, and damp weather succeed.

It is observed that there is a much greater variation in the seasons than formerly, and it may be expected, as the country becomes more drained and cleared of its forests, the temperature will be also more moderate.

But, after all, I am not inclined to regard the climate as presenting those obstacles or objections to a residence in the country which some do, and think the effects frequently ascribed to it, if they are not dependant upon other causes, might at least be greatly mitigated by a due attention to those simple but important matters, often altogether disregarded, and seldom sufficiently observed, viz. *temperance,* in every sense of the word, *cleanliness,* and *exercise.* Individually I can say that I landed in New York after an unusually cold passage, in the month of July last, the height of their summer, and a hotter summer than had been known for years, when the complaining of heat and indisposition was general; that I have subsequently travelled, first and last, nearly 1500 miles in the country, never, in consequence of the weather, having confined myself a single hour to the house; and that I have had nothing like illness throughout. The greatest annoyance I have experienced (and great it has been) has proceeded from bugs and musquetoes, the former especially. Opposed to this, however, I know there were instances of Englishmen coming over and wishing to return by the next sailing vessel; and one of these, with whom I am acquainted, was so grievously incommoded by the heat during the day, that at night, to refresh himself, he had recourse to the singular expedient of taking a boat, having previously reduced his clothing even to the extreme of republican toleration, and, with his hands depending in the water on either side, was rowed about to woo from the bosom of the Hudson the gentle zephyrs, in the absence of the sun's rays. And here I leave the gentleman and the climate to the kind consideration of the reader, and proceed to say a few words on the *Government.*—A Government which, in the short space of half a century from the issuing of their ever memorable *Declaration of Independence,* in 1776,*

---

* Only one of the distinguished individuals who signed this docu-ment is now in existence, namely, Charles Carroll, Esq., and hap-pening to meet with a description of, what I esteem, a most inte-resting interview, which lately took place between himself and two American gentlemen, I could scarcely feel satisfied without giving it to the reader; expressing the hope, however, that the enthu-siasm with which they regarded this relic of departed patriots, may have contributed not a little to induce a comparison less favourable to their statesmen of the present day than they really deserve. At all events, it is given as I found it.

" *Charles Carroll.*—This venerable representative of a former gene-ration, now in the ninety-third year of his age, and which he has almost completed, is in the full enjoyment of most of the faculties which appertain to the meridian of life. 'During a recent journey to the south,' observes the writer, 'I was fortunate enough to fall into the company of a respectable merchant at Baltimore, a parti-cular friend of Mr. Carroll, by whom I was introduced to the 'time honoured' patriot. As we entered his parlour, Mr. Carroll rose to salute us with the customary compliments, and offered chairs with almost as much ease and firmness as a man of fifty. His appearance indicated a high degree of health, which he affirmed he enjoyed without interruption. His under dress was a brown broad cloth; his waistcoat of the fashion of the last century. He wore no coat; but a gown of the same material as the waistcoat and smallclothes. His hair was of a silvery whiteness—his teeth apparently perfect— his eyes animated and sparkling, though, as he stated, they had be-come too dim for him to read. His sense of hearing did not seem to be in the least degree impaired. He spoke with ease, articulated with uncommon distinctness, and his voice possessed all the clear-ness of vigorous manhood. He seemed to be pleased with his friend for having introduced a stranger, and to be delighted in answering all our interrogatories respecting the incidents and the individuals to which he had sustained an interesting relation in the earlier part of his life. He spoke often of Jefferson, Hancock, the Adamses, and other members of the Congress of Seventy-six; but he seemed to take especial delight in talking of Dr. Franklin, whom he described as one of the most pleasing and fascinating men he however some of the *jura divina* tribe of other lands have been disposed to treat it, and whatever be its ultimate destiny, has already witnessed more

had ever known. He remarked that he and Franklin were commissioners to visit Canada, and endeavour to induce the inhabitants of that province to join the other colonies in declaring themselves independent of the mother country; and that the journey, though beset with difficulties and over bad roads, and sometimes through forests where there was no road, was rendered comparatively pleasant and agreeable by the wit and good humour of Dr. Franklin. He related many anecdotes of the Doctor illustrating these distinguishing traits in his character, and which made him a welcome and even a favourite companion in the politest circles of Paris. There was nothing in Mr. Carroll's manners or conversation that indicated the existence of that species of egotism which is usually the besetting infirmity of old age; and though he related in half an hour more anecdotes than we could write down in half a day, he was in no instance, that we recollect, the hero of his own story.— His reminiscences were of the mighty dead, and his commendations were bestowed with unlimited generosity on his cotemporaries who had gone before him to receive the ' recompense of reward,' and left him, as it were, to speak their epitaph.

" Mr. Carroll appeared to feel a lively interest in the ordinary topics of conversation ; made several inquiries of his friends respecting political affairs, the prospect of business, and the progress of the Baltimore and Ohio railroad ; and asked me many questions respecting Boston, its population, improvements, &c. He spoke more than once of the great invention of machinery for saving labour, of the improvements in the mode of travelling, and expressed a regret that the family of Robert Fulton had not been fortunate enough to obtain a greater share of the benefits resulting from his improvements in application of steam to navigation. He alluded several times to his own great age—attributed that as well as his health to the regularity and temperance he had always observed in his mode of living; said that some people thought he would live to be a hundred years old; but added, with a smile, that it was not his desire to live so long, unless his mental and physical faculties could be retained, which he could not expect to retain much longer. When we rose to leave him, Mr. Carroll walked down stairs with nearly as much elasticity of limb and firmness of step as either of his visitors. The time we spent with this delightful rapid advancement, and a greater increase of power, than was ever known in the infancy of any state, in ancient or modern times; and has given to the world a splendid spectacle of what may be accomplished by a people united in a good cause and determined to be free.

All *Legislative* power is vested in a Congress of the United States, which consists of a Senate and House of Representatives The House of Representatives is composed of members chosen every second year, by the people of the several States.* The Senate is com‑

---

old gentleman was short of an hour; but it was worth the fortnight we had then just wasted in the metropolis of the United States, where the lives of modern great men exhibit but few traits of character that entitle them to admiration, and their actions present but feeble claims to the gratitude of their countrymen. In the halls of Congress, or in the mansions of those who are elevated by the partiality of the people to places of power and dignity, one sees but little that can be remembered with real satisfaction, and is not unfrequently disgusted with much that he would take a pleasure in forgetting.

"The patriotism of the present day—at least that sort of patriotism which is of the most approved stamp, and which passes current in the capitol—seems to consist altogether in personal attachment to men in office, and to have no higher aim than the attainment of *a place;* its 'dirty assiduities are all levelled at the' treasury.

" But he who visits Charles Carroll will perceive in the sole survivor of those who signed our Declaration of Independence, a patriot of an opposite character, and may look back on such an interview as to one of the brightest spots on the tablet of memory. The character of this reverend patriot we shall not attempt to portray ; its sublime simplicity we feel our incompetency to describe. Nor is it in the compass of our ability to express the emotions we felt when our hand was cordially pressed in that which, more than half a century ago, set its signature to an instrument that certified the birth of a nation, and placed on the declaration of our freedom the seal of eternity."

* The State of New York returns thirty-four.

posed of two senators from each State, chosen by the legislature thereof, for six years.

The *Executive* power is vested in a President of the United States, elected for a term of four years, together with a Vice-President, chosen for the same period.—Being desirous, however, to confine myself as much as possible to a single State of the Union, it would be foreign to enter into detail on the general Government, and I would briefly speak of that of the State of New York, which "in all its departments is either mediately or immediately representative, reposing on the broad basis of the People, in whom exists an equality of Rights."

" The constitution has consecrated as inviolable the following, imposing restraints on its abuse :—

" 1st. No member of the State can be disfranchised, but by the law of the land, or the judgment of his peers.

" 2nd. The free use and enjoyment of religious profession and worship is secured to all mankind.

" 3rd. The privilege of the writ of habeas corpus is inhibited from being suspended, except in cases of invasion or rebellion.

"4th. No person can be held to answer for a capital or other infamous crime, but upon presentment or indictment of a grand jury, and counsel allowed to the accused.

" 5th. No person can be twice jeopardized for the same offence; can be compelled to give evidence against himself in a criminal case; nor be deprived of life, liberty, or property, without legal process.

" 6th. Private property cannot be taken for public use without just compensation.

" 7th. The right of freely speaking, writing, and publishing is secured, with ulterior responsibility for its abuse.

" 8th. In libel prosecutions the truth may be given in evidence; and if the matter published is true,— published with good intent and for justifiable ends, the defendant is to be acquitted.

" 9th. The right to determine on the law and the fact is reserved for the jury."

Inhibitions and Reservations.—To these articles it is added that the proceeds of all public lands, (with certain specified exceptions,) of the Salt Springs, and some other revenues, shall be inviolably devoted to the completion of the canals, and the repayment of the moneys borrowed for that purpose, with the interest thereon; the sale of the Salt Springs, and the establishment of Lotteries, are interdicted.

" The powers of the Government are divided into *Legislative, Executive,* and *Judiciary.* The *Legislature* consists of two Houses, the *Senate* and *Assembly.* The *Senate* consists of thirty-two Senators, who must be freeholders, elected for four years. The State is divided into eight *Senatorial Districts,* in each of which a Senator is elected every year, to supply the place of eight retiring members, who vacate their seats in the rotation prescribed by law. The Members of the Assembly are elected annually, and apportioned to the several Counties, in proportion to the number of inhabitants in each : every County to have at least

one ; and no new County to be established unless its
population entitle it to a Member.   A census to be
taken every ten years.   The two Houses of Legislature
are each authorized to originate or amend bills.   The
assent of two-thirds of all the members elected for
each House, is required to constitute a law for the
appropriation of public money or property to private
or local purposes, or for creating, continuing, or reviving any corporation.   No Member of the Legislature
can receive any civil appointment from the Governor
and Senate, or from the Legislature, during the time for
which he was elected : nor can any Member of Congress, or person holding a judicial or military office
under the United States, have a seat in the Legislature.   A Bill which has passed both Houses becomes
a law, if approved by the Governor.   If not approved,
he may return it to the Legislature, with his objections;
and if, upon reconsideration, two-thirds of the Members of each House present, agree to pass it, the bill
becomes a law, as it does also if the Governor neglect
to return it within ten days.

" The Right of Suffrage is extended to every white
male citizen of the age of twenty-one years, who shall
have been an inhabitant of the State one year preceding the election, and for the last six months a resident
of the town or county where he offers his vote, and
who shall, in the year next preceding such election,—
1st, have paid a County or State tax, assessed upon his
real or personal property ; or, 2nd, shall be by law
exempt from taxation ; or, 3rd, being armed and equipped according to law, shall have performed, in that

year, military duty in the militia of this State ; or, 4th, shall be exempt from doing military duty, in consequence of being a *fireman :* and every white male citizen of the age of twenty-one years, who shall have, for three years next preceding such election, been an inhabitant of this State, and for the last year a resident of the town or county where he may offer to vote, and shall have been assessed to labour on the public highway for the last year, and shall have performed the labour, or paid an equivalent therefor, according to law.—*Exception.*—But no man of colour shall be admitted to vote, unless he shall, for the last three years, have been a citizen of this State, and for one year preceding such election been seised and possessed of a freehold estate of the value of 250 dollars, and have paid a tax thereon. All persons of colour are exempted from taxation, unless so seised and possessed. All elections are to be by ballot. Annual election, first Monday in November ; and the Legislature meets on the first Tuesday in January. The political year commences on the 1st January.

" The *Executive* power is vested in a Governor, elected for two years, who is required to be a freeholder, a native of the United States, of the age of thirty years, and a resident of the State for five years, unless absent during the time on business of this State, or the United States. He exercises the following powers :—

" 1st. He is General and Commander-in-Chief of the militia of the State, and Admiral of its navy.

" 2nd. He convenes the Legislature, or the Senate only, on extraordinary occasions.

" 3rd. He communicates by Message to the Legisture the condition of the State, and recommends such measures as he deems expedient.

" 4th. He is to take care to enforce the execution of the laws.

" 5th. He may grant reprieves and pardons after conviction, in all cases excepting for treason, in which he may suspend execution, in order to refer the case to the Legislature.

" 6th. He nominates, and, with the consent of the Senate, appoints officers so designated to be appointed by the Constitution and laws, and commissions them ; and in like manner appoints Justices of the Peace, in cases of disagreement between the Judges of County Courts and the Supervisors.

" 7th. He recommends to the Senate the removal of officers, stating his reasons ; and, in some cases, removes them himself, giving them an opportunity of defence.

" 8th. He transacts all necessary business with the officers of Government, and the military.

" 9th. He expedites all measures resolved upon by the Legislature.

" The Lieutenant-Governor is elected for the same term as the Governor.   In case of an equality of votes, for either Governor or Lieutenant-Governor, the two Houses elect by joint ballot.   If the Governor is impeached, removes from office, dies, resigns, or is absent from the State, the powers and duties of his office devolve upon the Lieutenant-Governor, who is President of the Senate, where he has only a casting vote.

" The *Judiciary* is organized in regular gradation, from the Court for the Trial of Impeachments and the Correction of Errors, (which is constituted by the Senate, the Chancellor, and Justices of the Supreme Court,) to the Courts of Justices of the Peace of the several Counties. The Court for the trial of Impeachments and Correction of Errors, is the paramount tribunal of the State. It has original jurisdiction in all cases of impeachments preferred by the Assembly; and appellate jurisdiction in cases of appeal from the Court of Chancery, and from the Supreme Court on Writs of Error. Impeachments must be preferred by a majority of the Members of Assembly elected, and are limited to cases of mal or corrupt conduct of officers. Convictions can only be had with the concurrence of two-thirds of the members of the Court then present. Judgments on impeachments can only extend to removal from office, and disqualification to hold or enjoy any office of honour, trust, or emolument under the State; but the party convicted is still liable to indictment and presentment according to law.

" The Chancellor is the sole Judge of the Court of Chancery. He has a universal jurisdiction in all cases of equity, either original or appellate; on appeals from the equity side of the Circuit Courts; and on appeals from the Surrogates of the several Counties. The Supreme Court is the highest court of civil or criminal jurisdiction at common law. It is constituted

by a Chief and two other Justices, any one of whom
can hold the court: and they are authorized to hold
Circuit Courts, and preside in courts of Oyer and
Terminer, throughout the State. This court corrects
all errors in cases from the subordinate courts, and
has original jurisdiction in all common law cases, excepting those in which exclusive jurisdiction has by
law been given to inferior courts, on account of the
small value of the matters in controversy. There are
eight Circuit Judges, to each of whom a district is
assigned, who exercise an Equity jurisdiction in their
respective districts; hold Circuit Courts, for the trial
of issues from the Supreme Court; and, in the absence of the Justices of the Supreme Court, preside in
courts of Oyer and Terminer in their several districts.
The Chancellor, the Justices of the Supreme Court,
and the Judges of the Circuit Court, hold their offices
during good behaviour, or till they attain the age of
sixty years. Each County has a County Court, which
is a Court of Common Pleas, and a Court of Sessions;
and a Surrogate's Court, which has jurisdiction in all
testamentary intestacies, guardianships, and matters
incidental thereto. Five Judges are appointed for five
years, in each County Court, any three of whom hold
the Sessions, or any one or more of them, in the absence of the others, associated with Justices of the Peace,
not exceeding five. All other judicial officers, Justices
of the Peace excepted, are nominated by the Governor, and appointed by him, with the concurrence of
the Senate. The Justices of the Peace are appointed
by the separate nominations of the County Judges,

and the Supervisors of each County. If they accord, the appointment is of course: if not, the Governor selects the requisite number from the names on which they disagreed. The Sheriff, and Coroners in each County, are elected by the electors therein. An Attorney for the County, as prosecutor for the people, is appointed by the Judges of the County Court. The Secretary of State, Comptroller, Treasurer, Attorney-General, Surveyor-General, and Commissary-General, are appointed by the Legislature; the Adjutant-General, by the Governor."

I shall not enter into the *Jurisprudence* of the country, *wishing to steer clear of labyrinths*, although in this particular I might perhaps be in less danger of losing myself than at home, for the law *whereof the memory of man runneth not to the contrary*, is exploded here, and a *written* or *statute* law substituted in its place:—The Americans, however, may be said to have based much of their *statute* law upon the *common law* of England.

I have before spoken of *Taxes ;* exclusive of duties on foreign goods imported,* (which, by the bye, is a United States tax,) to *Englishmen* they are scarcely

---

* In round numbers, perhaps I shall not be far wide of the mark in estimating the aggregate average of duty on foreign goods imported at about thirty per cent., and I must be allowed to pass a few observations upon the unpleasant consequences which frequently result to the consignor of goods to this country, in consequence of the method pursued in the collection of their duties, which is as follows:—In lieu of the consignee at once advancing the amount of duties in cash, he gives his own bond together with that of a friend for the amount, payable by equal instalments, at eight, ten, and twelve months; which, by a little contrivance, in

worthy of notice; and the *Finances* of the State, as
well as the Union, are in a highly flourishing condition; in fact, the only fear of the holders of Government and State securities, yet unliquidated, in this

the course of trade, soon furnishes him with a capital of one-third
the value of his imports, and which is too often lost in hazardous
speculations, or expended in wanton extravagance; leaving the
bonds unprovided for, except by making use of the proceeds of the
goods, which ought to be remitted to the consignor; and, in case of
insolvency, the American Government, in order to protect itself,
gives the bond creditor a preference, to the prejudice of all others.
I cannot better corroborate and exemplify this statement than by
copying, *verbatim et literatim,* an advertisement, which an English
merchant, a particular friend of mine, had handed to him, the
other day, from his correspondent at Charleston, whom he had
intrusted with the collection of money for goods consigned to
another person, to the amount of nearly £800, and which unwelcome annunciation is all the satisfaction he ever did, or, most probably, ever will receive, and he preserves it as a memento of that
flagrant injustice which every honourable mind must execrate, and
which he grieves to think receives the protection of a Government,
in many respects so worthy of admiration, and professing to be
based upon the broad principle of justice between man and man.
The advertisement runs thus:—" *Notice*—Edward Brown, of
Charleston, merchant, having assigned over to the subscriber all
his outstanding debts, books of accounts, &c. he informs the creditors in general of the said Edward Brown, that the assignment is
in his possession and ready for their examination, and calls upon
such of them as are to receive dividends, *after satisfaction to the
preferred creditors,* to render in duly attested statements of their
demands within six months from the date hereof.

(Signed)   " O. L. Dobson."

I would willingly hope that this odious blot upon the statute law
of America, which gives a preference in cases of insolvency, will
not be suffered much longer to disgrace its pages.—And whilst advocating the cause of even-handed justice, there is another evil I
would remark upon, namely,—the great want of an effective treaty
between the British and American Governments for the capture,
and return to their country, of those miscreants, who basely ab-
scond with the embezzled property of their creditors, and the fre-

country is, that *they will be paid too soon,* and not, as
I am creditably informed is the case in a kingdom I
could name, where the *Debt* is somewhat larger, that
they will never be paid at all. The *Salaries* of all the
Officers of *Government* are moderate; altogether for the
State of New York scarcely exceeding the pay of a
British Ambassador at any of the principal courts of
Europe; and the stipends allowed to the members of
both Houses of its Legislature are not equal to twice
that sum.

Large appropriations are annually made for public
Schools, Roads, Bridges, &c., and the encouragement of
Arts, Sciences, and *Literature.* " The system devised
for public instruction embraces the establishment by
law of common schools, academies, and colleges.
Townships are divided into a convenient number of
parts, denominated *School Districts,* in each of which
schools are kept, regulated according to law."

The Militia constitutes the chief *Military Strength*
of the United States, and consists of every free able-
bodied white male citizen, between the ages of
eighteen and forty-five, comprehending the different
denominations of infantry, cavalry, and artillery.
The method of appointing the officers is perhaps
worthy of remark :—" The Major-Generals, Brigade
Inspectors, and Chiefs of departments are nominated

quency of which, by degenerate Englishmen, calls aloud for legislative interference. I can conceive *no* objection on the part of the
British Government to such a treaty, and any obstacle interposed
by the American must detract from that estimation which its best
friends would claim for it, and of which none more than myself
would wish to see it deserving.

and appointed by the Governor, with the consent of
the Senate. Brigadiers are chosen by the field
officers of their respective brigades: the Command-
ants of Regiments and Batallions, by the commissioned
officers of their corps: the Captains, Subalterns, and
Non-commissioned Officers, by the votes of their companies."

Of course, New York has no exclusive *Navy;* but
the navy of the United States, since the close of the
last war, has been progressively augmenting, and
now maintains a formidable position in the scale of
nations, whether we consider the size, the swiftness,
and number of their vessels, the ability of their commanders, or the valour of their men; and though I
hope the day may never arrive to interrupt the peaceable relations existing between America and Briton,
and Britons neither can, nor ought, nor need, to fear;
let them not therefore despise, but, as *prudence* has
been affirmed to be (I do not say that we should always
rely upon the authority) *the better part of courage,* it
behoves our Government not to overlook the advancement, towards maturity, of that force with which the
"*half a dozen fir frigates, with bits of striped bunt-
ing,*" (as a *great* man, in his *very littleness,* once
termed it) would now contrast but insignificantly.
I cannot dismiss this subject without further hoping
that Mr. Brougham, the powerful advocate of justice
to America, and who for years so nobly fought its
battles in the British Parliament, will use his well-
earned popularity in the States to bring about a still
more cordial feeling, and a less restricted inter-

course.—His *Lordship* will excuse my calling him *Mr.* Brougham—the appellation seems more familiar to me—I hate those *ships* by which the *aristocracry* contrive to *smuggle* talent and industry from the *people,* to the support of their *order*—these are the *ships,* after all, the most formidable to Briton—but I digress, and claim pardon.

In the City of New York, and throughout the State, *Banking Establishments* are very numerous. Silver is the legal tender—but each of these banks issue their own notes from large amount down to five dollars.* I pretend to no familiarity with the monetary system, but it does appear to me that whilst we are absolutely foundering on the rocks of Scylla, they are going almost within hail of Charybdis ;—or, in other words, whilst our lawgivers, either ignorantly or unjustly, or both, have returned to gold payments, without a due regard to the monied obligations of the country and individuals, they have rather a profusion of paper.

The legal *Interest* of the State of New York is *seven* per cent., but there are various modes of investment by which more can be frequently obtained : many of the banks, however, will discount unexceptionable paper at, or even below, *six* per cent.—They *keep their accounts* in dollars (equal, at par, to four shillings and sixpence of our money) and cents, or one hundredth parts of dollars; and their *Currency* is

* They were till lately allowed as low as one dollar, and great numbers of that amount still continue in circulation; but any re-issue under five dollars is now prohibited.

the dollar, the half dollar, the quarter dollar, the
tenth and twentieth of a dollar, in *silver;* and the
cent, in *copper.* The Spanish dollar is equally current, and is divided into one-half, one-quarter, one
eighth, and one-sixteenth; the one-eighth (or 12½
cents) is also called a shilling; but in consequence
of the more easy method of reckoning by decimals
their own subdivisions are greatly preferred.

In the extent of its *Foreign Commerce,* New York
stands pre-eminent to any port of the United States,
and, excepting those of London and Liverpool, is,
perhaps, not surpassed by any in the whole world.
It may be said to comprehend the foreign commerce
of its own State, as well as much of others, and its
inland traffic is also very great.

The *Manufactures* of the State are various and
thriving, as I have frequently noticed in passing
along, but in the aggregate they do not, at present,
vie with those of the Eastern States.

The *Post-office* department appears to be under
excellent regulations, and, for so infant a State, well
conducted; of course, in despatch and some other
respects, yielding to our own unrivalled establishment—which throughout reflects the highest credit
upon the directors and the country;—the rates of
postage are nearly the same.

I do not know that it remains for me in this
general, though very limited survey, to notice more
than the *Religion* of the country, and the *Character,
Manners,* and *Customs* of the people.—Of the *first,* I
may say, that although there is no *established reli-*

gion, as we term it, all religions being free alike, and
the conscience of every man amenable only to his
Maker, yet I must confess, with regret, that I have
too often witnessed an unbecoming degree of warmth,
and party spirit and feeling, frequently not unconnected with politics, on this momentous subject; a
disposition to introduce it as a topic of general, and
sometimes light conversation, and much divested of
that conciliatory spirit, that reverence and humility,
which, as they are its highest ornaments, are no less
its distinguishing and vital essence. Far be it from
me to judge any one : the foregoing remarks are
forced upon me by what struck me, as an unpre-
judiced stranger, as unpleasantly contrasting with
much that I admired, and wholly without seeking for.
I have no wish to enlarge, and shall merely observe,
that the ministers of all denominations (*Friends* excepted) are supported by the voluntary contributions
of their respective flocks :—the odious, iniquitous, and
unchristian extortion of *Tithe,* is unknown amongst
them, nor can any priest or clergyman hold an office
under the Government.*

Upon the subject of *Character,* &c., the shortness of
my stay in the country necessarily precludes my

---

* Whilst in Orange County, an elderly farmer, with whom I fell
into chat, mentioned to me a rebuff which a gentleman of this
order experienced the other day on applying to President Jackson
for an appointment to civil office. When introduced, the President's first inquiry was after the nature of his present avocation,
and being informed that he was exercising the profession of a
Minister of the Gospel, he briefly replied, "Then, Sir, I have nothing better to offer you ; go, and faithfully discharge the duties of
your calling." I cannot wish any trader in religion better success.

adding much to the observations I have already made. I may just put down a few particulars which have most arrested my attention.—In person the men are taller and less corpulent than the English; their complexions less clear and ruddy, often inclining to sallow; their hair, perhaps, evincing rather less disposition to curl; and their noses generally more prominent. The women in appearance very nearly resemble our own : their cheeks may not, do not, display quite so much of the lily and the rose, a matter with which the climate alone is chargeable ; but their figures are not wanting in elegance, or their features in animation and beauty. The latter, however, it has been observed, is of more premature decay; and transient as it is ever said to be, here seems indeed to fade too soon for such fair promise.

The leading characteristics of the men are a love of enterprise and independence, an ardent pursuit after wealth, (which, in the absence of titles and all acknowledged distinctions of rank, constitutes a primary contrast between individuals ;) and their Republican Constitution throwing all offices of Government open to them, many strive to attain pre-eminence in this way.

The spirit for *Electioneering* is frequently carried to a reprehensible excess, producing dissensions and animosities, and making sad inroads into the harmony which ought to exist in a well-regulated society ; and attached as I am to a purely representative system, and frequent appeals to the opinions of the people, I have been almost tempted to wish that they were either not so perpetually occurring as they are here, or that they were conducted with a temper and feeling which resulted in less unpleasant consequences. But even this state of things, bad as it is, I do not hesitate to pronounce far preferable to the abandonment of all control over our legislators for a period of seven years, which leaves them at liberty to play the game of corruption, regardless of the interests of their constituents, just at their pleasure.

It cannot be expected that in the higher branches of *Literature* and the *Classics,* in the *Arts* and *Sciences,* the Americans stand upon a par with some of the European States, yet they have made great progress, and have latterly evinced a growing taste for these refinements; and upon general subjects there are no people, taking them collectively, who are so well-informed. This I attribute, in a great measure, to their judicious system of education, and their *free press, unshackled as it is by duties or censorship.* This cheap and free press of America imparts to all a knowledge of every thing great and interesting which is passing in the world; and they are surprised when a foreigner is at a fault in any thing concerning themselves.

In their habits of social intercourse they are easy, polite, and obliging, that is, in towns, and in the better circles of society : in the country, in this respect, they are oftentimes boorish in the extreme; not that I have not seen them abundantly surpassed by some of my own countrymen who have settled amongst them, and who, copying a blunt independence of

manner, have fallen into a vulgarity and a disregard
to the common courtesies of behaviour, which few
Americans would practise, and which appear even
the more disgusting from being deemed an acquisition,
and worthy the effort of some study and application.

As a virtue conspicuous and common to all, I may
notice their genuine, disinterested hospitality, (the
only kind deserving of notice,) which is exercised
especially to strangers, almost as a thing of course;
and in humanity and generosity they yield to no
other nation. They are ever ready in their contributions to purposes of charity, and as prompt to
relieve distress and the unfortunate. Instances are
frequent, when a brother or sister dies, leaving children, of the surviving relatives adopting them into
their families, and treating them *entirely as their own.*
"This," observes a writer, speaking upon the subject, "is so common in America, that it meets with
no praise, and is considered merely as the performance of the most ordinary duty, and requiring
no effort."

In the towns, luxury is carried to a great excess.
It is said, indeed, that "the struggle for rank between different classes is productive of a very ruinous degree of ostentation, by increasing the expense
of living, and altering the public opinion with
regard to what constitutes easy circumstances, and
a competent fortune. Still, however, the inferior
classes of workmen entertain a higher opinion of
themselves than elsewhere. They find the road to
independence more practicable; and as the price of

their labour is high, their circumstances are easy, and they endeavour to throw aside, as far as possible, every appearance of rusticity. They see all ranks of men engaged in business, and do not, therefore, account themselves degraded by being compelled to labour; especially as they find their skill and industry sought after by others, while it is productive of affluence to themselves." Dress is much studied by all, and is esteemed as indispensable an appendage to the character of a gentleman as in the *bon ton* of either London or Paris, the fashions of which places may be said to prevail by turns.

Perhaps I saw too little of female society to hazard an opinion upon it. I think, however, I shall not err in saying that the women in America are much less domestic in their habits than those, at least, in the middle ranks of life in England; for which I must be permitted to think the men chiefly to blame. The almost exclusive attention which they every where pay to business and their public avocations, leaving the women too much to seek their own pleasures, and hence their predilection for the interchanging of visits amongst themselves—shopping—dress—music—novel reading, &c. I admit that many are more usefully and intellectually employed; but I must give them, I fear, rather as exceptions to, than as specimens of, the general character. The reserve and *"icy propriety"* which they evince also in mixed companies, and towards the other sex, and which appear so striking to Europeans, are doubtless to be ascribed to the same cause.* The latter, however, has at least the good effect of checking that sort of trifling and insincerity far too common with us, and which, however innocent and unexceptionable it *may sometimes be,* and is generally *professed* by those who practise it, is not unfrequently indulged in to a most culpable extent, and leads to consequences only to be reprobated and deplored. Here there must be no equivocating, no *double-entendering,* in *affairs of the heart;*—where ladies are unused to joking, gentlemen are expected to be in earnest; and in place of these matters lingering on for years, or any other indefinite period, as they do with us, one short month is often witness to their rise, meridian, and consummation, or decline, as the case may be.

I do not wish to be unnecessarily severe upon the gentlemen; but they must excuse my alluding to another custom, the renouncing of which would not only add to their opportunities of associating with

---

* A late writer, referring to this subject, makes the following observations:—" In place of that unreserved but innocent freedom of manners which forms one of the highest charms of polished society elsewhere, I must say that I seldom observed any thing in America but the most respectful and icy propriety upon all occasions when young people of different sexes were brought together. Positively I never, during the whole time that I was in that country, saw any thing approaching within many degrees of what we should call a *flirtation*; I mean that sedulous, exclusive attention paid to one person above all others, and which may by that person not be unkindly received. Without being called attachment, it often borders so closely upon it that mere proximity and frequency of intercourse tend to sustain a lambent fire beneath, which may be fanned into a flame, or be allowed to expire, according as circumstances upon further acquaintance prove suitable or otherwise."

the ladies, but surely could not fail to render them
more fit and agreeable companions,—I mean that
disgusting habit of *smoking* and *chewing* tobacco,
and of nearly *indiscriminate spitting*. Much as I
had heard of these practices, I was scarcely prepared to see them tolerated to the extent they are—
even in respectable society. In the first circles, I
am happy to add—I refer more particularly to the
two latter—they are very much discontinued, and
the sooner they are relinquished by all, and altogether, the better ; or, if there must be an exception, I
would leave the sailor with his quid, and the old
gentleman with his pipe, in the chimney corner :
if they can draw a solace, real or imaginary, from
such a source, let them freely, fully enjoy it; but
for landsmen with luxuries enough and to spare, and
upstarts with beardless chins, to smoke, and chew,
and spit, and in the presence of ladies, too, fie! fie!
I had surely forgotten myself when I said the gentlemen of America were polite and obliging; in deference to their fair countrywomen I must claim a
reservation here, and shall consider my title good
and valid whilst tobacco, whether in *smoke* or *solu-
tion,* is suffered for a moment to banish from the
drawing-room, or any other room, "the sex whose
presence civilizes ours."—There is not, I think, so
much disparity between the women resident in
towns and those of the country as I noticed in
speaking of the men; they, too, are willing to enjoy
whatever of recreation and leisure their circumstances may allow, and do not, I must say, so

fully harmonize with the character of *"helps meet,"* as the good housewives of the *old country.*

The domestic servants principally consist of coloured people, and emigrants from England, Ireland, &c. The native men, in particular, seem averse to servitude, and are rarely to be found in this capacity. The women are somewhat more ready to *help* out: but servants, whether white or black, native or foreign, entertain such notions of equality and independence as fit them but poorly for this station of life, and tend greatly to abridge the comforts of their employers. The white servants will not eat or drink with the coloured; and sometimes in towns, and very often in the country, they are dissatisfied if not allowed to take their meals with the families, fare precisely the same, and be well paid into the bargain. Wherever this is the case I am not surprised at its being urged as a drawback against a residence in the country, but there are exceptions, and the increasing influx of emigrants must gradually have the effect of lessening the evil complained of.

Pauperism is by no means unknown in the country, though I do not recollect having seen a beggar upon any occasion; and in a majority of cases where it exists, it may be traced to the too frequent use or abuse of ardent spirits; a circumstance which the Americans themselves are now fully aware of, and are using laudable endeavours to remedy.

Here I shall end this little digressional survey, which, imperfect as it is, I would fain hope may not be altogether uninteresting to my English readers;

and if these pages should be favoured with the perusal
of any of my transatlantic friends, let them judge of
me as one rather wishing to *extenuate,* than desirous
of *setting down aught in malice;* and if I have been
guilty of error or misrepresentation in any thing
I have advanced, I trust they will do me the justice
to believe it wholly unintentional, and attribute it to
the confined opportunities my hurried visit has afforded
me of judging correctly. I can assure them that on
a renewed and more extended intercourse and acquaintance, which it may probably be mine to enjoy,
I shall be as ready to correct and explain as they can
be to desire it; and with this confession I willingly
leave myself and the subject at the fair tribunal of
their candour and liberality.

It may be remembered that my last date of *September* 18, had landed me in New York, on my return
from my tour, from whence I was designing to embark
for England; but the vessel in which I had engaged
my passage not leaving till a fortnight afterwards, I
have had the pleasure of spending the interval amongst
a circle of the kindest friends in the neighbourhood,
and of seeing more of the city than I had an opportunity of doing upon my first landing. The notice
which I then purposely omitted I shall add now,
claiming permission, as on former occasions, to refer
for many particulars to the latest publications.

The *City of New York* is in lat. 40° 42′, long.
73° 59′. It is situated at the south end of an island of

the same name,* at the conflux of the Hudson and
East Rivers, extending along the former upwards of
two miles, and along the latter about four. Its width
varies from half a mile to two miles, and its circumference may be from ten to twelve. It was founded
by the Dutch in 1615, and then called New Amsterdam. In 1696 it was incorporated by the British.
During the revolutionary war it was the great rendez-
vous of the British fleet, and the frequent scene of
hostilities between the contending parties; and in
1776, a few days after its occupation by the British,
it was set on fire by persons attached to the American
cause, and one-fourth of the city consumed. From
that period, or rather from the acknowledgment of the
independence of the United States, its increase has
been rapid and progressive: the number of its inhabitants being then barely 20,000, and its present
population amounting to little less than 200,000.

"The streets of the ancient or lower part are irregular, many of them very narrow and crooked.
The northern part has been more recently laid out,
and with much better taste. Many of these streets
are very spacious, run in right lines, and are intersected by others at right angles. The ground is
now deprived of much of its original unevenness
by digging away hills, and filling up valleys and

* The island is fourteen and a half miles long, and from half a
mile to two miles broad, and comprises what is termed the County
of New York. It returns ten members to the Assembly of the State
of New York, and three representatives to the Congress of the
Union.

marshes, and some considerable ponds of water.
The quays and wharfs along the shores are far
extended into the original waters, that almost sur-
round the town. At present the surface has a gentle
ascent from the Hudson and East Rivers, which terminates in a handsome central elevation that every
where overlooks its gently sloping sides, and commands a fine view on the right and left of the
town, the rivers above named, and their crowds of
shipping."

Amongst the streets *Broadway* takes quite the
precedence. It commences at the *Battery,* at the
extreme south-west point of the island, and runs
through the centre of the city, along a height of
land, at about an equal distance from each river.
It is three miles long, and about eighty feet wide.
Here are many of the principal hotels, several
churches, and a great variety of shops or stores,
elegantly furnished with goods of every description and from every nation. It is one of the most
favourite resorts for citizens and strangers, and daily
displays much beauty and fashion. The next principal streets are *Pearl-street* and *Wall-street.* The
former branches from near the centre of Broadway,
on the east side, and winding through a populous
part of the city, terminates at the Battery. It is
almost entirely occupied with stores and counting-
houses, and is a scene of great bustle and business;
but the strange and unsightly practice of the merchants and storekeepers blocking up the causeways
with bales, cases, and merchandise of various de-

scriptions, and frequently throwing into the centre the straw, shavings, &c. which have been used in packing the goods, not only detracts greatly from the appearance of the street, but renders it very unpleasant, at all events to strangers, passing along it. Wall-street, commencing at the *Tontine Coffee-house*, East River, and continuing nearly in a straight line, crosses Pearl-street, and enters Broadway about a quarter of a mile from the Battery. In this street are situated the Exchange, Custom-house, most of the Banks, and many of the Brokers' and Insurance offices. Besides these, there are the Bowery, more spacious even than Broadway, Greenwich, Chatham, and Washington-streets, and several streets of nearly equal importance, with, of course, an infinity of others.

Of the general want of uniformity in the style of building, the impression which, at first sight, forced itself upon me, has been by no means removed by further observation. Excepting in the best streets, you will rarely find more than a few houses together which much resemble each other;—one, perhaps, may be built of brick, a good substantial-looking four or five story house; the next to it will probably be an old wooden one, of the moderate height of two stories, and 'tis well if it be not painted of various colours into the bargain; but the frequently occurring fires, and the prohibition against erecting a wooden house within the city, are gradually tending to remove these defects, and in a few years will, no doubt, much improve its appearance.

Of the *Public Buildings*, I shall pay the *City Hall* the justly merited compliment of a first notice. This is situated in a large open space, or *park*, as it is called, comprising about four acres of land, in the heart of the city, on the east side of Broadway. It is considered one of the most stately and elegant edifices in the Union. Its fronts and ends are of white marble, the rest of brown freestone. The whole length of the building is 216 feet, the breadth 105, and the height, including the attic story, 65. The roof is covered with copper, has a marble balustrade, and the centre is crowned by a handsome Cupola. In it are held the courts for the city and county of New York; and here are kept all the principal offices also. Many of the rooms are superbly fitted up, and that for holding the Mayor's court contains portraits of Washington, of the different Governors of the State, and many of the most celebrated Commanders of the Army and Navy of the United States. It was founded in 1803, and finished in 1812, at an expense of 500,000 dollars. I could not but regret, in inspecting this fine building, to observe such disgraceful evidence of an odious national habit, before alluded to: the, *otherwise*, beautiful flights of stairs, landings, and the floors of the rooms, being completely covered and stained with tobacco spittle, and the noisome smell of which was perceptible throughout the place.

Next to the City Hall ranks the *Exchange*, in Wall-street, a very handsome structure, also of white marble. Its front is 114 feet, and its depth 150 feet.

The main body of the building is two stories high, besides the basement, and attic story. The ascent is by an ample flight of marble steps, to a well-proportioned portico, ornamented with Ionic columns, 27 feet high, passing which you enter the Exchange. This is of an oval form, 85 feet by 55, and 45 feet high, surmounted with a dome, which supplies light to the place. From the Exchange are doors and passages leading to a commercial reading-room, and numerous newspaper and other offices. Underneath the Exchange, &c., on the basement story, is the Post-office, and its appendages. From the attic story a flight of stairs leads to the cupola, where is the Telegraph, which communicates with that of the *Narrows*, seven and a half miles distant. The height of the cupola above the attic story is sixty feet. The cost of the building, including the ground, was 230,000 dollars. It was commenced in 1824, and completed in 1827.

Amongst the *Banks*, situated in this street, I particularly noticed the *United States Branch Bank*, an elegant white marble building, sixty feet in front.*

The *Custom-house* is a four story brick building, but ill comporting with the magnitude of business transacted in it, or the general spirit of the place.

" The *Hospital* is a large establishment in Broad-

---

* There are at present no fewer than fifteen banking establishments in this city, exclusive of the Savings Bank, whose paper is at par, and several others, against which, in the Bank Note Table, published weekly, I observe such notices as the following : " Uncertain"—" Seventy per cent discount"—" No value"—" Broken"—and so on.

way, comprising also a *Lunatic Asylum,* and a *Lying-in Hospital.* It is erected on an area of 455 by 450 feet, inclosed by a high brick wall. The building is of stone, stands on elevated ground, and commands an extensive view of the city. The annual expenditure of the institution is about 40,000 dollars, and the annual number of its patients from 140 to 180."

" The *Alms-house* at Belle Vue, on the East River, is an elegant and costly establishment, exceedingly well endowed and regulated."

" *Columbia College,* above the City Hall, was chartered in 1750, under the name of ' King's College.' The edifice and grounds attached are extensive. The College contains a Chapel, Lecture-rooms, Hall, Library, Museum, and an extensive philosophical and astronomical apparatus.

"The *New York Institution* (formerly an alms-house) stands behind the City Hall, on the north side of the Park; is built of brick, three stories high, and a basement, 260 feet by 44. Its external appearance is rather forbidding, but the interior is richly stored with learning, learned men, and societies whose usefulness banish all recollections of the rusty appearance of the edifice, compared with the City Hall. Its apartments are occupied by the Literary and Philosophical Society, the Historical Society, the American Academy of the Fine Arts, the Lyceum of Natural History, and the American Museum. The Historical Society has a library of 10,000 volumes."

" The *New York Society Library,* in Nassau-street,

was commenced in 1740, and at the revolution contained 3,000 volumes, which were destroyed, or taken
away by the British troops. It was re-established
in 1789, and now consists of about 20,000 volumes, amongst which are many rare and valuable
works."

Though America abounds in *Churches* and *Chapels*,
many of them fully equal to any of our modern
edifices of this description, the venerable, the magnificent cathedrals, the immortal works of our Catholic ancestors, which so greatly embellish our own
country, and which, whatever may have been the
misapplication of them, one cannot still but admire,
it is, of course, in vain to look for here. The church
of the most antique appearance in New York is
Trinity Church, in Broadway. "The first built upon
this spot was in 1696. It was destroyed by the fire,
before mentioned, in 1776, and the present structure erected in 1788. It is of stone, in the Gothic
style, modelled after the old one, and has a steeple
198 feet high. It contains a chime of bells, the
only one in the city, and an excellent organ. The
Cemetery surrounding it is inclosed by a substantial
and costly iron railing. No interments have taken
place in this Cemetery for some years, owing to a
law prohibiting sepulture within the populous parts
of the city; but it has been ascertained by authentic
records kept, that more than 160,000 bodies have
been here deposited, (exclusive of the seven years
of the revolutionary war, when no records were

kept,) an amount approaching to the present population of the city."* Amongst the monuments is
one to General Hamilton, and one to Captain Lawrence, of the Chesapeake, the latter a broken column,
as emblematical of his death, which occurred in an
action with the British frigate *Shannon.*

"*St. Paul's Chapel* is a superb structure, further
up Broadway, near the Park. It contains a portico
of the Ionic order, consisting of four fluted pillars
of brown stone, supporting a pediment, with a niche
in the centre, containing a statue of St. Paul.
Under the portico is a handsome monument erected
by order of Congress to the memory of General
Montgomery, who fell at the storming of Quebec,
in 1775, and whose remains were brought to New
York, and interred beneath the monument in 1820.
The spire of this church is 234 feet high; and the
whole building is esteemed one of the best specimens
of architecture in the city. In the church-yard adjoining is an elegant monument, recently erected to
the memory of Thomas Addis Emmet, an eminent
counsellor at law, and brother to the unfortunate
Irish orator, Robert Emmet. The plinth of the
monument is one entire block, seven feet square,
and twelve inches thick. The Egyptian obelisk,

* The yellow fever has at times made great ravages here, but
latterly it has been much less frequent, and the thanks of the
inhabitants are due to the Board of Health, for the prompt and
spirited measures which they adopt, whenever this or other malig-
nant epedemic appears, to check its progress.

standing on its base, is also in a single piece, and is rising of thirty-two feet high. The face towards Broadway is embellished with the American eagle, sheltering a harp unstrung, with a medallion likeness of Emmet, and with his clasped hands, having stars around one wrist, and shamrocks around the other. On the north side is a Latin, and on the south an Irish inscription.

"*St. John's Chapel*, in Varick-street, opposite *Hudson-square*, is an elegant edifice, and the most expensive in the city, having cost more than 200,000 dollars. Its spire is 240 feet in height.

"*St. Patrick's Cathedral*, a Roman Catholic church, in Mott-street, is the largest religious edifice in New York. It is built of stone, is 120 feet long, eighty feet wide, and is a conspicuous object in approaching the city from the east."

There are nearly one hundred other churches in the city, belonging to eighteen or twenty different sects or denominations : all professing to be Christians, excepting one Synagogue of Jews. But Dr. Spafford tritely observes, he is persuaded *there are Christians amongst these Jews*, as well as *Jews amongst the Christians*. I dare say he is correct. At all events, it would be great presumption in me to question such authority.

The hospitalities of my friends, during my stay in New York, having left me no opportunity of visiting, I am, of course, unable to speak from experience of the internal arrangements and accommodations of

the *Hotels* and *Boarding-houses,* both of which are
abundant, and many of the former are upon a very
extensive scale, adding considerably to the beauty
of the city.   The principal are in Broadway, namely,
the *Adelphi,* fronting the Bowling-green, and in full
view of the Battery and Harbour.   It is a large brick
building, stuccoed, and six stories high.   The *City
Hotel,* near Trinity Church, one of the largest in the
city, containing more than one hundred parlours and
lodging-rooms, besides an Assembly or Concert-room.
The *American Hotel,* the *Mansion House,* the *Washington Hall,* the *Franklin House,* and the *National
Hotel,* are all splendid establishments, as are many
others in different parts of the town.

The good people of New York are neither wanting
in *Places of Public Amusement,* nor a disposition to
resort to them, as Theatres, Balls, Concerts, Panora-
mas, and the like ; and few towns can boast of more
fashionable promenades.   The *Battery,* as it is termed,
and which, I have before had occasion to state, is
situated immediately at the junction of the Hudson
and East Rivers, is one of the principal of these.   It
derives its name from its having been the site of early
fortifications and stockade forts, but now presents a
far more agreeable scene, thronged as it is with much
of the youth and gaiety of the city, attracted there for
the twofold purpose of inhaling the refreshing sea
breezes, and surveying the interesting and ever-varying scene around.   It commands a view of the port,
the egress and ingress of the ships, Governor's, Bed-

low's, and Ellis' Islands, Staten Island, the Narrows, &c.

The **Battery** itself is laid out with spacious walks, and very tastefully planted with shrubs and trees. At its eastern extremity is *Whitehall Slip,* from whence the North River and other steam-boats take their departure, as well as passengers for the European packets. From the Battery is a bridge conducting to *Castle Gardens,* called also *Castle Clinton* or *West Battery*—a spot selected for nightly displays of fireworks, and other public amusements, during the summer months.

Besides what I have noticed of the public buildings, there are the *State Prison,* the *Penitentiary, Bridewell,* and *Jail;* numerous humane and charitable institutions, two Museums, Marine Baths, Botanic Garden, Reading and News-rooms, Private Schools and Academies, Free Schools, a Philological Society, Printing Establishments, from which issue periodically several talented literary and scientific publications; and newspapers without end.

Of *Markets* there are, I think, not less than twelve —*Fulton, Washington, Duane, Franklin, Catharine, Spring, Centre,* and others I scarcely know by name. The first on the list I have repeatedly visited, and have no hesitation in saying that for the richness and abundance of its supply it surpasses any I ever saw, especially in fruits and vegetables; and in fish, flesh, and fowl, there is every profusion and excellence. I have been frequently asked by my American friends whether I considered their *beef* equal to " the roast beef of Old England ;" but I could only confess myself not epicure enough to tell the difference.*

* In reference to prices of various articles and other matters connected with housekeeping expenses in New York, I have been kindly furnished by a friend with the following particulars :

As regards *House-rent* in the city of New York, much depends upon situation. Remote from the business part of the city, a genteel two-story house can be obtained for 200 to 300 dollars per annum ; when at the same time, in the most desirable situation, near to the business part, a similar house would command from 400 to 600 dollars, and if of larger dimensions, with convenience of stables, &c. as high as 1000 dollars might be obtained. Such, however, as occupy these are generally the owners of the property. When houses are leased, the landlord, in most cases, pays the taxes.

The price of *Fuel* depends much upon the quantity in the market. Liverpool coal of the first quality, as used by many, varies from 9 to 12 dollars per chaldron of thirty-six bushels. The consumption of this is much curtailed by the introduction of Lehigh and Schuylkill coal, from its being cheaper than Liverpool. It is not, however, in such general use as was anticipated, nor is there any probability of its having the preference, unless at a materially lower price, the quality of it being so vastly inferior. *Wood* is from $1\frac{1}{2}$ to $2\frac{1}{2}$ dollars per load (about one-third of a cord) according to its quality. In severe winters the price runs up much higher, and those who have not had the prudence to lay in a good stock have often to pay about 50 per cent. more. Provisions may be quoted as under:

Fresh beef, first-rate cuts, 8 to 12 cents per lb. ;—Boiling and coarse pieces, 5 to 8 cents per lb. ;—Mutton, 6 to 8 cents per lb. ;—Pork, 5 to 7 cents per lb. ;—Veal and Lamb, 6 to 8 cents. per lb. ; —Turkeys, 75 to 125 cents each ,—Geese, 50 to 100 cents each ;—Ducks, 75 to 125 cents per couple. Other poultry in proportion.—Eggs about 1 cent each. Butter, 9 to 18 cents per lb. ;—Cheese, 6 to 12 cents per lb.

Of *Vegetables* there is a profusion of all kinds, the price varying much, influenced by seasons, &c. Potatoes may sometimes be bought as low as 30 to $37\frac{1}{2}$ cents per bushel, whilst at others they will sell for 50 or 70 cents per bushel.

Groceries.—Loaf or Lump Sugar, 14 to 19 cents per lb. ;—Moist ditto, 6 to 11 cents per lb. ;—Candles (Sperm) 20 to 22 cents per lb. ; —Ditto (Mould) 10 to 11 cents per lb. ;—White Soap, of best qua-

I have spoken of the frequency of fires in New York, and, as necessity is called the mother of invention, no efforts have been spared to render the *Fire Department,* which appears to be conducted upon an admirable system, as efficient as possible. One of its regulations is the enrolment of the young men of

lity. 12 cents per lb. ;—Yellow, 5 cents per lb ;—Green Tea, 90 to 130 cents per lb. ;—Black, 70 to 100 cents per lb. ;—Coffee (Java) 13 to 15 cents per lb. ;—Ditto (St. Domingo) 11 to 13 cents per lb.

Brandy, Rum, and Gin, 1 dollar to 1½ dollar per gallon;—Madeira Wine, 3 to 5 dollars per gallon;—Port (very little good) 2½ to 4 dollars per gallon;—Claret, 4 to 15 dollars per dozen;—Cider, 3 to 5 dollars per barrel (32 gallons);—Beer, 4 to 6 dollars per barrel: —these to be understood as the *retail* prices.

The article of *Bread,* of course, varies in price with the dearness or cheapness of flour, or rather, perhaps, I should say, the *size of the loaves* vary, the alteration being more commonly made in this way than in the price. As a general thing it may be stated full one-third lower than in England.

Servants' Wages.—For a good House or Chamber Maid (an adult) from 4 to 6 dollars per month is usual. Girls from thirteen to eighteen years of age are frequently obtainable for 3 to 4 four dollars per month. Good Cooks will command 6 to 8 dollars, and where the family is large much more is often given.—For first-rate men-servants, either as house-servants or to take care of horses, &c., 10 to 12 dollars per month is the usual price.

Clothing is something more expensive than in England ; that is, *men's.* For a good fine broad-cloth coat from 25 to 35 dollars are usually paid ; other articles in the same proportion : the fit and cut, however, are *incomparably* better than in England. Boots and shoes are also very neatly made, though the leather is inferior to the English, and, being much tanned with hemlock bark, has often the unpleasant effect of leaving a red stain upon the stockings, &c. Wellington Boots may be had from 3 to 5 dollars per pair ;—Shoes 2 to 3 dollars per pair.

Hats are not so well made as in England either in shape or quality ; they are sold from 3 to 6 dollars each : London Hats for 9 or 10 dollars.

Woollen and Cotton Stockings may be bought better and cheaper in England, and Silk Goods are now very little cheaper in America than in England, and no better.

the city, many of most respectable families who are
desirous of rendering personal services, and by such
enrolment are by law excused from militia duty;
these are supplied with the necessary dresses and ac-
coutrements, and upon an alarm of fire being given,
either by day or night, they repair with alacrity to
the spot, duly equipped, to assist in its suppression.
In the construction of their *Fire Engines*, too, they
have certainly combined the useful and ornamental
in a far greater degree than I ever witnessed elsewhere:—and though, perhaps, rather out of place,
the same remark may be well applied to their *Hack-
ney Coaches*, which are really elegant vehicles, drawn
by something better than *dog horses*, and presenting
an imposing contrast to the wretched conveyances
which we are accustomed to distinguish by that
name, and which (or the majority of them) are much
fitter to carry felons to Newgate, or *subjects* to the
dissecting room, than for any decent people to ride
in.   In addition to these, there are commodious
coaches passing to and fro, almost constantly along
the principal streets, and in which, for twelve and
a half cents, you may ride from one end of the
town to the other.

The *Fortifications* of New York have been greatly
strengthened and increased since the last war, and
are now next to impregnable. I may be spared the
enumeration of them, for there is hardly a spot,
either upon the shores or numerous islands, which
at all command the entrance, from Sandy Hook,
(sixteen miles distant,) to the city, but what is

planted with cannon. There are two arsenals, one belonging to the State, and the other to the Union.

The chief part of the *Shipping* lies in the East River, in what are called *Slips;* projections extending from the street to some distance into the water, admitting two or three vessels abreast, and where the largest may lie as securely as in Docks, with much greater facilities for passing in and out, as well as for loading and unloading. There are a considerable number of these projecting slips; several of them are constructed more in the form of a *dock* or *basin,* and are so termed; but they bear no resemblance to the docks of our sea-ports.

The *Bay* or *Harbour* of New York spreads in a southward direction, is about eight miles long, and from one and a half to five and a half miles broad, having Long Island on the east, and Staten Island and New Jersey on the west. It is connected with the Atlantic ocean by a short passage scarcely a mile in width, between Long Island and Staten Island, called " the *Narrows.*" The *tide* rises at New York about six feet, and " opposite the city ships of ninety guns have anchored, where they lie land-locked, well secured from wind and storms, with ample space for the largest fleets. The water in this Bay is very little less salt than in the open ocean, and its currents are very rapid and strong; circumstances that are of great importance in keeping the port of New York open, when others still further south are obstructed by frost. Philadelphia, Baltimore, and Alexandria are sometimes choked by ice, whilst New York is enjoying all the benefits of an open and free intercourse with the Atlantic."

The City and County of New York is now divided into fourteen Wards, in each of which is elected annually an Alderman and Assistant-Alderman; and these fourteen Aldermen, and fourteen Assistant-Aldermen, together with the Mayor and Recorder, constitute the Common Council of the City, or in the words of the original charter, "*The Mayor, Aldermen, and Commonality of the City of New York.*" The Wards also elect Assessors, Collectors, Constables, &c. The Mayor is elected by the Common Council, usually called the Corporation, and this body meet once a week throughout the year. No compensation is paid to the Aldermen or Assistants, it being considered they are well requited by the honour the office confers.

The *Nightly Watch* and *City Police* are highly spoken of, and the town is well lighted in every part: —but were I to notice all that is worthy of attention and remark in this great and enterprising city, which may well be termed *the young metropolis of the west,* I fear I should be trenching too much upon the patience of my readers, and instead of "getting under way" for England, almost induce them to believe that I was designing to tarry here. True I do not leave either place or people without many regrets; and the pleasing and varied incidents of the past fortnight will not speedily be effaced from my recollection. Most grateful to my feelings would it be to notice some most intimately connected with them, and whose

unremitting assiduities and exertions to add to my
pleasures, and assist me in my projects, entitle them
to my warmest thanks; but as naming these would
seem, in some sort, to exclude others, (and I know it
would be foreign to their wish,) all will be pleased to
accept of my very cordial and sincere acknowledg-
ments, and those to whom most are due may be assured
that I freely accord them the largest share.

For some days prior to my departure, my time was
too fully and too agreeably occupied to think much
of the *Robert Fulton,* the name of our vessel : it was
the only unpleasant subject which came across my
mind ; consequently it was not until the very morning
of sailing that I was aware of the great number of
passengers about to be taken. I was informed that
we were to be limited to *four* in the cabin, and about
forty in the steerage; in place of which, when I came
to embark, I found in the cabin *seven,* besides myself
and the captain; and, including men, women, and
children, about *ninety* in the steerage. Under these
circumstances I certainly should have declined going,
but the packet ship, *Caledonia,* had sailed two days
previously; and my principal reason for taking my
passage by the vessel at all, being a slight knowledge of the captain, (Britton,) still operating as a
stimulus ; and, not least, having passed through the
ordeal of a leave-taking, I concluded, truly unpleasant
as it was, to proceed.

It was about nine o'clock on the morning of the
3rd of October when a steam-boat was attached to
the ship, with the intention of towing us as far as

Sandy Hok, and in which several of my friends accompanied me; but the wind becoming favourable after it had conducted us a short distance, we hoisted sail and dispensed with the steamer much earlier than we had flattered ourselves we might have done.

For the first three days we had a fair wind, and made good progress, but afterwards it got nearly ahead, and with the exception of one day, on which we were becalmed, it continued to blow in that direction until the 15th of October. It then *chopped* round to the north-west, and carried us along in fine style, till the morning of the 18th, when, by an occurrence little looked for, all our buoyant prospects were suddenly and awfully dissipated, and the scene changed to one of aggravated horror—of hopeless and wild despair—when "shrieked the timid, and stood still the brave."—but one common destruction seemed to menace all.

As, however, the event which it is my painful task to narrate, may involve interests and property of serious amount, and occasion disputes to which I have no desire to become a party, I shall endeavour, in the most unbiassed and impartial manner, and with as much brevity as circumstances will admit of, to present it to the reader, and leave it to those better acquainted with the laws of sailing, and nautical technicalities than myself, to enlarge and refine upon it as they may think fit.

Upon going on deck at five in the morning, I found it blowing very fresh from the N.N.W. I continued on deck till about eight o'clock, when we

were summoned to breakfast, and shortly after we
received intimation of a sail being in sight, about
two and a half points on our larboard bow, (our
lat. being then 45° 10′ N. and our long. 44° 30′ W.)
upon which the Captain and the whole of the party,
excepting myself, went on deck, and from them I
learnt that it was a British barque with a signal of
distress at her mast head.   Our Captain, therefore,
altered his course, for the purpose of speaking her,
and rendering what assistance she might require, or
it was in our power to afford : previously he had
no intention of going near her.   By the time I went
on deck, we had neared almost within hailing distance.   Captain B.'s intention was to pass under the
lee of the barque; whether her Captain mistook this
movement, or was too close upon the wind to accommodate himself to it as expeditiously as was requisite, I am unable to determine ; be it as it may, the
position of the barque so completely becalmed our
sails, that our ship would not answer her helm, and
having her broadside exposed to the bows of the
barque, she came upon us with tremendous force,
running her bowsprit into our larboard fore-chains,
tearing them to pieces, with the fore-rigging, and
foretop-mast backstays, stove in the side under the
fore-chains, breaking several of the timbers, and one
of the upper deck beams, also the knees attached to
it, with the stanchions and rails.   Rebounding from
this concussion, she rose upon the next ruthless
wave, from the height of which she was furiously
driven upon us again, striking our main-chains, car-

rying them away, with the main-rigging, and one of the maintop-mast backstays, and tearing the bolts out of the side. In this shock the barque broke off her bowsprit close to the stem, and left some part of her rigging on board our ship. Dreadful as was the injury we had already sustained, we had yet to suffer another and a severer blow. Our vessel was now down in the trough of the sea, and ere she could rise, a heavy swell violently impelled the barque upon her for a third time, and, most unfortunately, brought her stem in contact with our mizen-chains; these "at one fell swoop" she tore away, with every rope and security attached to them, and, as if still unsatisfied, in passing off, struck, and stoved a large hole in our stern, and carried away our stern boat, and nearly all our oars, leaving us a complete wreck. The barque herself appeared to have sustained considerable injury, and the sea was running too high at the time to admit of her rendering us any assistance. We did not learn her name, or, in fact, exchange a word with her.*

In a few seconds after we had got clear of each other, our mizen-mast, all unprotected as it was,

* Since my landing in England, I am happy to say the barque has also arrived, and proves to be the *Standard*, of Whitby. At the time we met with her, she was bound to British America for a cargo of timber, and the chief injury she received being the loss of her bowsprit, she was not prevented continuing her voyage, from which, after repairing and loading as designed, she has returned in safety to the port of Liverpool. Thus, not a *single* individual on either vessel has perished by a catastrophe which threatened the destruction of *all*. —A miracle and a mercy none can too highly appreciate.

snapped short a little above the deck, and fell with
a dreadful crash over our starboard rail, the end of
it starting out, breaking our binacle and compasses
to atoms, and displacing the wheel.   Our situation
was now dangerous and appalling in the extreme;
and the cries of men, women, and children, added
not a little to the melancholy, the heart-rending
character of the scene.   Even the weather-beaten
tar, for a time, stood petrified with dread, or with a
reckless seeming of indifference, awaited the approach of his threatening destiny.   Seeing, however,
we still continued to float, the first faint stimulus
to effort was directed to the pumps, and inconceivable was our joy to find that, notwithstanding
all we had suffered, we had made comparatively but
little water.   This welcome gleam of hope afresh
renewed exertion, and as expeditiously as possible
the mizen-mast, which was hanging by its rigging
over the starboard side, was cut away; but whilst
thus engaged, we were fearfully apprehensive, from
the heavy rolling of the ship, that before any additional security could be given to the remaining masts,
they would share a similar fate, and extinguish
at once our scarce reviving hope.   Fortunately they
stood firm, and we had no sooner cleared the mizen-
mast, than all capable of rendering assistance directed
the most prompt attention to securing them to the
extent of our limited means, by setting up preventer
shrouds to the ring bolts in the water ways, and
every place that could tend to afford the least support.   We then righted the wheel, brought up our

only remaining compass, got the ship under snug
sail, and scudded her before the wind.

To think of pursuing our voyage, under the circum.
stances, was, however, utterly out of the question;
and the only choice or chance left us seemed to be to
run for the Western Islands, distant then about eight
hundred miles in a south-easterly direction; there we
accordingly endeavoured to shape our course; but, at
the same time, keeping a man at the mast head looking out for a sail, with the determination of abandoning our ship should any opportunity be afforded us,
not knowing at what moment she might founder, and
all our efforts prove abortive.   In this agonizing state
of anxiety and excitement the night closed upon us,
and by its impenetrable blackness added new horrors
to the scene.   The wind had now increased to a *heavy
gale;* the sea rose higher and higher, and ever and
anon seemed ready to break over us; whilst at every
roll we trembled for the fate of our masts.   Those of
the passengers who dared to venture on deck occasionally assisted at the pumps, but the greater part
remained below, stupified with terror, or imploring
the aid of that Almighty Power, to whose miraculous
interposition we yet owed our existence, and who
alone could succour in this dire extremity.   Slowly
and heavily the watches crept along, and every sound
of the bell which announced their termination struck
upon the ear as with the prophetic sadness of a knell.*

* Upon one of these occasions a poor fellow, who had heard the
Captain order the watch to " *strike eight bells,*" (usual on board a
ship at the expiration of every four hours,) half frantic with dread,

At length the morning dawned, or rather the pall of night was withdrawn : a fiery and portentous redness just announced its approach, and again the gloom of the tempest shrouded all. The gale continued as violent as ever, and with a furious impetuosity hurried us along : though in all the uncertainty of meeting with a sail, we scarcely wished it less. Since the time of the accident we had made upwards of two hundred miles, and if our masts stood, and the water did not increase upon us, there was every appearance of our accomplishing as much in the next twenty-four hours.—I will not trace the sad detail step by step ; descriptions of shipwrecks are familiar to most readers : those who wish to know more I refer to the pages of Falkner and Byron, which I never read with so deep an interest as when, upon an old hencoop, lashed to the side of our reeling vessel, I perused them upon this occasion : and though none of their most ardent admirers need ever covet a like experience, I must still think that it is only in the midst of the dread ordeal, and when every power of the soul is roused and rapt with the scene, that the fidelity and high-wrought energy of their colouring can be duly, fully appreciated. To proceed—on the evening of the 20th

came up and demanded of him, *if there was then no hope for us*, and on Captain Britton inquiring the cause of his increased anxiety, he replied, " Why, Sir, I thought I heard you tell them to *strike the dead bells*."—In the midst of all our fears it was difficult to suppress a smile. The man had probably heard the same directions given a hundred times before, without any misconception ; but the awakened and tortured imagination was now only alive to forebodings of evil, and ready to affix its own gloomy impress on all that transpired.

" the storm had spent its strength," and by the following morning it had become nearly a calm. We
availed ourselves of this opportunity of ascertain-
ing the extent of injury done to the vessel, and applying every remedy we could. The smaller open-
ings we filled with oakum, over which we nailed a
thick covering of tarred canvas. Into the large hole
in the stern, we stuffed a whole foresail, covering that
also with canvas and boards. We next turned our
attention to our long-boat, which we found shamefully
out of order, so bad, indeed, that though we spent
many hours in attempting to repair it, we could not
render it in a state fit to be depended upon. But with
the number which we had on board, however perfect
its condition, it could have been of no avail, except
in transferring us to another vessel, or upon the occasion of effecting a landing at a short distance.*

We did little or nothing at sailing throughout this
day, and many an anxious and inquiring glance was
cast around the wide horizon, and the wisdom of our
most *weather-wise* consulted, to divine, if possible,
from what quarter we must next expect a wind, and
dreading a change which would either compel us to
alter our *tack*, or our *course*. Happily, the next day
dissipated our fears, and brought us a gentle breeze
from the south. We crowded all the sail we could, and

* It appears to me highly imperative that some public enactment
should exist to compel the owners of vessels to provide good and
sufficient boats, in proportion to the number of passengers they
engage to convey ; and that none should be permitted to clear at
the Custom-house, until an agent appointed for the purpose had
satisfactorily ascertained the fact.

though the way we made was trifling in comparison with some previous days, we were thankful even to be holding on our course and nearing any land.

The principal occurrence which marked the succeeding day———23rd of October———I would willingly pass over altogether in silence, not wishing to indulge in personal reflections upon any one, and feeling that I cannot so far forget what is due to humanity—or at all events so appears to me, as to avoid it upon the present occasion :—with this premise, however, I leave the reader to form his own judgment, stating the circumstance very nearly as it is recorded in the Log Book.

At ten A. M. a sail appeared in sight, bearing directly towards us, upon which we immediately hoisted a signal of distress, and made every preparation for going on board of her; Capt. B. wishing to afford all an opportunity of leaving their present most perilous situation. We had scarcely done this when we were surprised to see the vessel altering her course, and continuing every moment to steer more out of our track ; this we construed into a determination to avoid speaking us, and after waiting for some time in a state of painful suspense, in order that there might be no misconception of our intention, we backed our main-yard, of which no notice still being taken, our former suspicions were confirmed, and we were just on the point of hauling down our signal, and making sail again, when the stranger tacked short about and came towards us. It proved to be the British barque " Mary Catharine," of Liverpool, bound for Charles-

ton. When within hail we lost no time in acquaint-
ing the Captain with our distress, though which indeed was but too sadly conspicuous, and requesting
him to take us on board. This he refused to do, on
the plea of insufficiency of provisions, which we
could only regard as futile, when he might have had
any requisite supply from our vessel. We next proposed to him to accompany us to one of the Western
Islands—the nearest being about 250 miles distant—
and for which we professed our willingness to re-
munerate him; but this he also objected to do. At
length, after much entreaty, he consented (rather an
advantage to him than otherwise, we presume) to take
three cabin passengers! which accordingly went on
board, having, at his request, been previously supplied with some stores by Capt. B ; he also offered us
a spar or two if we wished to attempt any repairs,
which, of course, we rejected, considering it, with the
the deplorable appearance which we presented, little
better than a mockery. He then made sail again and
left us to our fate.—If ever he should be placed in
a similar situation, ("what mortal his own doom may
guess?") and meet with the like treatment, however he
may feel its justice, he will not, perhaps, be disposed to
put a more favourable construction upon it than we
did upon his. To Capt. Britton, being an American,
it appeared even the more ungenerous and disgraceful, as our unfortunate situation was solely attributable to his humane endeavour to succour a British
vessel in distress. I shall only add that the individual who is the subject of these allusions is to me

a perfect stranger, and it is the *conduct*, and not the *man*, which I wish to expose, and hold up to that reprobation it so justly merits.*

The wind continued to favour us, and towards evening became more westerly, and blew fresher. We made excellent progress throughout the night, and by noon on the 24th, Captain B. having succeeded in getting an observation, we discovered that we had little more than one hundred miles to run to the most westerly of the Azores, the influence of the genial climate of which we were beginning sensibly to experience, and having proved how little we could depend upon any intermediate rescue, we looked towards them even with a more than intense eagerness.

At day-break on the 25th, being the eighth day since our accident, we first discovered the islands of Corvo and Flores, the former bearing E. by N., and the latter S. E. Shortly after the crew were summoned, and a consultation held as to the course it would be most eligible for us to pursue. After due deliberation,

---

* When speaking of this circumstance, it seems but impartial to mention the only possible extenuation which can be pleaded for such, otherwise, mysteriously unfeeling behaviour, which is, that in the present state of the insurance laws, if the captain of the " Mary Catharine" had deviated from the precise course specified in his policy, even though to save the lives of a hundred of his fellow-creatures, it would have vitiated his insurance for the remainder of the voyage, and, in case of accident, his owners would have been unable to obtain from the underwriters the slightest redress or recompense. It is high time that such an infamous inducement to evade the most sacred duties of humanity were removed; and I should little regret its operation in our case, if, in directing the public attention to it, it should in any way promote the accomplishment of so desirable and necessary an object.

and viewing the circumstances of the case in all its bearings, the shattered state of our vessel, the uncertainty of the wind continuing favourable, which, indeed, had already become less so, and the number of lives at stake, it was unanimously determined to make the first land we could. As the day advanced, the wind continued to back more to the southward, and notwithstanding we were once again in sight of land, we could not repress some unwelcome forebodings, conscious how much depended upon the next twelve hours. If, as appeared probable, the wind settled in its present quarter, or it came on to blow before we had made either of the islands now in view, we could have no hopes from the Azores, the remainder being situated still farther to the south, and to be exposed to another gale, which, even if we weathered, might drive us we knew not whither, was an alternative well calculated to excite our apprehensions. To leave nothing, however, unessayed on our part, we commenced clearing our anchors and cables, got our long-boat, such as it was, ready to hoist over, and with some barrels and spars constructed a raft, to be used in case of emergency. We had intended to have passed to the south of the Island of Flores, and thus round to Santa Cruz, (the principal town on the island, and situated on the eastern part of it,) hoping there to meet with anchorage and assistance ; but this we now found utterly impracticable, and, though we kept gradually nearing land, all we could anticipate was to touch at its north-western extremity. By two in the afternoon we supposed ourselves within twelve

or fifteen miles of this point, and hoisted a signal of
distress; after which we had very frequent recourse
to the telescope to discover the features of the unknown coast we were approaching, which had, indeed,
a most wild, rocky, and formidable aspect: here and
there we observed some patches of cultivation, but
no other evidence of the existence of a human being
was any where visible. In this forlorn and perplexing
situation, at five o'clock, we found ourselves close
in with the land, and a current setting us towards
it. To effect anchorage was impossible; in fact, the
very idea of anchoring at all in the state we were,
to put to sea again upon the first shift of wind, was
little better than preposterous; and to depend upon
our boat, at any distance from the shore, was equally
visionary. The night was coming on with unfavourable indications as to weather: the steerage part of
our cargo in particular " were mad for land," imploring that the chance might not be thrown away;
and, dreadful as was the alternative, there seemed to
be no other choice left us but to suffer the vessel to
drive upon the rocks. We accordingly selected a
small inlet between two immense projections rising
nearly perpendicularly out of the ocean to the height
of two or three hundred feet, as the most sheltered spot which presented itself for effecting a
landing. The moments which intervened between
this resolve and the striking of the ship may be
much better fancied than described : the most death-
like silence prevailed, or was only interrupted by
the wild clamours of the sea-gull and the breaking

surf before us. The frowning masses of rock between which we were entering seemed like two vast portals ready to close upon us; and to most, I doubt not, earnest as had been the desire for the adoption of the expedient, it appeared far more like an approach to destruction than deliverance. Our black steward, who had lived through one or two wrecks before, looked absolutely horrid with affright. A while previous I had observed him overpowered with anguish, and abandoning himself to despair: he knew, he said, that the vessel would go to pieces, that all could not be landed, and that he was sure to be last thought of. I endeavoured all I could to allay the poor fellow's apprehensions; told him that if we had not to swim for it, he should, at any rate, take his turn before me: but all would not do: a strange presentiment had seized upon him that he was destined to perish here, and it was not until he saw himself safe upon the rocks that he could be convinced to the contrary. I had certainly expected the masts, being so nearly unsupported on one side, to have fallen at the moment of the concussion; but the rocks in this inlet running out for some little distance under water, the keel of the ship ground along them, perhaps for more than half its length, which contributed much to lessen the violence of the final shock: this had no sooner occurred than we got our boat to the side, and commenced putting in the women and children. By this time several of the natives had made their appearance, and some in the most magnanimous manner swam off to our assistance. A rope was then attached

to each end of the boat; one we retained in the ship,
and the other passed to the people on the rocks; by
which means it was towed backwards and forwards
until all were landed, though leaking the whole time
to such a degree that three or four men were obliged
to be constantly baling to keep it afloat. Some of
our passengers seeing this, in the onset, and probably
thinking they stood as good a chance of reaching the shore by one means as another, had thrown
over the raft, but in their precipitation jumping all on
one side of it, it was, of course, upset, and two of the
number very nearly lost their lives:—one (by his own
account an ex-midshipman of the royal navy) it was
my happiness to rescue, just as he was giving over
the last struggle for existence. As soon as all were
safely on shore, our next care was to secure some provisions, and such of our luggage as could be most
conveniently come at; but the surf beginning to break
more violently, and our boat being in the wretched
plight alluded to, we were shortly obliged to forego
the attempt, and give up all until we could procure
some further assistance. We forthwith inquired if
there were any agent of the American Consul upon
the island, and being informed that a Vice-Consul
resided at Santa Cruz, we despatched a messenger to
that place, (a circuitous route of about twelve miles
over the mountains,) to acquaint him with our unfortunate situation, and requesting that he would lose
no time in repairing to the wreck. We then threw
ourselves down under the rocks, and overpowered
with long watching, fatigue, and anxiety, all wet as

we were, sank involuntarily to sleep. Our repose, however, was but of short duration, being broken in upon by the sound of a quarrel which had commenced between the crew and the natives; the former having contrived to bring on shore a part of a cask of spirits, and becoming completely intoxicated, sailor-like, were seeking with all possible avidity to " *kick up a row.*" Foreseeing the unpleasant consequences which such proceedings might lead to, for the natives had now flocked down from the mountains in considerable numbers, and many of them, too, had drank pretty freely from the same maddening source, an attempt was made to put an end to the contention by knocking in the head of the cask. This, though it effectually prevented a recurrence of the evil, for a time only added fuel to the flame; the crew especially, with the exception of one man, who conducted himself admirably, behaved in the most outrageous and infamous manner, even threatening our lives, and endeavouring all in their power to exasperate the natives against us, who, had they been left to themselves, would have manifested no disposition of the kind. As it was, from one, or the other, or both, we were every moment expecting an attack; and though none was made, it was chiefly the cause of adding one more to the many anxious and almost sleepless nights we had passed. In the midst of these disturbances, one or two boats made their appearance at the ship, for the purpose of plunder, which we had no means of preventing, though I do not imagine they carried off any thing of consequence. Before it was light a man in

authority arrived; that is to say, a description of
constable, armed with a black thorn stick nearly
as tall as himself, and who gave us to understand
that he was deputed by the Governor to protect the
property.   At first we were inclined to yield but
little credit to his representations ; but seeing that
by virtue of his *wand* and various official threaten-
ings he was able to keep his own countrymen, at
least, at a most respectful distance, we allowed him
to proceed as he would, and found him, contrary to
expectation, a very useful sort of personage.   In
this way we put on till near eight o'clock, when we
observed a number of boats approaching the ship,
(now rolling heavily, and appearing to be filling
fast with water,) one of which contained the Vice-
Consul, Mr. Borges, who immediately came on shore,
and in the most kind and feeling manner expressed
his concern for our misfortune, at the same time con-
gratulating us upon our truly miraculous escape
from a watery grave.   He then returned to the ship,
and commenced saving whatever he could.—It appeared that the nearest place of security was Ponte
del Gada, another and much larger inlet, lying
about six miles to the east of the present, and where
was also a small village.   Between this place and the
wreck the boats kept incessantly plying during the
day, and succeeded in getting off the greater part of
the passengers' luggage, the sails, cables, &c., and
about 200 barrels of flour, of which the cargo chiefly
consisted.   In the evening came our turn, and a
most formidable and perilous undertaking it was.

The surf now broke so high at the head of the inlet as to render it impossible to bring a boat up to that part; one or two were near being dashed to pieces in making the attempt, and it seemed every way probable that we must content ourselves with another night's lodging upon the rocks.   After various fruit-less endeavours, however, it was ascertained that a small cavity at the side of one of the projections would afford sufficient security to a boat, if we could manage to reach it; but with this proviso, the difficulty scarcely seemed less than before; the rock along which we must pass, about one-third of the way up, being, as I have stated, nearly perpen-dicular, with only a narrow shelving ledge, in some places scarcely wide enough for the feet, and where the slightest hesitation or faltering would have been irretrievably and instantly fatal.   Many, at once, determined to remain where they were, or get over the island how they could, rather than make the experiment; and few of those who undertook its per-formance would have been more readily prevailed upon to repeat it.   I am satisfied it never would have been accomplished at all, without the assistance of the natives, who are so habituated to scrambling amongst the rocks, that their feats in this way are absolutely incredible, and upon the present occasion, besides almost running along themselves without difficulty, they had to carry several of the passengers, and some bulky articles of luggage.   It was nearly dark before the first boat was freighted, (the last, I believe, did not get off till between nine and ten,)

and loaded it was to within a few inches of the
water's edge; the wind ahead, and blowing fresh.
In this state we pushed out, and had to pilot our
way through the most dreadful rocks and breakers
I ever beheld, oftentimes running close upon them
before they were perceptible.   On one side, and
nearly a mile distant, lay an iron-bound coast, like
one perpendicular wall of rock, and on the other
the open ocean, or with only the small Island of
Corvo intervening.   Our danger, indeed, seemed
scarcely less imminent than that from which we had
been so lately rescued, and though our boatmen
were familiar with the track, and managed the boat
skilfully, it was evident that they were by no means
charmed with their situation, and none of us felt
otherwise than perfectly satisfied to be landed in
safety at Ponte del Gada, and leave Santa Cruz for
daylight, or some more favourable opportunity.
After quitting the boat we had to ascend the rocks
by a most rugged road, and continued along the
summit until we reached the miserable huts where
we were to take up our quarters for the night.   For
our steerage company, a large room, being an appendage to the Mass-house, had been obligingly set
apart by the priest, who also entertained two or
three at his own house.   The rest of us disposed of
ourselves as we could, and upon the floors of the
different habitations, some with beds, and some with
none, full soon forgot the dangers and hardships
we had encountered, and, I'll answer for it, enjoyed
a night of as sweet, perhaps sweeter, repose than

any King in Christendom.—In the morning,———
27th of October,———Mr. Borges had been intending to return to the wreck, with the boats, and
renew his exertions at saving the cargo, but the *sea
had got up* so much during the night, and it was
blowing so fresh, that no one could be found willing to run the risk; and knowing that the vessel,
where she was stranded, must quickly go to pieces,
he considered it best to sell the whole, by auction,
without delay; and in all the uncertainty of being
able to save any thing further, the utmost bidding
that could be obtained amounted only to 261 dollars, for which sum our poor unfortunate ship, with
her remaining cargo, was accordingly knocked down.
A boat was afterwards sent off by the purchasers,
and lost; but all on board fortunately escaped.

The weather continuing very boisterous and unfavourable, we remained here until the 29th, when we
again set out in open boats for Santa Cruz, twelve
miles further to the S.E. Previous to our leaving,
there had been some further arrivals of flour from
the wreck, all of which had been under water, and
appeared much damaged. Our passage was about
as hazardous and unpleasant as upon the former
occasion, excepting that we had the day instead of
the night to perform it in, and being thus enabled
to discern danger before in immediate contact with it,
we were somewhat better prepared to guard against
it. Upon landing at Santa Cruz, as soon as arrangements could be made, there being no inn, or place of
public entertainment, we were variously billeted, the

crew, and the chief part of the steerage passengers, were housed in a building near the Fort; some got admission into the Convent, but were so terribly alarmed when its massy doors were closed upon them, that the poor friars were obliged to liberate them, to the no small relief of the one, and amusement of the other. Several were accommodated at a Scotchman's, who had settled in the place as a professor of physic.   Mr. Borges invited Captain B. and myself to his residence, and thus, by degrees, all were as well, and much better cared for, than shipwrecked men have any right to expect to be, or very commonly are.

Here, without anticipating the future, we were willing to consider our toils and troubles at an end, and though but upon a rock, as it were, in the midst of the wide Atlantic, felt thankful for the deliverance we had experienced, and rather wishing a transient interval of rest, than again to cast ourselves upon the treacherous waves of ocean : for the moment

> " Lovely seemed any object that should sweep
> Away the vast, salt, dread, eternal deep."

Such, at least, were my sentiments and impressions upon my safe arrival at Santa Cruz; and I was further gratified to find the detention we were likely to meet with would afford me an opportunity of rambling over the island, and contemplating scenes and objects of, to me, a novel and highly interesting character; as, however, before the period of our continuance here had expired, most, or all, excepting myself, began to be more or less troubled with *ennui*, and anxious for the hour of departure, perhaps, were

I to transcribe the detail of my Journal, I might run some risk of producing a like feeling in the mind of the reader, and I shall therefore extract, as I have frequently done, the very little which I find possessing general interest.

The *Island of Flores* is in latitude 39° 33′, and longitude 31° 8′. It is about twelve miles long from north to south, and six miles wide in the centre, from east to west, narrowing a little towards each end.* It is for the most part mountainous and rugged, every where demonstrating the existence of volcanic eruptions at a former period, although none have occurred within memory. Some of its slopes towards the sea, and portions also of the interior of the island, present small inclosures, walled with lava and pumicestone, and highly cultivated; with a soil of uncommon richness and fertility, producing Indian corn, wheat, yams, and potatoes, with a plentiful supply of herbage, amongst which I may include lupins, raised and cut for the cattle in a green state.

There is nothing that can be denominated timber upon the island; but besides a few orange plantations, apple, pear, and fig trees, there are trees and shrubs of various kinds, supplying all that is necessary for fuel and other purposes. The evergreens are chiefly the fir, box, juniper, laurel, and lauristinus, with some cedar, which grow luxuriantly, and

* When I have heretofore spoken of distances from place to place in this island, I must be understood as meaning the distance of land or water necessary to be passed over, to avoid the hills, or the rocks, as the case may be.

often conceal with their deep foliage the otherwise
barren rocks amongst which they spring. Water is
very abundant, and of the purest quality, intersect-
ing the valleys in small rapid streams, often in its
course turning the overshot wheel of a neat little
corn-mill. Sometimes it continues along the heights
until it reaches the rocks on the coast, from the
lofty elevations of which it is seen descending at
once in beautiful cascades into the ocean, and, in
some situations, vessels visiting the island for water
can obtain a supply by sending out their casks in a
boat, without having occasion to land.

The population of Flores is estimated at about
8,000, of which 1,500 may be resident in Santa Cruz,
and more than half that number at Lagens, another
small town to the south of Santa Cruz, also on the
eastern side of the island. The remainder is dispersed in several trifling villages, and detached dwellings, more properly denominated *huts* than *cottages.*

Of the chief town, Santa Cruz, little favourable
can be said. It consists pretty much of three narrow streets, leading from the sea, in parallel lines,
for a distance of near a quarter of a mile, to another
street, which runs from south-east to north-west, in
the direction of Ponte del Gada. Immediately behind the town is a high hill, with a very steep
ascent, cultivated almost to the summit, which is
chiefly overgrown with juniper. There was formerly a sort of *vigia,* or look-out, upon it; but only
a few yards of the wall are now remaining.

The better kind of houses are built of stone, the

walls very thick, never exceeding two stories high, and usually having a balcony from the upper rooms, with glazed folding doors opening into it : here the inmates are mostly to be seen lounging about in dishabille, with no other object or excitement save that of noticing occasional passing acquaintance, between whom and themselves a host of ceremonies and compliments is expected to take place. The lower rooms, if not used as cellars or store-rooms, are seldom furnished or inhabited. The mildness of the climate precludes the necessity of fires, and in no room, except the kitchen, is a fire-place ever seen. The rest, and by far the greater part, of the houses are mere cottages, rather roughly constructed and white-washed.—There are two small shops or stores in the town, at the principal of which I am told the receipts will not average more than two dollars per day, and even with that a twelvemonth's credit is frequently given; such, in fact, is the scarcity of money, that trading may almost be said to be carried on upon a system of barter. The rent of land is, I believe, universally paid in produce.

The public buildings are a Church and a Convent: the former very lofty and spacious, large enough to contain half the population of the island, but with grass growing in the interior on each side of the ile, just as on the outside, except at the upper end, where the arrangements are very similar to those of Catholic churches generally, and crosses, images of saints, &c. &c. occupy every little niche and situation in which it seems possible to place them.—The Convent is an irregular stone building, in size better corresponding with the magnitude of the Church than the insignificance of the town. It contains several roomy halls and other apartments, and is occupied by a few friars, who evidently take better care of themselves than the building; for whilst the former are well fed, sleek, and comely, the latter has but a neglected and dreary appearance. There are not any nuns in the island.

The Jail and the Custom-house are unworthy of notice; but there is a little edifice on the outskirts of the town which, for the novelty and ingenuity of its design and construction, must not be so passed over. It is a kind of Foundling Hospital, and one which, if secrecy be desirable, seems better adapted to meet the feelings of parties and the exigencies of the case than any thing I ever before heard of. The building is of stone, with windows only in the front. In the gable end is a small aperture, in which is affixed a barrel turning upon a pivot, in an upright position, with a few staves out on one side. In an ordinary way the perfect side of the barrel is outwards, but whenever any are desirous of availing themselves of the institution, upon arrival at the spot, a few slight taps immediately arrest the attention of the residents, who as promptly, without either having or seeking an opportunity of observation, present the open part of the barrel to receive the hapless consignment, which is no sooner made than the bearer decamps, the barrel is returned to its former position, and the little stranger being safely dislodged, receives at once, and during the first years of its infancy, such care and attention as are here deemed requisite ; after which, in the simple fashion of the country, it soon learns to cater for itself, and subsists in various ways. I was not a little amused with this unique establishment upon my first discovery of it, but good and evil are often too much blended together, and in this instance their connexion is obvious. It no doubt fully and effectually prevents the horrid crime of infanticide, but at the same time removes a very primary incentive to correct conduct and virtue in the female, and trenches fearfully upon the " chaste connubial tie," which is, amongst the peasantry, (to whom these remarks solely apply,) very generally dispensed with.

I have spoken of the Fort, but as may be supposed, it is rather a name than a reality. It is situated on a point of rock overlooking the sea, at the south-east of the town. There are not more than two or three guns mounted, and no regular soldier, I believe, in the island.

There is nothing like a bay or harbour at Santa Cruz. The coast about the town is low, and very rocky, so that only small vessels can approach near it, and these have sometimes to beat about for days, and even weeks, before it is safe to attempt it, and always upon their arrival are immediately hauled up, upon rollers, by main strength, out of the water, to the bottom of the street, leading down to the port, a distance of forty or fifty yards, to secure them from the surf, which frequently breaks here, as elsewhere, with great violence. There is anchorage

(the best the island affords) **at a mile** or two from
the town; but it is such as is altogether dependant
upon the wind, **and** vessels must be prepared to
put off to sea whenever that becomes unfavourable.
Two schooners belonging to individuals at Santa
Cruz comprise the shipping of Flores. They make
annually several trips to some of the other islands,
with grain, cattle, orchilla, and woollen stuffs—rather
of a rude manufacture—which they exchange for
wine and other commodities. A few schooners from
the other islands also occasionally visit Flores, beyond which it has little communication with them, or
the rest of the world, except an American whaler, or
other vessel puts in for refreshments, or like us, in a
case of dernier resort and distress.

The Government of the island is chiefly vested in
two authorities, called the Governor and the Judge,
every way worthy representatives of their wretched
master, Don Miguel, who having present possession
of the throne of Portugal, exercises dominion over
all the Azores, excepting Terceira, which espouses
the cause of Donna Maria. The power of these
petty tyrants appears of a summary and absolute
character, extending to the prevention of any one
launching a boat, or going to a vessel, although in
distress, without their permission; and to the impri-
sonment, during their own pleasure, of whoever upon
meeting them, or even passing their houses, omits the
ceremony of taking off the hat. With these specimens
of despotism, it were a farce to talk of jurisprudence,
and as superfluous to add that the people generally are

in a state of abject and degrading vassalage; but inured to subjection, they submit without repining, and, cultivating their fertile lands, or engaging themselves in fishing, obtain much more than a supply for their limited wants, and are contented and happy: —would that as much could be said of others under more enlightened and liberal systems!

Both men and women, for the most part, though rather short, are well made and healthy; their complexions clearer than those of the Portuguese on the continent of Europe; but their features are not unfrequently wanting in expression, if I except their fine black eyes, the beauty and brilliancy of which but render the contrast the greater. That class of society in the island whose means exempt them from the necessity of labour, lead a life of excessive indolence and supineness, scarcely relieved by amusements of any kind; even walking seems too great an exertion for them, and riding is out of the question, for there is scarcely either horse, mule, or ass in the island. Fourteen or fifteen hours, out of the twenty-four, they frequently spend in bed. The men, except when they appear in public, are almost slovenly in their dress, and no sooner enter the house, after having been out, no matter what the hour of the day, than their visiting attire is put off, and the undress resumed. The women are much more neat and cleanly in their dress and persons; their manners are unaffected, and their dispositions kind and obliging; but, destitute of those accomplishments, and, in fact, of opportunity of acquiring

them, which distinguish female society in polished
communities, they appear to great disadvantage to
strangers. They go even less frequently from home
than the men, and their seclusion scarcely differs, but
in name, from that of the convent. If, however, they
have not the refinements, they are at least exempt
from many of the follies and dissipations of a more
public and fashionable life, and, were there not a
medium in adjusting the balance between the good
and evil of the two, I, for one, must give the pre-
ponderance altogether in favour of the ladies of
Flores.

The dress of the peasantry has nothing very peculiar in it. They rarely wear either shoes or stockings;
nor, except when dressed for church, &c., any covering upon the head. On these occasions the women
completely envelop both head and face in the immense hoods of their cloaks, or in large white hand-
kerchiefs, which they hold out before them as far as
the arm can extend, keeping them closed in front,
except just so much as enables them to discern their
way; and the fingers with which they are held are
usually ornamented with a ring or two, which they
appear studious to display. They have a purple
flower, very common in the fields, which they call
" *the Nun,*" so exactly resembling this costume, that
one would almost think it had furnished them with
the hint for its adoption; but whilst the one is simply
natural and graceful, the other is equally unbecoming
and preposterous.

The style of living, that is, of cookery, amongst the

better class, embraces rather too much of soups, ra-
gouts, and *made-ups*, to relish with English taste.
Scarcely a joint appears at table that has not been
spoiled, in some way or other, of its fair proportions.
If it succeed to soup, it is nothing more than a collection of dry, insipid shreds. The soup, to be sure, is
all the better for it, and with rice, vermicelli, and such
like *et ceteras*, is excellent; but woe to those who
make reservation, or think to thrive upon the meat;
—it is about as nutritious and satisfying as the pith of
a bulrush. It is not the custom to help each person
separately, but to cut and hand round the table a
number of slices upon a plate, as we do cheese, and
no one commences until all are served; an etiquette
which is repeated with as many courses as may be
introduced, and becomes quite a tiresome and formal
observance. A little wine is drank during dinner,
but the American fashion obtains of rising and with-
drawing instantly afterwards. Three meals are taken
during the day:—breakfast on rising, often at a late
hour, of coffee, tea, eggs, &c.;—dinner, from one to
two; and tea, or some slight repast, at six or seven in
the evening, which is no sooner concluded than all
creep off to bed, seemingly wearied out with their day
of nothingness.

Yams and potatoes constitute the chief food of the
peasantry; sometimes a little fish; and water, or the
light wines imported from the other islands, their
only beverage. They are an industrious, inoffensive
race, though not quite free from a disposition to
pilfer when opportunity offers, or so we found them;

perhaps it may be more from strangers than amongst themselves. Any of the greater crimes are rarely known amongst them.

Provisions are very cheap. Beef, pork, and bacon,* excellent. Sheep are small, and seldom used for food, the wool being considered the most valuable part of the animal. Poultry and fish are in great plenty, as are also rabbits, quail, and pigeons; the latter precisely the same as our common blue dove-cote pigeon, but quite in a wild state. The pursuit of them afforded some of our party no little diversion, but they are rarely molested by the natives. The peasantry care nothing about them, and the gentry are too idle for sportsmen.

The roads of the island are of the most rugged kind, narrow, and, in many places, but mere passages worn amongst the rocks. I am not very ready to coin excuses for abridging the exercise of walking, but so intolerably bad did I find them, that, besides one or two severe falls, for some days after landing I was scarcely able to hobble along at all, and destroyed more boots and shoes in three weeks than would commonly serve me for as many months. The peasantry, however, travel over them

---

* A very singular custom prevails of shaving the backs of their hogs. I have asked them if the operation is performed in compliment to their friars; but the reason they assign for it is, that it has a tendency to make them spread in fattening. If it be so, the secret is worth knowing; but I am sceptical enough to believe that their yams and Indian corn, upon which the animals are plentifully fed, are much more concerned in producing the effect than the razor.

with their naked feet, thinking no more of inconve
nience than if pacing the turf of a bowling-green ; and
when their *betters* are inclined, or have occasion to
travel, for a mere trifle they will carry them in ham-
mocks, upon their shoulders, half over the island.

Goods and produce are conveyed upon a kind of
small dray, or oval platform, drawn by oxen. It is
a rudely-constructed thing, altogether of wood, and
when in motion the creaking of the wheels is, to un-
accustomed ears, beyond any patient endurance ; but
if ever I suggested the application of a little grease,
I was invariably assured that the noise had an enliven-
ing effect upon the oxen, and that it was the study of
the driver to produce it in the greatest possible degree : thus foiled, I could but let them creak on,
lamenting that the ears of their oxen were pitched to
no finer key, or that their own carelessness and indifference, to which I ascribed it, should so readily furnish them with an excuse for the non-suppression of
the nuisance.

Of one occurrence which took place during our
stay at Santa Cruz, namely, the interment of an infant
after the rites of the Catholic church,—a ceremony I
had never before witnessed in a strictly Catholic
country,—I have preserved this notice:—The father
of the child was baker-general to our company,
and upon going into his house I saw the little
thing *lying in state.* The coffin was placed upon a
table, in the middle of one of the rooms, which contained scarcely any other furniture, with a large cross
at the head of it, and surrounded by a number of wax

tapers. It was of very slight manufacture, not more
in substance than a bandbox, covered with marble
paper, and opening with hinges at each side; the
ends raised to a point in the centre, so that when
closed the upper part formed a kind of roof, which
was merely tied together in two places by ribbands.
The body was dressed with the nicest care, and depó-
sited in it, with a bunch of flowers in the hands,
which were joined upon its breast.   In a short
time as many friars as the room would well contain, with shaven crowns, and in long dirty cloaks,
made their appearance, and stationing themselves
around the table, lighted the tapers which were standing upon it, and each, besides, holding one lighted in
his hand, they commenced the loudest and most
inharmonious chanting, if such indeed it might be
termed, I ever heard.   This was continued for about
twenty minutes, when the priest and curate arrived,
and the former being presented with a pan of incense,
which, when ignited, filled the whole place with the
most odoriferous perfume, passed it three times over
the coffin; he then laid it down, and taking from
under his robe a long narrow phial, the top of which
appeared to be perforated much like that of a pepper-
cruet, thrice sprinkled the face of the child with the
holy water, which it was *said* to contain.   One or two
of the friars then took up the coffin to convey it to
the church, the cross being carried before it, and the
priest heading the procession.   The remainder of the
friars, with a few relatives and other attendants, without much observance of order, walked on each side

and in the rear; the former, at intervals, chanting as loudly and vociferously as before. When they arrived at the church, the body was taken to the upper part of it, and again placed upon a table, in the midst of lighted tapers, and nearly the same ceremony of chanting, sprinkling, and incense burning which took place in the house was repeated here, each friar holding a lighted taper, from three to five feet in length,—one similar to which, as a mark of respect to a stranger, was handed to me by the father of the child, which I held until the conclusion of the scene. The coffin, with its contents, was ultimately let down through a trap-door, into a vault by two friars, by means of a cord attached to each end of it, who, as they lowered it, swung it from side to side, bawling out a requiem well nigh sufficient to disturb the slumbering inhabitants beneath. On its reaching the bottom, the cords were thrown in, and the flaming incense having been passed three times over the opening, the trap-door was replaced, and the friars and others extinguishing their tapers, laid them upon the table, and the assemblage dispersed,—leaving upon my mind a mingled impression of pity and disgust for the deluded or designing actors in the scene, which to me displayed so much of the ludicrous as to divest it altogether of the solemnity which ought to attach to the occasion. But if even rites like these can be performed by men professing Christianity, and by rational beings, with sincerity, I am too much a friend to liberty of conscience, and universal toleration, to wish to treat them with levity and disrespect, and

willingly forego those comments I might otherwise
be tempted to indulge in, though I could not avoid
asking myself again and again, during the day,
*Is this really the nineteenth century, and can such
things be?*

On the 3rd of November, there was a sale by
auction of the various articles saved from our wreck,
namely, 200 barrels of flour, (or what remained of
that quantity, some having been used for bread for
the passengers,) the sails, rigging, cables, &c. It
had been generally notified throughout the island,
and also at Corvo, for some days previously, so that
we had little short of one hundred persons present.
The spot fixed upon for this *vendue* was an open
space about the centre of the town. The auctioneer
was a most uncouth character, much resembling the
constable that attended upon us under the rocks,
and like him carried a long black thorn stick, pacing
to and fro in front of the people, receiving their
biddings as he passed along. The sale occupied
nearly the whole of the day. The flour was purchased for exportation, not being allowed to be
consumed on the island, for the miserable price of
one dollar and seventy-five cents per barrel—the
other lots about in proportion. The Priest bought
the bell for church service, for eight dollars and
sixty cents. It was a galling consideration that
property should be thus sacrificed; but the case
seemed without remedy, as there were only a few
individuals with ability to make any purchases, and
the expense of conveying the goods elsewhere would

only have made bad worse, and the exertion used
to save them at all altogether thrown away.

I observe the following memorandum of the day :—
This day has been the most lovely and enchanting,
both in brilliancy and temperature, I ever experienced,
and were it not for the known anxiety of friends in
England, I could be well content to exchange its
dreary winter months for the spring-like softness of
this luxuriant clime, of which I begin to envy the
residents more and more.

It is with much pleasure that I speak of the great
kindness of Mr. Borges and his family to Captain B.
and myself, as well as of his care and attention, in
his official capacity, for the rest of the passengers and
crew, amounting absolutely to solicitude on their behalf; nor must I omit to mention the hospitality we
experienced from other of his relatives, as also from
a Spanish gentleman, Don Mariano H———, *the*
merchant of Flores.

Upon dining with Mr. L. Borges, the brother of
our friend, who entertained us with much generosity, I
was introduced to a new species of etiquette, namely,
that of the master of the house and one of his sons
assisting the domestics in waiting upon their guests,
who were put in possession of the top and the bottom
of the table, whilst his lady and the family, with the
rest of the company, were seated along the sides.
Whether our worthy host and his son dined before or
after us, or whether they dined at all, I know not; but
I do know, that, notwithstanding the marked attention
it was designed to evince, it would have been abun-

dantly more agreeable to me if they had dined with us.
Wine was taken at dinner much after the English
fashion, and our host did not fail, I believe, to drink
to the health of every one separately, and to wish us
a safe return to our native land.

This gentleman has a very fine orange plantation
at a short distance from the town. It is situated on
the side of a hill, which serves as a protection for the
trees in the violent gales which sometimes occur here,
and with serpentine walks leading from the bottom to
the top. Upon a platform about the centre is a capa-
cious summer-house, planted around with choice
shrubs and flowers, where the family usually spend
some portion of the year, and where, were I proprietor,
I should most gladly spend the whole, there being
no "pale concluding winter" here to "shut the scene,"
but now, in mid November, all is freshness, and
beauty, and odour. Most of the trees in the plantation
are young, but in a very thriving state, and in a few
years will yield a supply fully equal to exportation.
At present no fruit is exported from Flores.

The Island of Corvo, at the nearest point, is about
three leagues distant from Flores; but during my stay
I had not an opportunity of visiting it, nor did I feel
particularly anxious to do so, having seen a good deal
of it on our approach, and the description I received
of it holding out but few inducements. It is not more
than one-fourth the size of Flores, very mountainous
and rocky, and contains but about nine hundred inhabitants.

Since the time of our landing from the wreck we

had anticipated the necessity of proceeding to Fayal, (distant from Flores about one hundred and twenty miles in a south-easterly direction,) or some of the other islands having intercourse with England, where we might take passage by a trader, or charter a vessel of sufficient size to convey us to our ultimate destination; to facilitate which Mr. Borges was indefatigable in his exertions. The two schooners, before mentioned as belonging to Santa Cruz, of about thirty or forty tons burden, happening to be in port at the time, he immediately proceeded to treat with their owners for our transit in them to Fayal, and terms were no sooner agreed upon than we commenced preparing them for sea. It was not until the 10th of November that the first schooner was ready, nor until three days afterwards that the wind permitted us to get her off; but on that day——(the 13th)——we succeeded in launching her with thirty-seven of the passengers. Previously, however, another schooner arrived from Fayal, and, ultimately, it being considered that the number of passengers still remaining, together with the luggage, reduced as it had been, with great loss to the owners, was more than ought to be embarked on one of these little vessels, it was concluded to put her also in requisition. This we were enabled to despatch on the following day with forty more of the passengers, the remainder of us intending to set sail next morning in the third; but the wind changed, and stormy weather succeeded—so much so as to occasion many fears for the safety of those already on their way. Whilst we were thus detained, a schooner arrived from St. Michael's, for a cargo of *orchilla*,* consigned to Don Mariano, the owner of the remaining schooner we had engaged, who proposed to us to transfer the charter to the one from St. Michael's; assuring us that the orchilla, which would occupy but little space, was all ready to be put on board,—that she should take nothing else,—and immediately that was shipped should proceed with us to Fayal. At the time, seeing no objection to this proposition, and the state of the weather rendering it impossible to launch his schooner; the one from St. Michael's being already without the Bar, in the hope of avoiding delay we acceded to it. To our mortification, however, we soon found, that besides the orchilla they were detaining the vessel to complete her loading with wheat, whale oil, pigs, &c. &c., several casks of the oil being lashed upon deck. This infringement of the agreement, of course, caused remonstrance, and much unpleasant altercation, almost determining us to relinquish the idea of going by her at all, and obliging Mariano to send his own schooner with us as originally stipulated. Things continued in this state until the morning of the—17th,—when, in consideration of Mariano's previous kind offices to ourselves, and also of his being the friend of Mr. Borges, to whom we

* I have mentioned this amongst the exports. It is a weed of a grayish colour, valuable for producing a crimson dye, and monopolized by the Government. It grows principally amongst the rocks of the coast, from whence it is obtained by the peasants, oftentimes with extreme difficulty and risk. One of them had lost his life in attempting to procure it just before our arrival at the island. The price given to these poor creatures for collecting it does not exceed *threepence* per pound, whereas the Government obtains upwards of a *shilling* !

were so highly indebted, and who proposed accompanying us to Fayal, upon receiving a positive promise that nothing more should be sent off to the
schooner, we consented to go on board, and took our
leave of Santa Cruz and many of its kind-hearted
inhabitants, whom I shall long and gratefully remem-
ber.—It was about ten o'clock when we reached the
schooner, and we were then given to understand that
she was not cleared; nor was she ready, for presently
other boats appeared with a still further quantity of
loading, the property of the Governor. This was
something too bad to be borne, and the captain of the
schooner appearing to connive at the imposition,
anchor being weighed, one of our party took possession
of the helm; the sails were unfurled, and we set off,
regardless of the risk we run in not having our
clearances, and we had to thank Mr. L. Borges
for following us some distance in a boat to bring
them to us.—The abruptness of our departure from
a spot which had afforded us so welcome a shelter
I very much regretted, but am inclined to think
that Don Mariano had scarcely the option of refus-
ing to take the goods which the Governor wished to
send; and to this underling in " brief authority" I
attribute every thing of a disagreeable character connected with leaving, as well as the little occurring of
that nature whilst upon the island.

And now, "once more upon the waters, yet once
more," we had only to wish for a fair wind and
quick passage, the craft we were in, (formerly one of
Miguel's store ships,) being wholly devoid of accom-

modation, and much the worse for wear. Including
captain and crew, we numbered about fifty souls on
board;—as motley a group as is often seen: *videlicet*,
English, Scotch, Irish, American, Portuguese, two
Jews from Morocco,—the elder a Shylock personi-
fied,—pigs from Flores, and dogs from St. Michael's.

Until ten o'clock in the evening we had very
little wind, when it began to rain and blow fresh
from an unfavourable quarter, and so continued
for the most part of our voyage, which surpassed
in wretchedness, (excepting danger,) all previous
experience. For three days and nights, the whole
of the rest which I got was upon a coiled wet
cable on deck; the little box in the stern, denominated a cabin, being too insufferably offensive to
enter, stuffed with people and luggage, and literally
swarming with bugs. To add to the evils on deck, a
cask of whale oil got stoved in, and its contents
ran all about, so that, independent of the stench,
it was with difficulty we could move or stand:—but
I spare the reader a recital, loathsome even in reflection, and pass on to the morning of the——20th——
by day-break on which we were close in with the
west end of Fayal, the density of the atmosphere
not having permitted us to discern it before, and Pico
being wrapped in a mantle of cloud down to its very
base. The wind had now almost died away, and
the ocean began to assume a lake-like smoothness:
our sails were flapping idly against the masts, and
scarce a dying murmur of the waves was audible
upon the rocks of the coast. As the sun arose, the

mists gradually dispersed, and never shall I forget
the scene of beauty and of grandeur which then
unfolded itself to our view. On our left lay the
highly cultivated and luxuriant Fayal, a very Eden
of loveliness, and before us, in all its sublimity,
towered the mighty Pico. A few clouds still hung
upon the sides of the mountain, but the sun was
shining brilliantly upon the *peak*, which, from its
immense height, and the obstruction below, had
more the appearance of being suspended in ether,
than of any thing resting upon a basis of earth.
Its elevation above the level of the sea is not considered so little as 7,000 feet, and in clear weather
it can be discovered seventy, and, it is said, even
ninety miles off. But notwithstanding the sublime
and exciting scenery by which we were surrounded, such had been the miseries of this short
voyage, and such my eagerness to be again on
land, that (I almost write it with a blush) I
would have relinquished all for a few hours of
fair wind to have brought us to an anchor in the
Bay of Orta. We lay till noon almost becalmed,
when a light breeze sprang up; but, to our mortification, just against us. Being scarcely more
than a mile from land, often did I propose to
have recourse to our boat, or even to swim ashore,
rather than endure this very lazer-house of filth for
another night; but I was assured by those more
familiar with the arbitrary exercise of power than
myself, though merely passing from one island to
another, and our history and object well known,

that no one would be permitted to leave the vessel
until we had been visited by the officers of both the
revenue and health departments, and received their
sanction to land. There was, therefore, nothing left
us but submission to our fate, whatever it might be.
At length I did manage to get the boat over, and several
of our crew and others betaking themselves to the oars,
we commenced the towing process. At intervals the
wind so nearly died away, that, with great exertion,
we were able to effect something ; but again it vexa-
tiously thwarted us, and drove us backward farther
than we had advanced; and thus, hoping and fear-
ing, advancing and receding, we continued until
near six in the evening, when the tide turned in our
favour, and we found ourselves slowly entering the
channel between the islands of Fayal and Pico; and
as soon as we were discerned from the fort of Orta,
the capital of the former, several revenue officers
came off to us, bringing us the *agreeable* intelligence
that we should not be allowed to land before morn.
ing.   Owing to *eddy winds* and calms, which, from
the height and contiguity of the mountains, are very
frequent amongst these islands, we did not come to an
anchor until ten o'clock ; shortly after effecting which,
having lowered the sails, Mr. Borges and myself stowed
ourselves away amongst them, and I may almost
say *slept* for the first time since quitting Santa Cruz.
When we awoke in the morning, we found ourselves
safely moored within half a mile of the town, the
appearance of which from the Bay is uncommonly
fine and imposing, forming, with the projections of

high land at either end of it, the most perfect and
splendid amphitheatre. The town is built close to
the shore, from which it rises to a considerable
elevation, interspersed throughout with gardens,
orangeries, and other plantations. It contains a
great number of churches, convents, &c., which, "on
first appearing before the little city, give it an air
of architectural magnificence;" and viewing it altogether, you would be ready to estimate its extent
and population at, at least, double what it really is.

It was ten o'clock before the officers of the health
department came off to us, and near three hours after
that before boats were despatched to convey us
ashore. Some had been occupying this interval
in sundry attempts at purification, and, it must be
confessed, put on a rather more civilized aspect; but
as for me, though I felt myself one of the filthiest of
human beings, so I was determined to remain until
I could effect my escape from this abode of defile-
ment, and luxuriate in a thorough ablution. I have
before said, and heard it said, *that it is worth enduring
extremes for the sake of their opposites:*—I would not
endure filth for any thing,—but surely I never in my
life more highly estimated the value of soap and
fresh water, or arrayed myself in clean linen with a
more exquisite satisfaction, than when they were presented to me upon landing in the city of Orta:—I
seemed, indeed, as if I could scarcely have enough of
either the one or the other; and fervently hoped, if
this were a fair specimen, that I had for ever finished
my sailing under Portuguese colours.

I had scarcely *made my toilette* when the American
Consul, C. W. Dabney, Esq., most kindly called upon
Mr. Borges, Captain Britton, and myself, with an invitation to dinner, which we gladly accepted, and accompanied him to his residence,—an elegant mansion,
and which, for the magnificent beauty of its situation,
has seldom indeed a parallel.   It stands on the
acclivity of a hill, in the centre of a garden, delight-
fully overlooking the town and bay, whilst immediately in front lies the vine-covered Island of Pico,
with its lofty and majestic peak.   The garden, which
is most tastefully laid out, displays a rich variety of
tropical and European trees and plants;—the orange,
lemon, banana, fig, vine, apple, pear, myrtle, geranium,
rose, &c. growing luxuriantly together, with " flowers of
every scent and hue "   As contrasted with the scenes
which had been passing before us for some previous
days, it seemed rather like the work of enchantment
than reality, nor were such impressions in any degree
lessened when our kind *magician* introduced us to
the interior of his abode, and to the attractive family
circle by which he was surrounded.   It was one of
the quickest and most agreeable transitions in situation and feeling I ever experienced,—from a want of
the commonest comforts of existence, to the enjoyment
of its very luxuries; and from society of the lowest
grade, to that of those replete with every refinement,
and manifesting a truly generous and friendly interest
in our fate.—After thus enjoying ourselves for the
remainder of the day, in the evening, there being at
Orta, as at Santa Cruz, no hotel, or other establish-

ment of the kind, we retired to a vacant house on the outskirts of the town, which, upon landing, we had requested might be engaged, and partially furnished for our accommodation. Upon trial, however, it proved every way inconvenient and ineligible; so that betimes in the morning we sallied forth to reconnoitre the town in quest of a better, and succeeded, at last, in taking two small rooms in a house about mid-way along the main street, which, though nearly as destitute of cleanliness and comfort as those we had quitted, were much more agreeably situated, and, as we were assured, the best the town afforded—that strangers would be likely to gain admission into.

Before noon we were again honoured with a call from Mr. Dabney, repeating a kind invitation to dinner, which, gratified as we had been on the previous day, we were in no mood to refuse.

In the course of the morning I paid my respects to the British Vice-Consul, Mr. Walker, (a pleasant, gentlemanly man, but, unfortunately, blind,) who having taken charge of the British subjects, had written to Mr. Read, the Consul-General, residing at St. Michael's, for instructions how to proceed in conveying them home. He informed me of the steps which he had taken to provide, as far as possible, for their comfort; evident indications of which I had not failed to observe in the renovated attire of most I had met with, and some of whom, I doubt not, fared infinitely better at Santa Cruz and Orta than they ever did before, or, it is to be feared, ever will again. I received from this gentleman every polite attention, accompanied with offers of any assistance it was in his power to render me.

The afternoon of the day fully realized the agreeable anticipations of the morning in the intelligent and interesting society of the family at (what I shall term) *Fredonia House;* from whence we were not suffered to take our departure until, in the handsomest manner, I may say delicately so, to remove any diffidence on our part, Mr. Dabney desired us to consider the invitation extended to every day whilst we remained at Orta, and that, when not interfering with other engagements, we would visit them, without the least ceremony, upon all occasions.

For several succeeding days my mornings were spent in perambulating different parts of the island, and my afternoons chiefly at *Fredonia House;* or in walking, or riding out (for Mr. Dabney supplied us with most beautiful ponies) as inclinaton might prompt.—But were it not for the obligations I feel myself under to this gentleman and his family, I should be reluctant to intrude myself so much into the foreground of the picture. It is time also that I offer a few more general remarks upon the place and its people.

The Island of Fayal (which is said to derive its name from the *Faya,* a beautiful kind of beech-tree growing upon it) lies in latitude 38° 30′ and longitude 28° 41′ 2″. It is about the same size as Flores, though very differently formed, its length and breadth being nearly alike, It is also much less mountainous, and, of course, contains a far greater proportion of cultivated land, of equal richness and fertility. The climate is deliciously fine, said even to surpass that of the Azores generally:—but perhaps, in a few words, I cannot give a better description than I find in a valuable nautical work,* which I happen to have in my possession, and from which I shall take the liberty of making further extracts. It observes, " This island has been celebrated for its excellent pastures, fish, wood, &c. The air is always mild and pure; the cold of winter never felt, and the heat of summer always tempered by refreshing winds. Its inhabitants are computed at 17,000. The island produces wheat and maize, sufficient for itself and a part of Pico. The cattle reared here are not sufficient for the consumption of the island, and supplies are therefore sent from the neighbouring island of St. George, which produces a great number. The annual produce of wine is also scanty; for that which is exported hence is mostly from Pico, the opulent people of Fayal being owners of the best vineyards in that island; and they ship the wines from the port of Fayal for the different ports of Europe and America." Oranges are now cultivated to a considerable extent, and the flavour of the fruit is very fine, quite equal to that of St. Michael's. Several cargoes are annually exported to England; but I understand from those engaged in shipping them, that from the perishable nature of the fruit, the damage it often sustains on

* Purdy's Memoir, &c. for the Atlantic Ocean.

the passage, the uncertainty of a market, and various other causes, taking the average of years, they have found it a losing speculation. Fayal is not so well supplied with water as some of the other islands, nor is its quality equally pure and good. It contains, besides Orta, nine or ten villages; but as the first named could only prove of interest to strangers, I shall confine my remarks accordingly.

The *Villa Orta* (which I have before partially noticed) is situated on the south-east side of the island, and its population is estimated at more than 5000. The principal street, which runs nearly parallel with the shore, and extends throughout the whole length of the town, is irregular, in many parts narrow, and roughly paved. From this several small streets ascend to the level above the town, along which there is a pretty good road, though not adapted for carriages, to the village of Flamingo, about five miles distant, and other places. The houses, vastly superior as they are to most, even of the best in Santa Cruz, are built much after the same fashion, generally of limestone, two stories high, with glazed folding-doors, and balconies, of course,—essential, I conceive, to the very existence of their owners, as without them they would certainly either inadvertently precipitate themselves into the street, or expire for want of a lounging-place. The lower rooms, in the main street, are chiefly occupied as shops; amongst which those of tailors and shoemakers abound, who are to be seen sitting at their doors (the only part at which light is admitted) throughout the day in the exercise of their profession. Boots and shoes are remarkably cheap, and handsomely made, though they do not wear so well as the English. The other shops, equally dark and incommodious, are very variously furnished. I can not better designate them than as *little general stores.*

The public buildings, as said, are chiefly (or so styled) of a religious character,—monasteries, convents, &c.; appearing, like many other things, to the greatest advantage when viewed from a distance. They are then conspicuously ornamental to the place; a distinction of which a closer inspection very much divests them, the front being the only part displaying the least architectural taste. This is generally very lofty, and whitewashed, "terminating in the centre in a curved line pediment, containing some emblematic religious device; and a square tower at either side, with circular-headed windows, black quoins, cornices, belting courses, &c.; and surmounted by Turkish or Arabic turrets. The rear presents nothing more than a plain building of rough masonry." Amongst this description of edifices I may include one or two nunneries, several of the inmates of which I frequently observed peeping through their latticed windows, whether with

" Each flattering hope subdued, each wish resigned,"

I know not, but certainly without

"All beauty's treasure opening on the cheek."

The numbers of the pious sisterhood, I was informed, were much diminished a few years ago, during the sojourn in the place of a company of the gallant sons of Mars; since which but few votaries have offered themselves, and the *mania* (if I may so term it) appears altogether on the decline.

Orta is said formerly to have been a place of considerable strength, and in the hands of either the English or Americans would easily be rendered impregnable; but it is not now strongly fortified. The principal forts are at the south end of the town, and appear to be tolerably garrisoned; but the military force of the island is greater than common, the soldiers engaged in the unsuccessful attempt to reduce Terceira to the dominion of Miguel having been landed here, and for the present are quartered in Orta. A high and substantial stone wall is built along the whole front of the town; but I imagine as much to protect it from the tide, which often rolls and thunders against it with desperate fury, as for the purpose of defence in case of attack; at all events it would be found no very serious impediment to vigorous assailants.

Fayal, in the Bay of Orta, affords the best anchorage of any of the Azores, "excepting that it is open to the winds from north to north-east, and from south-east to south-west; and these winds are frequent in winter. That from the south-east is often very destructive, it blowing right in." So lately as last year Mr. Dabney had a fine brig driven ashore, the very morning she was prepared to start on her voyage, laden with wines, &c., and lost, with nearly all her cargo. The crew, I was told, were with difficulty saved, principally through his own very active exertions.

During the non-intercourse of America with England, preceding the late war, this was the principal depôt for American produce, and from whence a large amount found its way to England, which, I am sorry to say, greatly frustrated the justifiable and pacific intentions of the American Government to effect the rescinding of our iniquitous *Orders in Council*, as well as the prevention of the impressment of her seamen into the British service.

Here, as at Flores, provisions are exceedingly cheap. Beef, though not the largest, without any exception the finest flavoured I ever partook of, selling only for 2d. sterling a pound. Fish and poultry are also very plentiful, and equally good. Some quantity of cheese is made upon the island, but the quality of that is inferior; nor can I say any thing in favour of the bread ; it is brown, tough, and insipid. The style of living, as well as the society of the better class in Orta, I should suppose only differs in its degree from that of Flores; but as I visited with no Portuguese family during my brief stay, I am unable to speak to particulars. Besides Mr. Walker, there are several respectable English residents.

The peasantry are just the same sort of people,—a quiet, hardy, and industrious race, and possess all the necessaries of life in great abundance: but they will perform the heaviest labour for the most trifling consideration in money. Numbers of them I saw carrying boxes of oranges, weighing two to three hundred weight, from the gardens at Flamingo, where they were packed, to Orta, (five miles,) for a *pistareen,* or tenpence ; and you will generally meet them attended by dogs, so remarkable for their fatness that

you are ready to query what they can have been fed
upon to produce such an effect; but I am satisfied there
is something in the climate very congenial to these animals, since, if they are brought upon the island from
other places, ever so lean, in a month or six weeks,
without any extraordinary feeding, they become as
fat as those bred on the island; and the dreadful disease of hydrophobia is wholly unknown.   Oxen and
asses are the principal beasts of burden; but I saw
even fewer carriages, of any description, than in
Flores; nor are the roads much better adapted for
them.   Ploughing at both places is always performed
by oxen, and the soil is so uncommonly rich and fine
that the ploughs have not a particle of iron about
them, (excepting, perhaps, the few nails which may
be used in putting them together;) and I observed
the peasants merely ran them through the ground,
turning nearly an equal furrow on either side.   But
little art is requisite to raise crops on the cultivated
lands of the Azores; such is their fertility, that seed
would almost grow if thrown on the surface.   There
are fewer stone or pumice-stone walls in Fayal than
in Flores, the fields often being fenced with a sort of
cane reeds, which grow twelve or fifteen feet high,
and form excellent hedges; they are used also for
thatching the cottages, and various other purposes.
The peasants manufacture very handsome baskets
from willows that grow upon the island, and great
quantities of them are exported to the other islands,
as well as to the Brazils.   They are generally red
and white, a part of the willows being dyed a scarlet

colour. A *nest* of them, as it is termed, (fifteen or twenty of intermediate sizes, fitting within each other, the largest capable of containing three bushels, and the smallest scarcely a goose's egg,) may be purchased for about two dollars.

I omit other things which might seem of more importance, as it is my intention presently to devote a few pages to those of the Azores which I have not already spoken of, and as in many respects so great a similarity exists between them, it is unnecessary to indulge in general comments upon each.

November 27th.—Before we had risen from breakfast this morning we received a very polite note from Mr. Dabney, proposing, if agreeable, as the morning was particularly favourable, that we would avail ourselves of it to visit *the Caldera,* an immense, though now exhausted crater, upon the extreme height of the island. There was, of course, little reluctance on our part to comply with the kind suggestion, and equipping ourselves for the excursion, we proceeded to Mr. D.'s, where we found Mr. Frederic Dabney, a younger brother of the Consul, with asses and attendants prepared to accompany us, and soon after nine o'clock we commenced the ascent. The distance, by the route we had to pursue, was about ten miles; for the first two or three of which the road was nearly level and of little interest, but afterwards it began to rise considerably, and winding along over a high ridge of hills, commanded a view

of the most transcendant beauty. A richly-cultivated
plain, with orange groves and ever-verdant fields,
interspersed with the neat white cottages of the peasantry, extended for some miles on either side, and
at the foot, gracefully retiring from its lovely bay,
appeared the convent-crowned Orta. Pico was uncommonly clear, from base to summit, which I had
scarcely seen it before since our landing, and an
object of inconceivable grandeur. Though the day
was comparatively calm, the surf was breaking high
upon its rocky shores, forming around them a girdle
of the most snowy whiteness, and the sound being to
us perfectly inaudible, tended to favour the deception ; while to the west, serenely slumbering, and as
if never more to be awoke by storm or tempest, lay
the blue and boundless ocean. Again and again did
I pause enraptured with the scene,—in all its variety,
richness, beauty, splendour, and extent, the most
transporting I ever beheld. I felt, if it would but
have remained the same, as if I could have gazed
upon it for ever ; and had I not been reminded by
my companions of the object which had induced the
excursion, *the Caldera,* much as I had desired to see
it, might have stood over for future opportunity,—I
must have lingered out my day of admiration here.
Moments like these are the purchase of years, and
they are worth it,—sweet in possession, still sweeter
in retrospect : the bright spots on the dark ground
of our existence : once realized they can never cease
to charm ; the mind recals them in its happiest

musings through after years; they create its happiest musings, and " pass like spirits of the past," bringing

> " The day, the hour, the sunshine, and the shade,
> All things pertaining to that place and hour"

in fair review before us.   The scene itself may vanish, —the recollection never.

Pursuing our route we continued at every step mounting higher and higher, and at length arriving within three miles of the summit, we dispensed with our steeds, and one of our attendants returning with them to the village of Flamingo, which we had left about two miles in the rear, the other with a basket of refreshments accompanied us on foot.   The remaining distance, alternately bog and rock, (not the most desirable footing for pedestrians,) was of much less arduous ascent than I had anticipated, and before one o'clock we had gained the southern edge of the crater; of the magnitude of which, having purposely been kept a little in the dark, I had formed no conception, and stood for some time on the brink in almost speechless astonishment.   The form of the immense cavity, as the name, *Caldera,* may imply, is very similar to that of a caldron or basin.   Its circumference at the top is about six miles,—the diameter consequently two,—gradually contracting in its descent to a circumference, at the bottom, of perhaps two miles.   The entire depth of it is estimated at 4000 feet, and it is even thought by some to be on a level with the sea.

When the first overwhelming sensations of amazement had a little subsided, the day being now on the

wane, I proposed to my companions to make the
descent; but neither appearing to manifest any such
disposition, without a guide, and almost without direction, I determined to undertake it myself. For the
first part of the way down I pursued nearly a direct
course, sometimes scrambling through bushes, and at
others rolling over rank and slippery beds of moss, as
wet as rain or dew could render it, and in which
I frequently sank more than a yard deep. But
afterwards it became fatiguing in no small degree,
the only passage I could discover being a rocky and
most tortuous water-course, often seeming to terminate in abrupt projections, from which I had to
jump or fall, as the case might be, until I found it
again amongst the thickly interwoven shrubs which
were arched over it. At length, however, with jumping, tumbling, and rolling, soaked to the skin, I
arrived at the bottom, and confess my sensations
were not of the most agreeable character, when,
after *descending* experience, on first casting my eyes
upwards, I contemplated the difficulty of a *re-ascent*,
a reflection, too, which in addition to the advanced
hour of the day, left me little opportunity for observation—none worth recording;—nor do I imagine
from the period which has elapsed since the crater
was in a state of conflagration, that, except in the
peculiarity of its form, its appearance is strikingly
dissimilar from that which it might have presented
had it been occasioned by other violent convulsion
of nature;—a question, however, fitter for geologists
than me. The surface at the bottom is nearly level;

for the most part very wet and boggy; the centre is
wholly covered with water, though of no great depth,
and containing quantities of gold and silver fish.
Near the part where I descended, but quite detached from it, there is a huge mass of rock and
earth of considerable height, which has also a large
cavity on its summit.

The whole scene is calculated to inspire the most
sombre ideas and impressions; even the water, from
the great depth of the crater, and the dark foliage
which hangs upon its sides, assumes an inky blackness. No kindly sunbeam penetrates to exhale the
heavy vapours which stagnate in the air; but the
atmosphere is chill and damp. The storm may
howl its fury; but it is heard not. The roar of
ocean never reaches here. Solitude reigns supreme,
and all is mute and motionless, save the sea birds,
which, wheeling around you in rapid eddies, keep
up a loud and incessant screaming as if to scare
you from their dreary retreat. It requires almost
an effort of mind to believe that such things as
cities, and the busy hum of men, have any where
an existence, or that you can ever again behold
them. You are lost in conjecture at the mysterious
agency which once filled this mighty vacuum with
sulphureous matter—how it has so totally disappeared—by what unknown causes it may be again
produced—or where it may be still raging;—but
speculate and ponder as you will, all is doubt and
mystery, and you end but where you began, in
knowing, in determining—nothing. Had I allowed

myself, however, much farther to indulge the reverie
into which my situation, so full of the novel and
exciting was leading me, I must have been content
to amuse myself with it during the night, for which
various cogent reasons disinclining, I turned at once
to the somewhat more feasible, but still vastly perplexing proposition of a re-assent, which, wherever
meditated, put on a most formidable aspect. I had
unwisely determined, supposing I could not change
for the worse, to make the attempt in another quarter
from that in which I descended; and after surveying
the crater around, awfully precipitous as it appeared, fixed upon the northern side. I accordingly
floundered on through bog and water, until I had
gained what appeared the most eligible part, and
here—for nothing less I found it—commenced the
arduous struggle. For the first 500 feet or so it
was difficult and dangerous in the extreme; the
rocks, steep as they were, being in addition, in consequence of the water which was perpetually trick-
ling down from the top upon the moss that grew
in their fissures, excessively slippery, and up these
I had frequently to pull myself as high as I could
reach, and cling till I could gain a fresh footing,
conscious the while that one false step would have
been inevitably fatal; and that, after all, however
fearful the alternative, finding it impracticable to
proceed, I might be compelled to return. The last
reflection had perhaps the good effect of stimulating
me to still greater exertion to accomplish my purpose, and thus struggling on, with but little im-

provement for one-third of the way up, at that distance I had the good fortune to stumble upon a
sort of track, as rugged as you please, but still a
track, and worn by human feet.—I afterwards discovered that the peasants had proceeded thus far
down the side of the crater for the purpose of cutting
wood, which accounted for the abrupt commencement of the path, as well as for there being no
communication between it and the bottom.—Such
as it was, however, I pursued it, until, by a most
circuitous and wearying course, it landed me at
length on the summit, a position which I regained
with feelings of no ordinary satisfaction, exhausted
as I was both by long fasting, and the severe exertion I had used. I had then to continue winding
round the edge of the crater, for about three miles,
until I reached the spot from whence I started, and
where, instead of meeting with my friends, I found
the servant left with a note, informing me of their
having sought for me in vain, and that almost in
despair of seeing me again, they had taken their departure for Flamingo, where, if I were fortunate
enough to escape from my perilous exploit, I should
find them awaiting my arrival.—Here then was a
trudge of five miles further; but having rested a
moment, and refreshed myself with a draught of
excellent wine, pleased to be thus far landed, I
again set forward, and quickly arrived at the village, and the orange garden of our kind friend,
Mr. Dabney, who, accompanied by Mr. Borges and
members of his own family, had rode out thus far

to give us the meeting, and with my morning's companions did not fail to congratulate me upon the feat which I had performed, assuring me that he had never before heard of any individual attempting the ascent of the crater on the northern side, and, in fact, that it had been deemed impossible:—I would not willingly be again called upon to demonstrate its practicability.—After partaking of a bountiful repast, which our generous host had provided us, we mounted our steeds, and returned to his residence at Orta, adding one more to the many charming evenings we had passed there, and I retired not a whit the worse for my ten hours' toil, (estimating it, however, equal to a *ramble* of fifty miles on level ground,) and with a feeling of interest in the excursion and events of the day which I shall long retain.

On the following morning, in company with Mr. Frederic D., I ascended one of the projecting mounts at the south of the town, which is fortified, and very finely commands the entrance of the bay. On the top of it, to which the ascent is pretty steep, is a hermitage, dedicated to *Our Lady of Guia.* (N.S. de la Guia.)   At its southern extremity, which is altogether rock, there is a tremendous cavern, called *the Devil's Hole,* and where, in a storm, Mr. D. informs me, the roar of the surge is truly appalling.

Connected with this mount is a smaller one, the soil of which is of a deep red colour, exactly resembling that of Pico, and in appearance as if it had been burnt for ages, which it most probably has. It is totally unlike any other to be found upon the island, and is the only land in it devoted to the cultivation of the vine. To the west of this is a sandy cove, called *Port Pin*, where small vessels frequently anchor, in favourable weather; but it is quite open to winds from the south-west.

The nearest point of Pico from Fayal is but about four miles, and I very much regretted that I had not an opportunity of visiting the island, and ascending the peak; but during the early part of my stay in Fayal, the surf was breaking so violently upon its shores, that it was not thought prudent for a boat to venture, and afterwards being in daily expectation of sailing, I could not absent myself from Orta. I must, therefore, be content very briefly to notice it with the other islands.

December 1st.—Captain B. and myself having determined upon pursuing our course to England by the first possible chance, soon after our arrival at Orta engaged the cabin of a small schooner, which had been some time waiting for a cargo of oranges, and was to have sailed on this day, but frequent showers preventing the loading of the fruit, she was detained until the following afternoon;—when, bidding adieu to our kind friends at Fredonia House, &c., we were conveyed on board *the Kitty*, such the nomenclature of our little vessel, William Johns, master, bound for Plymouth;—and rarely indeed have I taken my departure from a scene and from friends with a heavier heart than I quitted Orta. Mingled was the association of ideas and feelings which crowded upon me: but ten days ago I had landed here, and place and people were alike unknown and indifferent to me; now I regarded the former with a high degree of interest, and my acquaintance with one family at least, had ripened into the warmest sentiments of gratitude, regard, and esteem. I could leave both with the most lively and unfeigned regret; the more so, from the possibility, (I will not write probability,) which existed of my never meeting them again. Such is the ever-varying, the checkered allotment of life! how transient, how uncertain is all that it presents to us! how little of the morrow can we read to-day! What mere chances, as they would seem to us, serve to bring parties together who may never even have heard each other's names before:—to form friendships which you would deem a real acquisition, and wish to cultivate and enjoy:—to open some of those fairy scenes of nature, lovelier than fancy had painted them; and just when all is beginning most to charm and rivet itself upon you, and, rather than resign it for ever, you are tempted to wish you had never known it, the spell is rudely broken, and the harsh sentence of separation sounds in the ear, and saddens on the heart! You feel—but I check myself: if there is pain, there is also pleasure in the retrospect. Most have passed the ordeal: I envy not those who cannot.

I would be the last to offend with panegyric, but I must be forgiven in saying that it never was my lot to be introduced to a more interesting or agreeable

family circle than that of the Dabney's—one in which
a stranger would, or ought, sooner to feel himself at
home. Mr. Dabney is, in all respects, the finished
gentleman, well-informed and intelligent above the
common, of highly fascinating manners, with a disposition nobly generous, and kind and courteous to all,
one whom but to know, must be to respect and admire :—I will not, however, particularize where all are
so truly amiable and deserving—where all alike demand my ardent and devoted thanks. Most gratifying
to me was it to witness the delightful harmony which
reigned throughout this establishment. Truly might
each be said *to share the bliss of others.* There
seemed, as it were, to be no division of interest or
feeling,—none of those petty envyings and dissensions
which are *just* enough to ruffle the surface of social
pleasures, but mutual good will and affection predo-
minant in every breast; refinement, without affecta-
tion; and polish, without display. Though, in every
domestic arrangement, the nicest taste was observable, the useful and convenient were not therefore
thrown heedlessly into the back ground, as things of
no moment. Whether alone, or surrounded by guests,
an elegant table alike was spread, but there was no insipid, hackneyed observance of etiquette or formality;
and, to crown the whole, you felt fully assured of the
hearty sincerity of the welcome. The very words of
obligation, intrusion, and so forth, seemed as unin-
telligible sounds to the whole household.—Such was
the circle into which, with no other recommendation
than that of an unfortunate stranger, I was here

unexpectedly introduced. I ask the reader's pardon
for the insertion of the following effusion,* which I
penned upon taking my leave :—it might not, indeed,
be worth transcribing, but as a record of emotions
which the past had inspired, and which the future
can never obliterate;—a sense of the deepest gratitude
for favours received, and the sincerest desires for the
happiness and welfare of my generous benefactors.
Long may Heaven preserve them, and crown their lives
with the best and choicest of her blessings !

TO MR. AND MRS. DABNEY,

AND THE MEMBERS OF THEIR WORTHY FAMILY,

UPON MY LEAVING ORTA FOR ENGLAND.

My worthy friends ! or ere we part
And I, with no exulting heart,
    Pronounce the word adieu !
(Although from off a foreign strand,
I steer towards my native land,)
    My grateful thanks are due.

And thanks e'en more than I can pay,
Or more than feeble words may say,
    Or feebler pen express ;
Yet trust me, where engraven deep
The record stands for time to keep,
    I shall not feel it less.

---

* Originally very hastily written, and not intended to meet the
public eye.

No, oft will memory seek to dwell
O'er scenes that I have prized full well,
    Nor leave without regret;
And though my fate hath seemed severe,
And wreck and peril cast me here,
    I grieve not we have met.

So fair an isle from ocean's wave,
As if by Heaven decreed to save,
    And wrest his greedy prey:
What, though in fancy I might trace
Semblance of such a resting place,
    I thought not to survey.

And not alone a land I've found,
With nature's beauties richly crown'd,—
    Nor blooms the year in vain:
But safe within a genial zone,
Our wintry blasts are all unknown,
    To sweep the smiling plain.

Here Flora holds her lovely court,
And with Pomona seems to sport
    In ever gay costume.—
Here Pico rears his monarch head,
And rocks and mountains wildly spread,
    And wilder billows boom.

What transport, Nature for our guide!
Conductress fair! who asks beside,
    Or whether grave or gay,
But just to mark thy footsteps free,
And rove, as here I've followed thee,
    Along the devious way?

Yet still I've found what charms me more—
The kindest hearts—the open door—
    The welcome all sincere ;
Warm, generous, sympathizing friends,
Prompt to devise each fair amends
    And make e'en exile dear.

I've seen *one* social circle meet,
In harmony and union sweet,
    Each other's bliss to prove.
Seen brothers own " the kindred band,"
(Too oft destroyed by discord's brand,)
    " Of Friendship, Truth, and Love."

And elegance, that innate grace,
Apart from pride, which may deface
    Her all-attractive mien ;
And minds with each endowment fraught,
And gay luxuriance of thought,
    With sportive wit between.

These have I found—these have I priz'd—
These have I fondly realized,
    Nor ever deem'd to find :
And *Orta's* name, and *Dabney's* worth,
Where'er I rove, or rest on earth,
    I never leave behind.

We part, indeed, and Heaven can say,
Alone, when next our meeting-day,
    And seas may roll between ;
But seas nor time can e'er erase
The cherish'd memory of this place,
    Or banish what hath been.

Peace to thine house, thrice honour'd host!
I pledge thee with as warm a toast
 As parting guest e'er gave:
And would that it might e'er be mine
To pay the debt to thee or thine,
 No happier boon I'll crave.

Peace—and *Farewell!* and if that word
Were ever uttered, ever heard,
 All honest from the heart,
I speak it now,—may time fulfil
The prayer responsive to my will,—
 And with that wish depart.

Orta, December 2nd.

AZORES.

And here, in place of presenting the dry detail of a sea journal, let me be allowed to fill up the interval, and fulfil my promise, by adding such general notice of the Azores, and of the remaining particular islands, as I find in the work already referred to.

"The Azores, (originally Ilhas dos Açores, or Isles of Hawks,) or Western Islands, are nine in number, and named *Santa Maria*, or *St. Mary's, St. Miguel*, or *St. Michael's, Terceira*, or *Tercera, St. Jorge*, or *St. George's, Graciosa, Fayal, Pico, Flores*, and *Corvo*. The land is, in general, high; the coasts steep and rocky.

" These islands are said to have been discovered about the middle of the fifteenth century by Joshua Vanderberg, of Bruges, in Flanders, who, in a voyage to Lisbon, was driven to them by stress of weather. At Lisbon he boasted of his discovery; on which the Portuguese, in that spirit of enterprise so strongly manifested by them at this period, set sail and took possession of them, calling them *Azores*, from the many hawks and falcons found amongst them.

" Antonio Gonzalo says that the great Don Henry, Prince of Portugal, considered these islands as so considerable an acquisition, that he went in person to take possession in 1449. This was forty-three years before Columbus landed in America: and it has been affirmed that the Flemish merchants, on the part of their countrymen, sent a colony thither, many of whose descendants continue in Fayal to this day. Hence the islands have been also called *Flamingos*, or *Flemish Islands*.

" The capital of the Azores is (or was) *Angra*, in Terceira.

" The inhabitants generally are an innocent, good, and honest people, who prefer the olive to the laurel, and who would seek for distinction rather by industry than by arms. The climate is delightful; the air generally clear and serene; the soil so prolific that both European and tropical plants arrive at the greatest perfection: the face of the earth is, however, so diversified as in some places to exhibit, within a small extent, volcanic hills and productions, gardens of aromatic plants, pastures, vineyards, orangeries, &c.

The greatest inconvenience of these isles is their having been subject to eruptions and earthquakes, and in some parts, where the coasts are low, the sea has, at times, overflowed the land, and occasioned considerable mischief. Yet in the cultivated parts, the lava, once a stream of fire, is planted with oranges, lemons, and vines; and the land, formed from the decomposition of volcanic substances, is sown with Indian corn, small beans, and wheat. The islands still abound in waste lands, fit for the cultivation of hemp, the vine, &c."

The following description of the appearances of St. Michael's will apply generally to the other islands:

" The *Island of St. Michael* appears to have been originally a plain, covered with beautiful trees, rich verdure, and aromatic plants: at the present time, however, it consists of a number of mountains, hills, and declivities, none of which are primitive, but evidently the production of volcanic eruptions. The mountains and hills clearly indicate, by their conical figure and the cavity at their summits, their being the production of fire, and bear unequivocal marks of the effects of this destructive agent in an accumulation of lava, scoriæ, and volcanic sand. Externally, the volcanoes appear extinguished, but they are supposed still to burn internally and invisibly : of this *Caldeiras,* or fountains of boiling water, in the valley of Furnas and other parts, are evident symptoms. Circumstances also afford strong reasons for believing that there have existed three principal craters, whose vertex now form three great lakes, situate towards the centre and the northern and southern portions of the islands. From these craters vast mountains have been thrown up; and, in proportion as these ceased to vomit forth the matter, partial eruptions burst out, and formed the lateral hills and declivities which extend themselves in every direction from the mountains surrounding the lakes. The cessation of fire from the different craters has been attributed to water, which appears to have gained access to each, and suddenly extinguished the effervescence of its mineral contents; and the fire now seems confined to stations, where it operates only in boiling water, with various degrees of activity and force.

"Exclusive of the remains of burning volcanoes, the island presents decisive evidence of its having been the theatre of repeated earthquakes and convulsive shocks. In most countries, earthquakes are produced by sulphur and nitre, or by sulphur sublimed from pyrites, and ignited, in subterraneous caverns, by a fermentation of vapours, which gives an appulse to the neighbouring combustible matter, and causes it to be discharged with a noise like thunder, and sometimes with an eruption of water and wind: but here the earthquakes seem to have been occasioned by a contrary cause; by the bursting in of the waters upon the mineral fires; an agency which must have instantly produced sudden blasts, violent explosions, rumbling in the bowels of the earth, and that lifting up of the ground above it, which occasions havoc and devastation till it gets vent or discharge. That this is the case, appears incontrovertible; for many

of the existing extinguished volcanoes, which served
as so many spiracles for the discharge of subterraneous fire, are rent and torn asunder by the violent
effervescence caused by the sudden conjunction of
the two opposing elements.

"The effect produced by this unnatural confluence
of fire and water is not confined to fissures in the
craters, and rents in the cliffs ; some mountains have
been precipitated into the adjacent valleys; others
upset from their base; and some swallowed up in the
bosom of that earth whence they originally rose in
lava, scoriæ, and sand. The bases of the precipitated
mountains exhibit palpable remains of decomposed
substances originally produced on the surface of the
globe; the strata of the mountains nearly upset is
displayed perpendicularly, and not horizontally; and
those mountains which have been swallowed up have
left behind them some frightful chasms, tremendous
precipices, or form the beds of beautiful lakes. The
more perfect mountains are of a conical or hemi-
spherical figure, as formed by continued eruptions,
and their exterior is distinguished by characters which
denote the nature, and, in some measure, the date of
the conflagration. The lava, on some, appears in
craggy eminences; and on others is in a state of
decomposition, forming a soil highly fertile and productive. The various features of the ground show
where the lava ran without interruption, only filling
up inequalities in a lovely champaign country; and
where its course was impeded so as to leave insulated
spots or oases, covered with all the bloom of luxuriant

vegetation, while encompassed by mountainous ridges
of volcanic ashes, with ferruginous and pumice stone.

"The island, at length, seems to be of such a structure and conformation that the waters pass freely
throughout its volcanic caverns, and are easily forced
out without shaking or disturbing the earth. One hundred years have elapsed since the inhabitants have
been terrified by volcanic explosions of a terrific
nature;* and what is now heard, and that perpetually
in several places, resembles the flowing and ebullition
of waters, with a dull noise like that of a heavy carriage rolling along in rapid motion; and it seems that
in consequence of the introduction of the waters into
the subterraneous caverns, and of the washing away
of the sulphur and nitre from their arches, the fire
has ceased to appear in frequent eruptions as formerly, yet it operates invisibly on the waters contained in the caverns beneath.

"These observations, which were previously written,
have been corroborated by a remarkable event. In
the early part of the year 1811 a most awful and tremendous explosion of smoke and flames issued from

* "The approximation to an eruption has, however, at times,
appeared to have been very close. On the 11th of August, 1810, at
the hour of ten, p.m. slight shocks of an earthquake were felt, which
continued, at intervals of a few minutes, for four hours. Between
two and three o'clock next morning, a dreadful rocking was experienced throughout the whole island; several houses, unable to
resist its violence, were thrown down, and many others were greatly
damaged; and such persons as sought safety in the open air were
dashed to the ground. On the eastern side of the island an orifice
was discovered resembling the crater of a volcano, and out of which
flames occasionally burst forth; but they do not appear to have
been accompanied by any ejection of volcanic matter."

the sea, at the distance of half a league from the shore, at the western end of the island. From the depth of about forty fathoms in the ocean issued smoke, fire, cinders, ashes, and stones of an immense size. Innumerable quantities of fish, some nearly roasted, and others as if boiled, floated on the surface of the sea towards the shore. Thus a dangerous shoal gradually formed.* On the 16th of June the crew of the Sabrina, British sloop of war, observed two columns of white smoke arising from the sea, which they supposed to arise from an engagement, and made sail towards it, but were disappointed by the wind's dying away. The smoke continued to ascend, with volumes of flame, and they then concluded it was a volcano· Next day they were close in with the land of St. Michael's, and found the volcano still raging. They learned, on the island, that smoke was first discovered on the 13th of June; two or three days previous to which there had been felt repeated shocks of earthquakes in the capital of St. Michael's, which threw down several cottages and portions of the cliff towards the north-west, so that destruction was feared on the island; but these ceased so soon as the volcano broke out.

" On the 18th the Sabrina went so near to the

" * The flames were first seen in the night of the 1st of of February, but invisible indications of its operation had been felt in shocks on the island from the middle of the preceding year. Its observed situation was south-west of Point Ferraria and due west from the Pico de Ginetes, at about a mile and a quarter from the nearest shore.—The ship Swift, with all her crew, were lost on this spot before the existence of the shoal was known."

volcano as she could with safety, and found it still
raging with unabated violence, throwing up, from under
the water, large stones, cinders, ashes, &c., accompanied
with several severe concussions. About noon, on the
same day, they observed the mouth of the crater just
showing itself above the surface of the sea, where
there were formerly forty fathoms of water. At three,
p. m , same day, it was about thirty feet above the
surface of the water, and about a furlong in length.
On the 19th, they were within five or six miles of
the volcano, and found it about fifty feet in height,
and two-thirds of a mile in length; still raging
as before, and throwing up large quantities of
stones, some of which fell a mile distant from the
volcano. The smoke drew up several water-spouts,
which, spreading in the air, fell in heavy rain, accompanied with vast quantities of fine black sand, that
completely covered the Sabrina's decks, at the distance of three or four miles. On the 20th they proceeded on a cruise, leaving the volcano about 150 feet
high, and still raging as formerly, and continuing to
increase in size. On the 4th of July they again visited
it, and found that a complete island was formed,
and perfectly quiet. The captain and several officers
landed upon it, and found it very steep, and its height
from 200 to 300 feet. It was with difficulty they were
able to reach the top, which they at last effected in a
quarter where there was a gentle declivity; but the
ground, or rather the ashes, composed of sulphurous
matter, dross of iron, &c., was so very hot to their
feet that they were obliged to return. They, however,

took possession of the islet, in the name of his Britannic Majesty, and left an English union-jack flying on it.

" The form was nearly circular, and the circumference of the isle, at this time, about a mile. In the middle was a large basin of boiling water, whence a stream, of about six yards across, ran into the sea, on the side facing St. Michael's; and at the distance of fifty yards from the island, the water, although thirty fathoms deep, was too hot to hold the hand in : in short, the whole isle appeared as a crater : the cliff on the outside as walls, steep within and without ; the basin of boiling water being the mouth, from which the smoke, &c. issued.

" On the 17th of June, Captain Tillard, of the Sabrina, accompanied by Mr. Read, the British Consul, with two other gentlemen, proceeded over land to the cliff nearest to the volcano, and which was between 300 and 400 feet above the level of the sea. The first appearance it presented was that of an immense body of smoke revolving in the water almost horizontally, in varied involutions ; when suddenly would shoot up a column of the blackest cinders, ashes, and stones, in form like a spire, and rising to windward at an angle of from ten to twenty degrees from a perpendicular line. This was rapidly succeeded by a second, third, and fourth, each having greater velocity, and overtopping the preceding one, till they had attained an altitude as much above the level of the eye on the cliff, as the sea was below it. The columns of ashes, &c.

at their greatest height, formed into branches resembling magnificent pines; and, as they fell, mixing with the festoons of white feathery smoke, at one time assumed the appearance of vast plumes of black and white ostrich feathers; at another, that of light wavy branches of a weeping willow. These bursts were accompanied by explosions of the most vivid lightning, with a noise like the continual firing of cannon and musketry intermixed; and as the cloud of smoke rolled off to leeward, it drew up the waterspouts, above-mentioned, which formed a beautiful and striking addition to the scene.

" Subsequently, this islet fell, by degrees, into the sea; and in the middle of October no part was left above water; but a dangerous shoal remained in the place which it had occupied. In February, 1812, smoke was discovered still issuing out of the sea near the spot.*

" St. Michael's is about thirty-five miles long, and from four to eight wide, and contains one city, five principal towns, fifty-four parishes, and about 80,000 inhabitants The coast is very bold, and may be approached without fear in almost every part, the north-west side excepted. Its military strength consists of 300 or 400 troops, with a militia of several thousand peasantry, whose arms are the pikes with which they drive their cattle. The prin-

---

* " About fifteen leagues to the westward, a volcano, which had appeared in 1638, broke out from the sea in 1719, and disappeared in 1723. A depth of eighty fathoms was afterwards found on the spot which it had occupied."

cipal fortification is the castle of St. Bras, which is
close to the sea, at the western end of the city of Ponta
del Gada. It is mounted with twenty-four pieces
of cannon, but few of which are capable of service.
A league to the eastward are two small three-gun
forts, inefficient from decay and neglect. The island,
notwithstanding, has many strong local holds; and
several of the hills and passes, if judiciously fortified, would be impregnable. The rich level country is properly adapted for wheat, Indian corn, and
beans, or callivances. In the lava districts are cultivated the vine and orange, which yield most abundantly. It is generally understood that the lava in
the south-east region of the island is older, softer,
and becomes fertile sooner, than that of the north-
west, which retains such a degree of hardness as to
be, in many parts, altogether incapable of yielding
to human industry. In the intermediate parts, between the volcanic lands and the level country, the
surface exhibits volcanic sand, metallic slag, pumice-
stone, &c.

" The inhabitants of this and the other islands were
formerly compelled by law to confine their trade to
the port of Lisbon; but latterly they have been allowed a wider range, and maintain a considerable
commerce not only with Lisbon, but with England,
Russia, America, &c. From England they are entirely supplied with woollens, hardware, earthenware,
and various other necessaries, sending in exchange
about seventy vessels annually with fruit. To Portugal are sent corn, pulse, poultry, cattle, and vege-

tables, which are paid for in returns of tobacco, sugar, coffee, trinkets, dispensations, indulgences, images of saints, relics, &c.   From America they receive boards, staves, lumber, rice, pitch, tar, iron in pots and bars, and a variety of Indian goods, which are paid for, in exchange, by wines.   The intercourse with Russia is similar to that with America, but on a more contracted scale.   There exists, also, a ready-money trade with vessels which make the island (or islands) for refreshments, the crews of which are furnished with cattle and provisions equal to the English, and to any in the world beside; and also with wine, pleasant and peculiarly suited to the health of seamen.

"The city of *Ponta del Gada* is the chief seat of commerce.   It is situated in the narrowest part of the island, on the south-west side, in lat. 37° 45′ 10″ N., and long. 25° 41′ 15″ W.   This town appears exceedingly pleasant from the offing, and derives an air of dignity from its numerous convents, &c.   There is a mole for the protection of small vessels, but those of greater burden are compelled to ride in an open roadstead.   By deepening and enlarging the harbour, it might be rendered capable of receiving vessels of a considerable draught; and, by excavating the square of St. Francis, and cutting a canal between it and the mole, a large number of vessels might be accommodated.   As it is, vessels of burden cannot safely use it; for they would risk the danger of slipping their cables, while loading or unloading, and, perhaps, not be able to recover their station for several weeks; or, at least, not dare to attempt its recovery during the prevalence of strong southerly gales.

The roadstead and harbour of Ponta del Gada are, however, the best that the island affords. The place of next consequence is that called *Ribeira Grande,* on the north side of the island; but here is no anchorage; and having no harbour, it is dependent for its commercial supplies on the towns on the south side. Villa Franca, which is on the latter, has a very inferior anchorage, and that for small vessels only.

" The disadvantages arising from the want of naval conveniences are greatly aggravated by the customs of the country and its government; but with all these disadvantages the country has improved, and exports annually about 15,000 tons of fruit, wine, and provisions, the amount of its surplus produce. Yet the arts, agriculture, and commerce are not carried to more than a twentieth part of the extent to which they might be; nor is the population by any means proportioned to the extent of territory.

" On approaching the north-west end of the island, from the westward, the appearance is very unpromising, as it presents barren mountains of stupendous bulk, with a coast like many ramified pillars of basaltes, exhibiting at the top a few trees of stunted growth. The impression made by a scene of rough and craggy cliffs is, however, soon dissipated by a pleasing contrast on the southern coast, as this presents a beautiful acclivity adorned by luxuriant vegetation. Open pastures, bounded by woods, vineyards, and corn-fields, interspersed with orange and lemon trees, every where meet the eye, and afford a landscape extensive and various, that will always, in clear weather, be seen with delight."

———————

The *Island of St. Mary* lies to the south of St. Michael's, and is the most southerly of the Azores. Its principal town is of the same name, and is situated on the south-west side, in lat. 36° 58′ N, and long. 25° 12′ 18″ W. Besides this there are three villages containing together about 4,500 inhabitants. "The chief productions of the island are wheat and barley of the first quality, with some wine and cattle, but only sufficient for its own consumption. It has water in abundance, but of wood little, and a scanty proportion of fruit and vegetables. The *Road of St. Mary's* is open, and exposed to southern gales; on this account it is resorted to in summer by small vessels only. The best anchorage known to the pilots is about a mile from the coast, in a depth of thirty-six fathoms, bottom of sand ; but at a short distance eastward the ground is foul. Hence it is that *Port San Lorenzo*, on the north-east side, is considered as the best anchorage about the island. At either place refreshments may be obtained as at the other islands, with the addition of partridges, which abound here."—In size, the island is rather less than Fayal.

" The *Formigas*, or *Ants*, which lie to the north-eastward of St. Mary's, in lat. 37° 16′ 50″ N. and

long. 24° 54′ W., are a range of seven or eight high
rocks, extending N.N.E and S.S.W. (N. and S.)
about three-quarters of a mile, and among which
there are other rocks under water. The highest,
which is nearly sixty feet in height, bears, from a
distance, some resemblance to the sails of a ship, and
lies two-thirds of the length of the range towards the
north. At the north part are many rocks under
water. Close along-side is a depth of seven fathoms.
—The Formigas have a dreadful appearance, the
breakers commonly flying higher than a ship's mast-
head. At a time when the sea ran from the westward,
no soundings could be found off the eastern side, with
a line of fifty fathoms, until within thirty yards of the
rocks.

" Between the Formigas and the Island of St. Mary
no bottom was found with a line of 120 fathoms, until
within a quarter of a mile from the island."

" The *Island of Terceira* is from eighteen to twenty
miles long, and from eight to eleven wide. It is
fertile, pleasant, and healthy. The lava districts here,
as at St. Michael's, produce excellent vines, although
not equal to those of the Canaries and Madeira The
land yields large crops of wheat and other grain,
pasture for cattle, and a prodigious quantity of lemons,
oranges, and all those fruits of hot and cold climates
which are propagated to the greatest advantage in
temperate countries.

" The capital, as already noticed, is *Angra*, situated
on the south side of the island, in lat. 38° 38′ 33″ N. and
long. 27° 12, 33″ W., and having a harbour, defended
by a fortress, in which *was wont* to reside the Governor of the Azores.   It is distinguished by several
handsome churches, convents, &c.   Besides this there
is another town, *Praya*, and fifteen villages, all of
which contain about 30,000 inhabitants.   In the Bay
of Angra, and around the island, fish of good quality
are abundant.

" The coasts are high, and so surrounded with
craggy rocks as to render the island almost impregnable; every accessible part being defended by bat-
teries, with heavy cannon, and a numerous garrison.
The interior is, in general, moderately high, but the
western side is higher than the eastern, and is distinguished by a rugged mountain, extending nearly east
and west, and of which the western extremity, *Pico
de la Serreta,* is the most elevated.   This peak may
be known, at a short distance, by a great break on
the eastern side.

The *Bay of Angra* is open to all winds from the
S.S.W., by the south to the east.   The swell from the
south-west, in particular, which sets round *Mount
Brasil,* (a remarkable forked hill near the sea, on the
western side,) is tremendous.   Vessels may safely remain in the road in June, July, August, and September, when the winds are light, and prevail from
between west and north-west; but on the commencement of winter the winds from the offing rage so

violently that upon the least appearance of bad weather it is requisite to put off to sea, the coast affording no shelter.

" The boats of the island come out so soon as any vessel is seen to anchor, and by them supplies may easily be óbtained, even while keeping under weigh, tacking in and out, as they will bring water, wood, and all kinds of provisions."

This, of course, refers to the state of things prior to Miguel's dominion in Portugal.

REMARKS ON TERCEIRA, BY CAPTAIN LIVINGSTON.

" The *City of Angra* is generally very regular, the situation beautiful, and the streets have regularly excellent flagged footpaths. The houses are commonly of three stories.

" At about six and a half or seven miles north of Angra, in a valley near the summit of the mountains, a great deal of steam issues from crevices of the earth, or rather clay, which clay, I am informed by a scientific gentleman here, is actually lava, decomposed by the action of sulphuric acid. Some of the clay looks, when cut by a knife, much like Castile soap : it is of various hues, and the natives of Terceira use it as paint. There are small quantities of sulphur formed around some of the apertures. The steam which rises is very hot: we cooked some eggs by laying them among the clay, at mere cracks whence the steam issued. My thermometer ranged only to 152° of Fahrenheit's scale. I exposed it to the steam at the first aperture I reached, but the mercury rose so rapidly that, from fear of bursting the tube, I was obliged to withdraw it in, I think, about three or four seconds. Persons visiting *Angra,* who have any curiosity in their composition, should see this *furnaso,* or *souffriere.* The access to it is by no means very difficult, though if you ask any of the Portuguese, (I dare vouch for Captain Livingston's accuracy,) they will describe it as accessible only at some periods of the year. One may ride to within less than half a mile of it. Ponies or asses, and guides, may readily be hired.

" No vessels should go to Angra without two good chain-cables; the bottom of the bay being generally too foul for any to trust in hempen cables.

" The better sort of people in Angra (natives) are very hospitable and kind, but full of ceremony. The poor people are generally very clean, and none seem in want of the necessaries of life. None of that wretchedness which we so often see in this country is visible ; but many of the older peasants have their clothes, though clean, so industriously patched, that it is next to, or altogether, impossible even to conjecture of what colour they originally were.

" There are some fine pine woods in the island ; a good deal of boxwood, and some cedar. Plenty of juniper, the berries of which are so very strong as to leave, for a long time, a very unpleasant flavour in the mouth after chewing them. There is plenty of pumice-stone, but of a coarse quality, in the island, and every where marks of volcanic agency are apparent. Water is good, but not so easily procured as might be supposed.

" The Terceira fruit (oranges) has improved much of late years ; more attention having been paid to its culture, and it is now little, if at all, inferior to the St Michael's.

" Very good linen is made in the island, and they manufacture a coarse earthenware, the clay of which it is made being imported from St. Mary's. No noxious animal is known; nor, though there are many dogs, has hydrophobia ever made its appearance. The natives rear a great many swine, most of which are remarkably broad-backed. Their backs are generally shorn, which, it is alleged, allows them to spread in fattening.

" Bloody flux is very frequent, both among strangers and natives, and is often fatal. A Scottish surgeon there told me it was the worst disease he met with in the island.*

" Vegetables are excellent and cheap : poultry and eggs good and reasonable : beef and mutton tolerable, the former about threepence per pound. Some of the island wine is tolerably good.

" I was surprised to see a pretty fair bunch of bananas one day carried by a peasant. They have apples, pears, figs, chesnuts, and walnuts, and, I have

* " It deserves to be known that the size of a hazel-nut of Castile soap, scraped fine and dissolved in about three wine glasses of boiling water, to which add half a wine glass of good spirits and a few lumps of white sugar, scarcely ever fails of curing bloody flux. Two or three doses may be required. I have tried it on myself and others with perfect success.—*A. L.*"

heard, some olives, with abundance of grapes. Goose-
berries and currants, I am told, have been tried, but
have not succeeded.   They have a very fine tough
willow, which makes excellent hoops and baskets;
also plenty of yams, Indian corn, wheat, and excellent barley, also tolerable potatoes.   The market is
generally well supplied with good and cheap fish.
Rabbits and quail are plentiful : thousands of black-
birds, fine turkeys, few or no geese; no peacocks and
no pheasants; a few red-legged partridges; and I
have heard it positively asserted that there are some
grouse on the mountains, yet I doubt the fact.   There
is a great deal of orchilla weed—monopolized by the
Government.

"The north coast of Terceira should not be approached by a stranger, as it is rocky and dangerous.
The western coast is also inaccessible."

————

Pico.—" This island derives its name from the remarkable peak or volcanic mountain which stands
upon it; the summit of which is in lat. 38° 26′ 15″ N.,
and long. 28° 27′ 58″ W., and terminated by a small
sugar-loaf, so very regular that one would think it
had been made by art.   The height of the peak above
the level of the sea, according to the geometrical operations of the French astronomers, is 1100 French
toises, (about 1172 English fathoms;) and, consequently, in clear weather, it can be seen twenty-
four or twenty-five leagues off; but it is frequently

so obscured by clouds as not to be seen at any distance.*

" The peak has been described as filled with dark volcanic caverns, which have frequently emitted smoke, flames, and ashes, to a considerable distance. At the foot of the mountain, towards the east, is a spring of fresh water, generally cold, but sometimes so heated with the subterraneous fire as to rush forth in torrents, in a boiling state, and sending forth a stream of sulphureous vapours, vitrified stones, &c."

Pico, exclusive of the great inequalities of its surface, may be about twenty-five miles long, and from six to nine miles wide, though narrowing to the south-east, where it terminates in an obtuse angle: " it contains about 22,000 inhabitants, who occupy three towns and eleven villages. The soil being stony little grain is produced, and the greater part of the wheat and maize, for consumption, is imported from the neighbouring islands. The wine is the staple commodity, and is reputed the best in the Azores. This, with brandy, is exported in considerable quantities. The cattle are various, numerous, and excellent; fruit is abundant, and equally fine.† They

* " The Spanish surveyors have since given the height of the peak, from its observed altitude, above the level of the sea, as 1212½ Spanish toises, (1103 English fathoms only.) The mountain, they observe, covers the whole of the western part of the island; its skirts, and even half way up, are cultivated with vines; the next fourth part by shrubs; and the last and highest part seems all of rock, covered with a very short grass. An ascent to the summit may be made, though not without difficulty, and some caverns afford occasional shelter."

† Pico, I believe, produces no oranges.

have cedar and other timber, including a beautiful
kind of yew, called *Teixo*, which is remarkably solid
and fine; but which is monopolized by, and felled
only by order of, the Government.

The *vino tinto* of Pico, made from the Oporto vine,
propagated in Pico, Captain Livingston thinks excellent; but it is not plentiful. The teixo wood, he
says, is the same as our yew.

" The principal towns and villages are *Lagens,
Pico, Santa Cruz, St. Sebastian, Pesquin, S. Rocca,
La Playa,* and *Magdalena.*" The island affords no
anchorage, and nothing but coasters can approach its
shores.

" Off the most prominent part of the western coast
is the little port and isles of La Magdalena. From
the town which stands here, the greater part of the
produce of the island, for exportation, is shipped off
for Fayal in small row-boats. The islets are surrounded with rocks; but very near the latter the
depths are six, seven, and eight fathoms, rocky
ground."

" *St. George's* lies at a distance of three leagues from
Pico, and is separated from Graciosa by a channel
eight leagues in breadth. It is a long narrow island,
about nine leagues long, and not more than one in its
average breadth. Its most easterly point, Ponta del
Topo, lies W. ¼ N., (W.S.W. ¼ W.,) 30¾ miles from
the summit of *Mount Brasil,* in Terceira, and in lat.
38° 29′ 22″ N., and long. 27° 50′ 27″ W.

" On its south coast is the little town called *Villa das Velas,* or *Vellas,* with a port where small vessels may lie sheltered from all winds.

" This island, when Tofino described it, contained more than 11,000 persons, in three towns and seven villages. He says that it produces much wine of a good quality. It has been famous for its cattle, with which it supplies other islands, and its cheese is said to be fine. The produce of wheat and maize is equal only to the consumption of a part of the inhabitants, as the lower class substitute the root of iname. Wood and fresh water are abundant.

" On the 1st May, 1808, a dreadful volcano, seen from Fayal, burst out about the centre of the island, in the midst of fertile pastures, about three leagues south-east of Vellas. On the 3rd, a crater was formed, in size about twenty-four acres. In two days, it had thrown out cinders or small pumice-stones, which a strong north-east wind had propelled southerly; and which, independent of the mass accumulated around the crater, had covered the earth from one to four feet in depth, half a league in width, and three miles in length: then, passing the channel, did some injury to the eastern end of Pico. The fire of this large crater had nearly subsided on the 3rd of May; but, in the preceding evening, another small crater had opened, one league to the northward of the large one, and only two leagues from Vellas. The sulphureous smoke of the new crater rendered impracticable an approach to the large one. Within a mile of the crater, the earth

was rent in every direction. The Fredonian Consul
of Fayal, who, with some friends, visited this place,
stated that "they at length arrived within 200 yards
of the spot, and saw it in the midst of a pasture,
distinctly, at intervals, when the thick smoke, which
swept the earth, lighted up a little. The mouth of
it was only about fifty yards in circumference, and
the fire seemed struggling for vent. The force with
which a pale blue flame issued forth resembled a
powerful steam engine, multipled a hundred-fold—
the noise was deafening—the earth where they stood
had a tremulous motion—the whole island seemed
convulsed; hollow bellowings were occasionally heard
from the bowels of the earth, and earthquakes were
frequent. After remaining here about ten minutes,
they returned to town; the inhabitants had mostly
quitted their houses, and remained in the open air,
or under tents. They passed the night at Vellas,
and next morning went by water to *Ursulina,* a
small sea-port town, two leagues south of Vellas,
and viewed that part of the country covered with
cinders before mentioned, and which had changed
the most valuable vineyards in the island into a
frightful desert.

" On the same day, (May 4th,) the party returned
to Fayal ; and, on the 5th and succeeding days, from
twelve to fifteen small volcanoes broke out in the
fields they had traversed on the 3rd, from the chasms
above described, and threw out a quantity of lava,
which travelled on slowly towards Vellas. The fire
of these small craters subsided, and the lava ceased

running about the 11th of May; on which day the large volcano, that had lain dormant for nine days, burst forth again, like a roaring lion, with horrid belchings, distinctly heard at ten leagues distant, throwing up prodigious large stones, with an immense quantity of lava, illuminating at night the whole island. This continued with tremendous force until the 5th of June, exhibiting the awful, yet magnificent, spectacle of a perfect river of fire, (distinctly seen from Fayal,) running into the sea. On that day, the 5th, its force began to fail, and, in a few days after, it ceased entirely. The elevation of the crater from the sea was about 3,500 feet. The lava inundated and swept away the town of Ursulina, and country houses, and cottages adjacent, as well as the farm-houses, throughout its course. It, as usual, gave timely notice of its approach, and most of the inhabitants fled; some few, however, remaining in the vicinity too long, endeavouring to save their effects, were scalded by flashes of steam, which, without injuring their clothes, took off not only their skin but their flesh. About sixty persons were thus miserably scalded, some of them died on the spot, or in a few days after. Numbers of cattle shared the same fate. The consternation and anxiety were so great among the people, that even their domestic concerns were abandoned; and, amidst plenty, they were in danger of starving. Supplies of ready-baked bread were sent from Fayal for their relief, and large boats to bring away the inhabitants who had lost their dwellings. In short, the island,

heretofore rich in cattle, corn, and wine, presented
such a scene of desolation and distress as has rarely
been witnessed in any country."

———

" *Graciosa* is said to take its name from its beauty
and fertility in corn, fruit, pasture, and cattle; supplying Terceira and several of the other islands with
a great part of its produce. It is the most fertile
of all the Azores, and has about 8,000 inhabitants
distributed in two towns and two villages. The
greatest extent of the island is only eight miles and
a half; but, in this extent, the quantity of barley
which is produced is almost incredible, together with
wheat, maize, wine, and all kinds of fruit and vegetables. Of sheep, hogs, and fowls, the inhabitants
have more than they can consume. The only scarce
article is wood, which is obtained from St. George's
and Pico. The chief town is *Santa Cruz,* on the
north-east side; but the anchorage is to the south-east
near *Ponta del Carapacho,* which is situated in latitude 39° 0′ 0″ N. and longitude 27° 57′ 45″ W. Here
vessels load and unload, and are ready to be off
with any winds; but they lie sheltered only from
south by the west, nearly to north. All the goods
from the town of Santa Cruz are brought to this
anchorage to be shipped, as they have no other.

" The *Channels* among the *Azores* are, in general,
clear and deep, and may be navigated at all times:
that, however, between St. George and Pico should
not be attempted, unless in settled weather, or with

a steady breeze, for a sudden calm may prove fatal; as a strong current runs through the channel, according to the state of the tide."*

To these observations and extracts it is unnecessary for me now to make farther addition : should future opportunities (shipwreck always excepted) reland me amongst the very interesting group of islands to which they refer, perhaps I may be able to offer something better worthy of notice than any thing at least which I have said myself respecting them; and would that I might find them from under the dominion of the detested tyrant who now holds them in subjection— Terceira excepted, which, I have before noticed, has espoused the cause of Donna Maria; but this I am inclined to attribute much more to foreign agency and example than to any ambition of the Portuguese themselves: they appear to me a people altogether without energy or enterprise, content to lead a life of the most worthless and degrading indolence, and, if that be only conceded, ready to crouch to any tyrant who may chance to usurp supremacy over them. Terceira, for some time past, has been cut off from all communication with the other islands, or elsewhere, having been closely blockaded by Miguel, and we have frigates there acknowledging the blockade, whilst the pitiful tyrant is suffered to rob and plunder our merchants with impunity; and yet we call ourselves *Britons!* It was in reference to this subject that I

* " And we suspect, too, according to the state of the Florida Stream, especially when it flows from a high northern parallel."

was addressed by a foreigner nearly as follows:—
" Sir, formerly if *England* said or did a thing, we
knew, and the world knew, at once, what she meant
by it, but now there is so much assumed mystery,
tampering, equivocation, and insincerity in her foreign
policy, that it is difficult to comprehend, and still
more difficult to trust any thing she says or does.
How is it, Sir? We ascribe much of it to the military Duke who now presides in your Cabinet, and
who, however familiar he may be with the *ruses* and
artifices which war may sanction, displays none of
those qualifications which are necessary to direct the
affairs, and uphold the renown of a great nation like
England. And did he not, at the time of Mr. Can-
ning's coming into office, acknowledge his own utter
incompetency to fill the situation? It would have
been well, indeed, if his conscious inability—very
commendable diffidence—or any thing else had kept
him out of it."—I could but own the justice of the
gentleman's observations, and arrive at the like conclusion.* As to Terceira, however, she will carry

---

* Since penning these remarks a new era has dawned upon us,
and but for the benefit of contrast I would most gladly cancel them.
Wellington and Peel, and the old Tory boroughmongering faction
are gone, I trust, for ever;—we have a patriot king,—an enlightened
and liberal ministry willing to keep pace with the growing intelligence and enterprise of the times;—we are upon the point of
obtaining a second *Magna Charta*, a *Bill of Rights*, which even
eclipses the first:—and, as regards Miguel, had not the dastard
wretch fallen on his knees and sued for mercy, the British thunder
would have shaken his citadel to atoms. I am thankful to have
lived to see this day. I shall not now blush, as I have done, on a
foreign shore, for the sullied and suffering honour of my native
country.

her point against either, sufficient is produced upon the island for its consumption, and nature has supplied impregnable barriers of defence, of which every advantage is taken.

The established religion of the Azores is, of course, Catholic, and *priestly* and *kingly* dominion much upon a par.   At St. Michael's, where British residents are numerous, I am informed a church has been erected, in which service is performed upon the principles (as it is styled) of *the Church of England.* Here, too, I am told, there are tolerable roads; carriages and horses, or ponies, (the latter remarkable for their beauty,) in abundance; and asses, also very fine ones, so numerous that there is said to be one for every inhabitant in the island.

I must not omit to mention that there is excellent shooting at the Azores, *without the slightest interference or restriction.*   Quail, rabbits, and pigeons plentiful, I believe, on all the islands.   Partridge on some, and woodcocks; and, as Captain Livingston remarks, it is said, grouse.   Of the existence of the latter, like him, I am rather dubious; but I scarcely know why, excepting that I saw none on two of the islands, (and I rambled pretty much over them,) but I saw some of the finest heath I ever met with, three or four feet high, and cover enough for all the grouse in Scotland.

PLYMOUTH, *December* 14, 1830.—After a voyage of twelve days, during the latter part of which we suffered severely from cold—our fruit cargo prohibiting us the use of fire—and various inconveniences incident to the smallness of our vessel, (though obliged to Captain Johns for the disposition he evinced to accommodate us in every possible respect,) with a fair proportion of favourable and head winds, gales, laying to, &c., we anchored safely in this port about two o'clock this afternoon, the coast being almost strewed with wrecks which had occurred a few days previously; and thankful do I feel not only to have escaped the number of these, but for my preservation through the many trying scenes of difficulty and peril to which I have been exposed since quitting my native land. May I never forget the goodness of that beneficent Being to whom I owe so much; *whose tender mercies are over all his works;* and to whom, for favours and blessings, past and present, I would ascribe the homage of a reverently grateful heart!

A day or two passed at Plymouth, recovering from our fatigues and retracing a file of adventures now so happily consummated, and far from unpleasing in retrospect, I again set out with Capt. B. for Liverpool, whence he was designing to take a passage by the earliest packet leaving for New York. Our ride, though for the most part, and for December, a fine, was a very cold one, and oftentimes had I occasion to contrast the nipping severity of our *winter* climate with the mild and spring-like temperature of the one we had so recently quitted,—drawing all my comparisons in favour of the latter. It was difficult, indeed, to believe, with the cheerless evidences of the season around us,—the whitened and frost-bound plain,—the current stiffened in its course,—the "naked shoots, barren as lances,"—and the hollow wind, as sighing nature's dirge,—that but a fortnight ago we were ranging the orange groves, and surveying the ever-living verdure and beauty of a sunny Fayal. But I hasten to a close:—the reader has, doubtless, thought me too much of a laggard already.

Arriving at Liverpool I was welcomed by many kind friends and acquaintance as one arisen from the dead; but few amongst them not having long since consigned me to an ocean grave:—and for the truly affectionate interest evinced by them, and the numerous other congratulations which I have received, I take this opportunity of returning my very sincere thanks.

With heartfelt pleasure I have subsequently heard of the safe arrival at their various destinations of all on board our unfortunate vessel ;—for whom, as for myself, I cannot indulge or conclude with a better wish than that upon every future embarkation we may be favoured with a more propitious voyage, or, if cast away, be driven upon the like hospitable and friendly shores we found at Flores and Fayal.

FINIS.